Thomas F. Waters

THE RIVERS OF MINNESOTA

The Gorge of the Temperance River.

THOMAS F. WATERS

The Rivers of Minnesota

Foreword by Tom Helgeson

Recreation ▪ *Conservation*

RIPARIAN PRESS
St. Paul, Minnesota
2010

Published by RIPARIAN PRESS
                5887 Carlson Street
                Saint Paul, Minnesota 55126
                651-486-6471

Text set in 12-point Garamond.
Printed in the United States of America.
Substantive editing and cover design by Elizabeth L. Waters.
Book manufactured by Bang Printing, Brainerd, Minnesota.
Photographs by author, except where credited.
Photographs by author previously published are reprinted herein
   courtesy of the University of Minnesota Press.

Publisher's Cataloging-in-Publication data

Waters, Thomas F.
      The rivers of Minnesota : recreation and conservation /
   Thomas F. Waters.
      A p. cm.
      ISBN 978-0-9637616-2-0
      Includes index and bibliographical references.
1. Rivers --Recreational use --Minnesota. 2. Boats and boating --
Minnesota. 3. Minnesota --Description and travel. 4. Wild and scenic
rivers --Minnesota. 5. Rivers --Minnesota. 6. Outdoor recreation --
Minnesota. 7. Stream conservation --Minnesota. I. Title.

GV770.4.U55 W38 2010
917.76045—dc22   2010902474

FIRST EDITION 2010
FIRST PRINTING 2010

Cover photograph: Snake River, Minnesota, by Thomas F. Waters

FOREWORD

HIS FRIENDS CALL HIM "DOC." He is steely eyed, even as he wades into his 80s, but disarmingly courteous to those who seek him out, and many do. He is a scientist, precise and calculating in word and deed, but he savors his friendships and loves a story told well.

His university graduate fisheries students — now at work across the country in employment usually having to do with protecting this earth's aquatic environment — remember him with affection.

"Doc. How is Doc?" they ask.

They fondly recall nights by a campfire on the banks of a little creek near the Twin Cities, and a toast amongst themselves to the star-filled sky while they evaluate the contents of the drift nets they set out to capture invertebrates. He was their mentor, their friend and co-conspirator, the professor with a coaxing smile who gave them passage into the world he loved, a world of statistics, graphs, of bugs and fish, and water moving over rocks and sand.

Thomas F. Waters: professor emeritus at the University of Minnesota where he taught for more than three decades, conservationist, author of five praised books (this is his sixth), and much honored river ecologist — if you care about rivers,

7

about clean waters and robust ecosystems, and about their future, this man is your good friend.

You may have read his landmark book *Streams and Rivers of Minnesota.* I did, not long after it was published in 1977. With deft descriptions of this state's major watersheds, *Streams and Rivers* illuminated our river corridors and their recreation values. With it in hand, I plotted my own fly fishing future — where I'd go to fish, and what I'd look for when I got there.

This latest book, *The Rivers of Minnesota,* flows clear and easily, just as *Streams and Rivers* does, almost a companion text for lovers of moving waters, for canoeists, anglers and walkers of paths and woodlands.

There are descriptions of Dr. Waters's many accomplishments elsewhere in this book. In fact, it is slightly daunting to read about all he has accomplished, in print and through his teaching. My sense of the man, however, is derived from other sources, more personal but no less meaningful.

Dr. Waters and I go back a ways, our friendship spawned by a shared interest in and a concern for rivers. We first met to create an organization that would protect them, and our relationship grew as a result of an acknowledgment that rivers are sacred in our lives, and in our times.

I wrote an article about him for the magazine I publish, *Midwest Fly Fishing.* During interviews, I listened to his stories of growing up in Michigan, of fishing its rivers with his father as a young boy, especially his favorite, the Pine.

I felt called out to remember my own growing up along rivers in southwestern Minnesota. I was beginning to appreciate the depth of his wisdom, of his "looking back," and the warmth of his vision.

His storytelling was joyful, bubbling along with remembrances of relatives and loved ones, of trout hooked and lost or kept, of woodland sounds and the hushed sliding of water taken downstream to other rivers, to finally the ocean.

Throughout his years at the University of Minnesota and after his retirement, Dr. Waters has been a tough advocate for clean rivers and unmolested ecosystems. It has been a crusade all along.

His vigilance has been steadfast and he has been roused to outcry over ATV trails that threaten river habitats, encroaching agriculture that defiles the sanctity of forest and valley, the risks of sediment created by erosion and runoff, and the dangers of unwise planning and development.

It is important that you know that Dr. Waters has always been willing to speak out, to take a stand. We need such people in our world more than ever.

Two summers ago, Dr Waters and I sat together on the bank of a river filled with shimmering puzzles of light and feeding trout. We had stopped fishing to watch the river and the evening emergence of mayflies.

There was a gentle breeze that seemed to bring the evening's coolness with it from the west and up the valley.

"I appreciate that we could come here today," he said. "Being beside a river like this at dusk is truly remarkable, something everyone should see."

No words can sum up adequately the work of a man who recognizes so profoundly that life is at once a revelation of the sacred and an opportunity to communicate those revelations to new generations and new audiences.

Dr. Waters has meant so much to so many of us. His life and this book are gifts of the highest order.

Tom Helgeson

Tom Helgeson
Editor/ Publisher
Midwest Fly Fishing magazine

ABOUT THE AUTHOR

IN HIS EARLY YEARS, Tom Waters explored the local creeks around his home in southwestern Michigan, an area of many lakes, streams, and wooded hills. Alone he fished for chubs and shiners in a creek and, farther afield with his father, for brook trout. He soon fell in love with streams and rivers and maintained an addiction to flowing water for his lifetime.

After high school and service in the U.S. Navy, 1944–1946, he entered college and, some years later, received his doctorate from Michigan State University in 1956 in Fisheries and Wildlife.

Waters took a position with the Michigan Department of Conservation, in charge of a field trout research station, 1956–1957, and after that he joined the fisheries faculty at the University of Minnesota, 1958–1991, for a total scientific career of thirty-five years. As a professor of Fisheries, he taught fisheries biology and management and did extensive research within the field of stream ecology, concentrating on invertebrate and fish dynamics, publishing in the journals *Ecology, Transactions of the American Fisheries Society, Canadian Journal of Fisheries and Aquatic Sciences,* and *Limnology and Oceanography,* among others. He has received numerous awards for his research and became widely known internationally. His professional affiliations have included the American Fisheries Society, the Ecological Society of America, and the North American Benthological Society. He is now an emeritus Fellow of the American Institute of Fisheries Research Biologists.

He has maintained a strong activism in the protection of rivers. His many popular works have provided sound scientific information with writing that is both accurate and easily readable, mostly on the rivers of Minnesota.

His mission now, Waters says, is to encourage more people on the water, to learn about the ecology of rivers, and become advocates of good conservation of our natural resources.

This is his sixth book.

ALSO BY THOMAS F. WATERS:

The Streams and Rivers of Minnesota
University of Minnesota Press,
Minneapolis, Minnesota
1977

The Superior North Shore
*A Natural History of Lake Superior's
Northern Lands and Waters*
University of Minnesota Press,
Minneapolis, Minnesota
1987

Timberdoodle Tales
Adventures of a Minnesota Woodcock Hunter
Riparian Press, St. Paul, Minnesota
1993

Sediment in Streams
Sources, Biological Effects, and Control
American Fisheries Society,
Bethesda, Maryland
1995

Wildstream
A Natural History of the Free-flowing River
Riparian Press, St. Paul, Minnesota
2000

RIVERSONG

I hear the song the river sings
That makes a gray day brighter,
I hear a rapids 'round the bend,
And grip the paddle tighter.

When sundown shrouds upon the stream,
A cloud of mayfly spinners,
The bats and trout alike appear,
To claim their evening dinners.

A nice brown trout then takes my fly,
My bamboo rod a-quiver,
Forming waves of golden foam
Upon the swirling river.

And when at last in net he lies,
Two pounds, I guess I'd say,
I gently take my fly and hook,
And watch him swim away.

An errant sunbeam strikes a spark
In the dark of a cedar's shadow
To light the depths of a deep green pool,
'Neath a young kingfisher's rattle.

With end of day when shadows fall,
On friends, and fire, and river,
And softly then the currents sing,
A song that sings forever.

To the memory of

CAROL YONKER WATERS

For nearly five decades,
with pencil and paint she shared
with me the beauty of Minnesota's
rivers, forests, and wild shores

THE RIVERS
OF MINNESOTA

Recreation · Conservation

TABLE OF CONTENTS

PREFACE

I<small>T'S NOT DIFFICULT FOR ME TO PINPOINT</small> when I was first attracted to rivers—to one river especially. I came close to growing up on its banks.

That revered stream was the Pine River, a trout stream in Michigan, the major tributary of the Manistee. It was also the major trout fishing stream of my father who, with my mother, camped there often. He said I caught my first trout in the Pine when I was two years old, but I'm skeptical. I don't think he lied; he was just overanxious to make that claim. He may have hooked a fish, clasped my chubby, little fingers around the cork rod handle and pulled a flopping, brightly colored, little brook trout up on a sandy bar. For the record, my first trout.

*   *   *

W<small>HAT I REALLY BEGAN TO REMEMBER</small> included the long trip up north from home in southern Michigan to the Pine, more than 100 miles of gravel. This was not too long after the great harvest of white pine from the forests of north central Michigan. So the gray pine stumps that spread to the horizon resembled gravestones in huge cemeteries. The fields of stumps were indeed cemeteries, of a sort. And, finally, the bumpy track down into the river valley.

The time was in the early 1930s, in the middle of the Great Depression, which of course made no impression on me. But the noisy ribbon of rapids and pools in the Pine River, although

21

scary, pulled me to its edges like moths to a Coleman lantern. The deep pools, green and mysterious with unseen monster trout surely hidden in the dark bottoms, invaded my young brain to create indelible memory, and I became thoroughly and permanently enmeshed in the Pine River.

I'll skip many years here. Having received my PhD degree in fisheries and wildlife at Michigan State University in 1956 and having spent a couple of years with the Michigan Department of Conservation, I was invited to join the fisheries faculty at the University of Minnesota.

I immediately dove into research on the mysteries of Minnesota's streams and rivers, and in a few years, ten or twelve I suppose, I had been around Minnesota pretty well and had acquired a good overall appreciation of the rivers around the state.

My department head, Dr. Alexander Hodson, and I had become good friends, and one day over a couple of beers we were talking about books. I said something about my ambition to someday write a book about the rivers of Minnesota. He told me he was on a faculty committee that reviewed book proposals for the University of Minnesota Press. He said I should pursue my aspiration and that he would drop a word to the assistant director of the press, William (Chip) Wood.

A few more years of preparation—studying some books about writing a book, more traveling around the state, taking lots of photographs, consulting often with many members of the state Department of Conservation, who also made available to me their records of past stream and river surveys and published studies—and I was ready to submit my typed manuscript. I had written it all with pencil and paper, then translated it into type with an old portable machine from my teenage years. (This was well before the age of personal computers.)

The next step was editing. The Press appointed Margaret Ewing, whom I already knew as having been a student in one of my fisheries courses. (It was then I learned that she had a PhD degree, in limnology, a perfect choice.) It was a new experience for me, a long, drawn-out process. I would give her one chapter, she worked it over for a few days, then we got together and fine-tuned that chapter. So through the entire book, chapter by chapter, I don't think a single sentence was spared. In the end, it was a new book, greatly improved. In the process I learned more about book writing from Dr. Margaret Ewing than I would have from any manual of instruction or formal coursework, and I've loved her for that ever since.

The Streams and Rivers of Minnesota turned out to be popular with stream anglers and canoeists, now thirty years later in its sixth printing. Robert Redford's movie, *A River Runs Through It,* stimulated an enormous increase in fly fishing for trout, across the country—and (I think) in sales of my book as well, in Minnesota. At one point a few years ago, the University Press asked me to write a second edition, but I declined. Too much time and trouble, and I was working on other books.

I had included a final chapter in "streams and rivers" entitled *Minnesota's Streams—A Call for Stewardship*, almost as an after-thought. It was seminal for me, as I soon became passionate about protection of our streams and rivers, and additional books that I wrote dealt more and more about river conservation. I did a lot of other writing, articles and such, gave oral presentations and seminars, and got involved in a number of court cases dealing with threats to Minnesota's rivers. During my retirement now, I have come to feel more responsibility as a stream and river advocate.

Yes, my professional interest in rivers grew out of my avocation of fishing. I admit it. But that has caused me to realize that those who fish and otherwise use our outdoor resources also have an obligation: to practice good stewardship. Thus I connect using and enjoying the resource with protecting and conserving it.

A new book, *The Rivers of Minnesota,* with a subtitle of *Recreation and Conservation* was the obvious choice, emphasizing both use and protection, in other words, *recreation* and *conservation.* They must go together.

You will find some short essays on conservation and stewardship of streams and rivers at the end of each river chapter.

They are not intended to relate directly to the preceding chapter. (I hope you don't mind if they seem to favor trout streams a bit.)

One time a member of my reading public suggested that, with my vast knowledge of trout and trout streams, I must know where every fish lay in a stream and how to catch it. I replied, "No, but when I don't catch anything, I know the best excuses."

THE RIVERS OF MINNESOTA

Recreation · *Conservation*

INTRODUCTION — A RICHNESS OF RIVERS

Among its more than ten thousand lakes, five million acres in fifty-eight state forests, two huge national forests adding three million more, sixty-eight state parks, hundreds of county parks, 1,380 Wildlife Management Areas with a total of over a million acres, and thirteen National Wildlife Refuges with a million more—run some 70,000 miles of flowing water, hundreds of rivers, streams, and creeks.

Almost all are open to the public for recreation. Thirty rivers with outstanding character are designated as special canoe streams with individual management. Excellent maps for each river, available from the Department of Natural Resources, are free for the asking.

In diverse ways, rivers connect us to the natural world that surrounds us every day. The rain that falls on our sidewalks and streets somewhere enters a river. The hills that we may see outside our kitchen window were carved by running water that eventually became a river. On a weekend drive or longer vacation we will cross a river and somewhere enjoy a landscape that has been sculpted by a river.

Rivers can afford us gentle recreation or wild, exhilarating adventure. They give us places to listen to the music of the riffle

—a balm to quell the raucous noise of the traffic, telephones, and computer beeps and whistles that fill our commercial day-to-days.

Rivers offer us adventure. For fishing, paddling canoe or kayak, or hiking a wilderness valley trail, each bend in the river presents us a picture-window glimpse of a new riverscape, a quiet float with your family, a pool that in its mysterious depths must harbor big fish, or the challenge of whitewater rapids. The list goes on.

Mysteries of running waters intrigue us and urge contemplation (while sitting on a sunny riverbank?). Where does all that water come from? Where does it go? What does it do and see on its journey far around the bend?

Holling Clancy Holling, in his delightful kids' book, *Minn of the Mississippi*, recounts the adventures of a small snapping turtle launched by an Indian boy in the quiet headwaters of the big river Mississippi, and its long journey to the Louisiana bayous.

In fact, a few brave souls—grown-up kids we must suppose —have dared to reprise that journey in a canoe, from Lake Itasca to the Gulf of Mexico.

Perhaps for many of us, rivers offer the opportunity to submerge ourselves into the natural environment. That can transform us into an elemental, functional segment of the natural ecosystem. Like the adventure of Minn of the Mississippi. Each day on the river is new. The noise of unseen rapids, somewhere ahead, may give us an adrenalin charge, but the thought of a quiet camp at the end of day will bring a pleasant anticipation to the heart.

The vital signs and dynamics of rivers inspire many of us to wonder what chemical and biological processes happen in its clear water. What living creatures crawl about and swim beneath the riffle's surface, on the gravelly bottom, and in the unseen depths of a quiet pool? Actually, a whole science of stream ecology has developed—professional and amateur alike—to observe and study the plants, insects, and fishes, and the struggles they must endure to complete their life cycles adapted to a swiftly-flowing environment.

There are many more—the passing and ever-changing scenery of the riverbank during a float, wade, or hike down a river; the thrill of a wild ride in canoe or kayak through whitewater; or battling a large fish on light tackle. For the birder, the sight of a new species may be special, while we wonder what relationship holds between a particular bird and the river's currents.

The whispering of a river as twilight descends to darkness, with its unseen and mysterious night voices, can bring a delicious, spooky shiver down our backs. And that sudden, explosive splash out in the darkness may simply be the tail-slap of a playful beaver, or the gulping rise of a monster trout.

As we venture forth to enjoy the pleasures of our streams and rivers, we should be reminded that there are some cautions. We must learn to preserve places that give us quietude of mind and spirit, free from the intrusions of civilization. Here we can replace our commercial world with its motors and shrieks with the music and images of the natural river— morning mists over a river rapids, the rattle of a kingfisher on a sunny afternoon, the quick dash of a trout in a limpid pool, the grumble of diving nighthawks, and the flurry of night-feeding bats over the water with its swarm of newly-emerged mayflies against a fading evening sky. Add the glow and crackle of the campfire, among friends, with the music of the river in the shadows, that can leave us with memories to last a lifetime.

If we value these pleasures for other days, for our kids growing up, for new friends we have yet to meet on other rivers, for the future, then as custodians we must savor them carefully, as treasures to cherish and protect.

*   *   *

WE ALL KNOW OF MINNESOTA'S plentitude of lakes. We enjoy these wonderful resources for fishing, swimming, boating, water skiing, and just drifting about at sunset in a rowboat. We also know that most of our privately owned lakeshores are crowded with cottages and homes, often too close together, nevertheless bringing much pleasure to open water lovers. Mention that you're going up to the cabin for the weekend, and a friend may ask, "What lake are you on?"

We also are aware of seriously degraded lake waters that once were clear but now are turbid with algae and sediment, the result of development that produces lawn fertilizer and seepage from private sewage systems. And all this despite many lake associations that actively work to protect the environmental quality of their water.

Such is not the case with Minnesota's rivers—yet. Fortunately, a large proportion of our streams and rivers flow through public lands—county, state, and national forests, state parks, and wildlife management areas. New shoreland rules help shelter the river landscape and maintain water quality. Most private tracts along streams are large enough that cabin and cottage development is sparse and located well away from the river's edge—for now.

Still, many potential threats hover over our rivers. With increased pressure, private land may be subject to dense residential construction. Polluting industries, old and new, can emit more wastes into air and water, the result of perceived increased needs for manufacture and waste treatment. Even our public agencies, in charge of our natural resources, can slip over the edge and allow the development of inappropriate woodland roads, logging, motorized recreation trails, or too many variances from environmental rules.

One example: the proliferation of thousands of animal feedlots in Minnesota. Although more profitable for large landowners than traditional family farms, poorly designed or constructed feedlots threaten breakage or overflowing in floods with animal manure. Then at risk are groundwaters, drainageways, and nearby streams and rivers.

Constant vigilance will be required. Needed, will be increased insistence by Minnesota citizens for strict protection by our state agencies and election of environment-friendly officials and politicians.

Most important is the inclusion of ordinary citizens in policy and management decisions.

*   *   *

THREE MAJOR RIVER SYSTEMS drain Minnesota's excess water to the Atlantic Ocean. To bring some order to our recreational opportunities, this book is divided into three major groups of chapters according to these three major watersheds: the North Shore of Lake Superior, where tributary waters flow eastward through the Great Lakes and on to the North Atlantic; the huge watershed of the Mississippi River, draining to the Gulf of Mexico and the South Atlantic; and, lastly, the western plains and the northern border lakes, whose waters flow to Canada and Hudson Bay, itself part of the North Atlantic.

In the far southwestern corner of Minnesota lies a tiny portion of the Missouri River watershed. It contains several small streams, including the Rock River and Pipestone Creek. So, in addition to the three major watersheds, a small part of this book will be devoted to the recreation potential of this little corner of southwestern Minnesota, draining to the wide Missouri (also, of course, draining into the Mississippi).

Obviously, we cannot include all of Minnesota's hundreds of streams. So I have been selective, with my own choices, and these may not match your choices. For that, I apologize. On the other hand, I think it is important to leave some exploration of missing rivers on your own. They just might give you the greatest satisfaction of all.

*   *   *

THE GEOLOGIC ORIGINS OF MINNESOTA landscapes are greatly diverse—and so are the kinds and sizes of our rivers. The major geologic factor, long ago setting the final stage for the evolution of our river systems, was the glaciation of the Pleistocene Epoch, continuing for two million years. In Minnesota-land, the southward movement of the glaciers came to a halt about 18,000 years ago and, by melting, left our region clear of ice about 8,000 years ago. Through this period there were times of fluctuating global temperatures, when glaciers crept forward across the state as temperatures dropped, only to melt back when warmth returned.

What we see today from all that freezing and melting is the deposition of *glacial drift*—materials like gravel, sand, silt, and clay—left behind when the glaciers' loads were dumped. When the front edge of ice melted back at the same rate as the glaciers were moving forward, huge piles of sand and gravel accumulated in place, formed into the mounds and high hills we see commonly around the state, which we call *moraines*. Naturally, the locations of streams were determined by all those moraines laid down in a wondrous diversity of orientation. Flowing waters running over the moraine formations developed into a network of streams and rivers, finding their ways into the three major watersheds. The diversity in moraine formations thus led to the great diversity of the streams and rivers we see today in Minnesota.

Pleistocene glaciers approached the land that was to become our state from two different directions: one from the northwest and one from the northeast. We call these intruding masses of ice *glacial lobes*. The Wadena Lobe from the northwest covered most of western and southern Minnesota, the Superior Lobe from the northeast covered our Arrowhead country and east-central Minnesota. These major lobes had many sublobes, and they came across the state at different times. And in some places lobes from one direction superimposed drift over that of a lobe from a different direction. Small wonder that our rivers seem to be running in many different directions!

Glaciers were also responsible for our many lakes. Many of these have streams running through them, from lake to lake, like the chain of lakes we call the First through Eleventh (going upstream) in the headwaters of the Crow Wing River. Other lakes were formed from the melting of large blocks of ice buried in glacial drift and have no connecting streams. Some were formed by the scouring of moving glaciers, such as the lakes in the

Arrowhead region north of Lake Superior. Minnesota and other northern states are fortunate indeed for their glacial heritage; southern states that were not glaciated essentially have no natural lakes at all.

A second major geological factor affecting the quality of our rivers is the type of bedrock beneath glacial drift. Of course, such rock formations had been created long before the Pleistocene glaciation—hundreds of millions of years before. The kinds of bedrock we have today are largely responsible for the chemistry of our river waters, resulting from the scrubbing of glaciers over bedrock. The Wadena Lobe, from the northwest, advanced over sedimentary bedrock, formed by deposition of silt, sand and marl on the bottoms of ancient oceans, whereas the Superior Lobe from the northeast scoured igneous rock, the Precambrian Shield with its lava and granite.

The chemistry of groundwater emanating from sedimentary rock is alkaline in nature, whereas groundwater from the igneous rock in the northeast is acidic. This difference in water chemistry had great importance on the biology of today's surface waters, with alkaline waters being more productive than acidic waters. These differences in productivity account for the fact that fish in western and southern Minnesota are more abundant than in our northeastern region.

*   *   *

How MANY STREAMS AND RIVERS do we have? Minnesota is known as the land of ten thousand lakes (there are actually many more than that). Lakes are relatively easy to count. But how do we measure the abundance of our streams and rivers? The best yardstick, we find, is the distance of stream flow; for example, the Minnesota Department of Natural Resources (DNR) has given us a figure of about 70,000 miles of streams and rivers within or bordering the state. Thus, Minnesota supplies a lot of water to other states and the Atlantic Ocean. We have a great responsibility to see that all that water is clean and unpolluted when it leaves Minnesota.

*   *   *

A WEALTH OF RESOURCES is available to us with the outdoor recreational opportunities in Minnesota. They help us find, plan, and enjoy some of the finest outdoor experiences anywhere. And a great proportion of that is on streams and rivers. Information from the Minnesota Department of Natural Resources (DNR) is abundant, generally free, and available simply with a telephone call 651-296-6157, that will reach the DNR Information Center where you can request what you want. Of course, you have to know what to ask for, and this book will help you do that.

Throughout these pages you will find the major treatments of river recreation that emphasize fishing, paddling, hiking, and camping on rivers, pretty much in that order. There exist many excellent books available that treat these four subjects, and others, in more detail. Some are listed as you go along in separate chapters, and others are also included in the back matter labeled FURTHER READING.

Start with the canoe maps prepared by the DNR's Division of Trails and Waterways. Thirty of our most favored streams are included. The maps include county locations, canoe accesses, campsites both drive-in and remote, water availability, state parks, public and private lands along the streams, and much more. Each one folds into pocket size; take one on each of your river trips. Just call the DNR Information Center and ask (651-296-6157). These maps are referred to frequently in this book.

Another extremely helpful set of publications available from the DNR are the Public Recreation Information Maps (PRIM). These are large and not very suitable for spreading out in a canoe or on the trail, but immensely helpful in planning. These include all kinds of outdoor recreation information—state and national forests, state parks, Wildlife Management Areas, Scientific and Natural Areas, lakes and streams, and much, much more. The entire state is covered, in more than fifty regional areas, with a separate map for each. To order, call the Minnesota's Bookstore at 651-297-3000; there's a modest cost. PRIM maps are cited in this book's chapters, by name, for each river and stream.

Don't forget the internet. The Minnesota DNR website is so large you'll be tempted to spend too much time on it (instead of getting out on the river). And its extremely helpful. Of course, there's a lot more on the web, such as the state parks and state forests, two large national forests (Chippewa and Superior), National Wild and Scenic rivers, National Wildlife Refuges, and hundreds of county parks and recreation areas. Many websites are listed throughout this book.

And speaking of books. Mentioning just a few, there are several excellent volumes on canoeing, fishing, and hiking on or along rivers. For canoeing and kayaking, Greg Breining's *Paddling Minnesota* is classic, and Lynne Smith Diebel's recent two volumes, *Paddling Northern Minnesota* and *Paddling Southern Minnesota* (by Lynne and Robert) give us a literal encyclopedia on our state's canoeing rivers, with much valuable detail. The Diebels introduce an extremely valuable element to their books: the information on a river is organized so that each segment completes a day's trip, with put-in access and take-out landing, and everything you need to know in between.

Join the Minnesota Canoe Association, get their *Minnesota Paddler*, full of trips, tips, and river conviviality.

On fishing: there are probably more volumes here than you want to know, but here are a few. Mickey Johnson's *A Flyfisher's Guide to Minnesota* is a must for learning about the subject on all of Minnesota's waters. The premier trout fishing guide by Jim Humphrey and Bill Shogren, *Trout Streams of Wisconsin and Minnesota*, should keep your line wet from here on. Shawn Perich's books on the North Shore, *Fly-fishing the North Country*, and *The North Shore, A Four-Season Guide*, are certain to get you up there. Tim Holschlag's two volumes on smallmouth bass fishing, *Stream Smallmouth Fishing* and *Smallmouth Fly Fishing*, are not restricted to Minnesota but essential for pursuing this acrobat-on-a-line in our state's streams. I include here my older *The Streams and Rivers of*

Minnesota that covers the geology, history, ecology, and a lot of other river stuff. It's pretty fishy, too.

On hiking and biking: John Pukite's *Hiking Minnesota* should be in every hiker's backpack. Trails are described in detail throughout Minnesota's forests and plains, many along rivers. Available in all bookstores.

Now there are some great new books with special treatments of hiking trails, with a host of maps on the trails and bike paths of Minnesota.

Join the Superior Hiking Trail Association for superb maps along the most spectacular river trails in Minnesota. Their book, *Guide to the Superior Hiking Trail,* covers Minnesota's entire North Shore, continuously for 240 miles, including side loops for special places, especially along rivers. Ron Morton and Judy Gibbs team up to present a new book with additional details and views of the Superior Hiking Trail, with emphasis on specific "walks" that include special scenes and sites, in *A Walking Guide to the Superior Hiking Trail: Natural history, scenery, and other trail features.* Like the Association's treatment, this book crosses and follows many streams and rivers. It's particularly heavy on geology, but fortunately the authors include a glossary of geologic terms and features. They also include an extensive list of wildflowers, names and descriptions that you will find along the trail.

Farther inland, the North Shore State Trail runs approximately parallel to the Superior Hiking Trail, remote and wild, with dense cedar and spruce forest, mountainous hills, sweeping valleys, and many rivers and small trout streams to cross. Brook trout water. The trail totals 146 miles, Duluth to Grand Marais, but recommended for hiking from the town of Finland to Grand Marais, 70 miles. See a description at the DNR's website: www.dnr.state.mn.us/state_trails/north_shore.

If you're hiking in the Driftless Area (southeast Minnesota), don't miss the Blufflands State Trail. It's in two connected segments: Root River and Harmony-Preston Valley. Both segments wind around in the valley of the Root River, beneath towering bluffs and cliffs of limestone and dolomite. Some of the best trout and smallmouth bass streams flow through the Driftless Area.

The Harmony-Preston segment, eighteen miles, crosses several trout streams in the valley but climbs up topside, too. The Root River segment, however, almost totally follows the river for forty-two miles under limestone cliffs that seem to bend right over the stream. The trail follows up the South Branch of the Root, some of the best trout fishing in the state.

See the DNR website for more: www.dnr.state.mn.us/state _trails/blufflands.

*   *   *

IN AND AROUND THE TWIN CITES, Tom Watson's *60 Hikes within 60 Miles* is stuffed with detailed information that will get you out there with all the dope you might want. The covered area centers on St. Paul and Minneapolis but stretches out for around sixty miles in all four corners of your compass, north to near North Branch, west past Buffalo, south as far as Mankato, and east into Wisconsin. Greatly detailed descriptions of each trail; maps are complete and easy to read. Included are lists of hikes by length (three miles and less, three miles to five, five to ten, and longer than ten; lists of flat terrain and some hilly; some suitable for young children, some with historic sites, some best for fall color, some best in springtime for birding, some with special geographic features; each with the page number in the book. Lots of rivers and waterfalls. Each hike includes a phone number for more information.

Ask the DNR Information Center, 651-296-6157, for information on Minnesota's State Trail System.

Contact the National Park Service's Mississippi National River and Recreation Area for their new Trail Guide along the Mississippi River—miles and miles in the metro area. Call for a copy, 651-293-0200, and check out www.nps.gov/miss.

Don't forget trails in our state parks—all have trails, hundreds of miles along streams and rivers. The state park guidebook by Anne Arthur, *Minnesota's State Parks*, includes many details on the sixty-seven Minnesota state parks, including trails along rivers. Ron Morton and Steve Morse present an extremely detailed treatment of the eight North Shore state parks, *Gooseberry Falls to Grand Portage: A walking guide to the hiking trails in Minnesota's North Shore state parks*. Like Morton and Gibbs's book on the Superior Hiking Trail (previous page), this one is also heavy on geology, and includes a glossary of geologic terms and a similar list of wildflowers.

An older set of small books, individual by region, is *The Minnesota Walk Book*, in six volumes covering the major regions of the state, by James W. Buchanan, literally a seminal guidebook to the states' outdoor recreation. Finding them may require an extensive search.

Many county parks offer excellent hiking trails, and camping as well. A new, very welcome guidebook, *County Parks of Minnesota*, by Timothy J. Engrav, details 300 county parks, ranging from simple waysides to large, extensive parks with full facilities. Not all have hiking trails, but many do, often along a river. Available in bookstores.

On camping: there are literally thousands of campsites along rivers in Minnesota, but no definitive book on all. Most available information you will find is in our state parks where camping is the main activity. See *Minnesota's State Parks,* detailed on previous page. (Have you noticed that most of our state parks are on rivers?) There's also a wealth of county parks with camping facilities, some specifically on streams and rivers (for example, the many riverside parks in Anoka County). Again, see *County Parks of Minnesota* for more details.

Minnesota's system of fifty-eight state forests contains a treasure chest of wildland camping opportunities. Twenty-eight of these have developed campgrounds, many on rivers or lakes. However, "dispersed camping" is allowed almost anywhere in the forests; campers are expected to use common-sense and take care of their chosen sites, such as removal of trash, burial of human waste, and no cutting of trees. Special caution in the use of fire is of greatest concern; be positive that it's out. Motto: "leave no

trace." See the DNR forestry website—www.dnr.state.mn.us/
state_forests/camping—and its links for details on each
campground.

Our two national forests, Chippewa and Superior, boast
many campgrounds, but almost all are on lakes. Two river
campgrounds are located in the Superior National Forest, no
river camps in the Chippewa. The South Kawishiwi River Campground, in the Superior forest, is on a diverted loop of the Kawishiwi where currents are slow. This diverted loop will eventually
come back to join the main stream. Great northwoods scenery,
and the fishing's good for walleyes and northern pike. The other
one in the Superior forest, the Little Isabella River Campground,
is located on the river of the same name and is notable for brook
trout fishing. The Little Isabella was one of Sigurd Olson's favorite trout streams.

Although not a guidebook in the strict sense, John Tester's
treatment of the diversity of Minnesota's natural resources is not
to be missed, *Minnesota's Natural Heritage: An Ecological Perspective*.
He covers forests, lakes, wetlands, prairies, and streams and rivers, with a broad brush but at the same time with a rich lode of
fascinating details. Available from the University of Minnesota
Press or practically any bookstore.

And don't forget the DNR's marvelous bimonthly magazine,
the *Minnesota Conservation Volunteer*. Hardly an issue comes out
without at least something special on our state's streams and
rivers.

One book documents camping with tents ans picking out
campgrounds that rate the best for quietude: *The Best in Tent
Camping: Minnesota* by Tom Watson. A small-type subtitle reads,
"A Guide for Car Campers who Hate RVs, Concrete Slabs, and
Loud Portable Stereos." Fifty park campgrounds are described
with good maps of the campsites and rating scales for beauty,
privacy, and quiet. The author breaks the fifty into three regions,
Northern, Central, and Southern; campgrounds were selected
mostly from state parks and state forests. All told, twenty-some
parks are on rivers.

It's a book intended for campers who want to camp out with their bedding on the good earth and in the quiet of nature, the whispers of nighttime in the woods or by the murmur of a river.

*   *   *

DID YOU EVER WONDER how all those creeks, streams, and rivers got their names?

By and large, our rivers were named through the diversity of our history, both geological and cultural. Stony Brook, for example, and the French River. Many names came from our Native American peoples—like the Mississippi. Some from proper name places, some from early explorers and fur traders, many from the local fauna—lots of Beaver and Deer creeks and rivers. Some, small, have no name at all. Throughout this book, the origins of stream names are explained, when possible.

Stay tuned.

CONSERVATION NOTE

SOME VIEWS ON " CONSERVATION"

WHEN I WAS A YOUNG LAD deeply into fishing, I joined the local Conservation Club in my home town, Hastings, Michigan.

The club was really into only fishing and hunting, and that was OK with me. But for some years I thought conservation *meant* fishing and hunting. After all, the state agency dealing with fish and game was called the Department of Conservation.

To some extent, we still use it today; for example, I belong to a County Conservation Club, but only active in shooting sports and hunting.

Eventually, "conservation" came into lesser use in the limited meaning of fish and wildlife, although some states still use it for their natural resources agency.

But professionally, it has come more to mean the science and stewardship of rare, threatened, and endangered species, that is, *conserving species*. And there's now a major scientific journal entitled *Conservation Biology*. My department at the University of Minnesota changed its name from Fisheries and Wildlife to Fisheries, Wildlife, and Conservation Biology.

Here I use the word conservation primarily to mean *stewardship*, based on our love for rivers.

Since the value of streams includes many aesthetics to those of us who use and love them, I write these notes in the first person style, which allows me to interject some personal thoughts and perceptions.

Part One

THE
NORTH SHORE

A Crown of Waterfalls

THE RIVERS OF MINNESOTA

Recreation · Conservation

INTRODUCTION TO PART ONE
THE NORTH SHORE

MINNESOTA'S NORTH SHORE lines about two hundred miles of Lake Superior's northern coastline, from Duluth to the Pigeon River. Rocky, tumbling streams all drain into the big lake, the largest expanse of fresh water in the world. Here, flowing waters mingle among all the lake's tributaries and later with the waters of all the other Great Lakes, to eventually flow as the St. Lawrence River into the North Atlantic Ocean.

Recreational opportunities in our North Shore streams abound with fishing, some rough-and-tumble canoe/kayak paddling, and the most scenic landscapes for hiking and photography in Minnesota. A top guidebook is Shawn Perich's *The North Shore: A Four-season Guide to Minnesota's Favorite Destination.*

Originating more than a thousand feet above Lake Superior, they tumble and drop in their last few miles to create myriad, spectacular waterfalls and whitewater cascades. Eve and Gary Wallinga's outstanding *Waterfalls of Minnesota's North Shore* will guide you to more than 130 falls, cascades, and thundering drops of up to 100 feet.

*   *   *

ANGLING IN NORTH SHORE STREAMS can be separated into two major categories: fishing for the steelhead (migratory rainbow trout) in the lower reaches of most streams, and for brook trout in almost all upper headwaters and small tributaries.

The rainbow was introduced into Lake Superior from western rivers in the late 1800s. The exact river and location of the source of the very first introduction are of some confusion, but somewhere the transferred fish included the migratory strain, because sometime over the past century the Lake Superior rainbows exhibited the migratory behavior, spawning in spring in almost all North Shore rivers as far as it can go, continuing an anadromous strain we know as steelhead. Although migrating steelhead try to get as far upstream as they can, in most North Shore streams, their passage is soon blocked by high waterfalls. The steelhead is a great "leaper," ascending small falls and rugged cascades with ease.

On the end of a fishing line the steelhead is likewise a leaper, literally a supercharged aerobatic, repeatedly jumping several feet into the air to the great admiration of the angler. But there's a limit to how high it can jump, and so the accessible reaches of rivers are limited to relatively short stretches from Lake Superior up to the first high falls. At the upper end of this reach is a legal, marked boundary; regulations differ between below and above this point. A few Lake Superior streams have a Fish Sanctuary established, usually near the mouth, where angling is prohibited during certain times, protecting spawning steelheads. These are identified in a book of fishing regulations.

Brook trout were native to Lake Superior and its tributary rivers, but only as far upstream as the first high waterfalls, which were barriers to further extension of its early range. However, brook trout have been introduced into all North Shore streams above the barriers where they have flourished in small headwaters and tributaries. The beauty of the brook trout is remarkable, with bright red spots on its flanks, often with a blue halo, yellow worm-like spots on an olive-colored back, and bright white edges to its black fins. Approaching its fall spawning coloration, the male brook trout's flanks become a flaming scarlet. Its size is small in small streams, but larger in remote beaver ponds and lakes with stocked stream trout. Fishing pressure is light, and its range extends over a broad area of its headwater environment throughout the North Shore. The "brookie" is admired wherever it is found.

This book is not a fishing guide, but many other published works are available to give you the basics of North Shore angling. Perich's, *Fishing Lake Superior* and *Fly-fishing the North Country,* along with Bob Linsenman's *Best Streams for Great Lakes Steelhead,* are excellent examples.

The new angler should exert some caution: fishing regulations may be different here from the rest of the state, changing in time, from river to river, and even with the particular reach of stream. Posted boundaries (usually at a blocking waterfall) divide streams into two major reaches with different regulations. For example, below the boundaries brook trout must be at least twenty inches in length. Angling is open only during the regular state-wide trout season, and only one may be kept; above the boundaries, brook trout may be of any size but only one over 16 inches may be kept. Rainbow trout angling below the boundaries is continuous year-round, but only fin-clipped fish (hatchery origin) and at least sixteen inches long may be kept. Unclipped rainbows (wild fish) must be released. Study your current book of rules carefully. Maintain a respect for the quality of water you visit, for yourself the next time, and for the next angler who follows you.

*   *   *

THE ROUGH AND RUGGED NORTH SHORE watershed is the product of its geologic origins: a combination of volcanic activity a billion years ago and the much more recent glaciation of only a few thousand years. When volcanoes spewed forth molten rock upon the primordial landscape, hard lava remained, almost too hard to be erodible at all, and even today the sharp edges of lava rock are visible along the shore in almost their original character. Later, mile-high glaciers scoured the Superior basin and its near topography into an immense diversity of lakes, streams, and rocky crags. The resulting tumbling riverine landscapes of the North Shore provide an infinity of adventures to be explored. The beauty of native brook trout that inhabit the wilderness headwaters of cool streams and rivers bring delight to anglers who search them out.

Of course, Minnesota can claim only part of the Superior North Shore; the geologic forces that created the Superior basin and its northern coast were not limited to national boundaries. Canada's Ontario holds by far the largest portion of the entire North Shore. Minnesota's part is a fairly straight 200 miles from Duluth to the border stream, the Pigeon River; Ontario's share is some 800 to 900 miles, depending on whether you follow exactly the much more irregular shoreline.

*   *   *

THE NORTHERN WATERSHED of Lake Superior with its many trails is uniquely worth exploring for its access to fishing and hiking, especially in state parks and forests. If you're a history buff, visiting the area's many historic sites will be especially rewarding, for it is through here that early explorers and fur traders passed on their way to the far Northwest and the Pacific Ocean, in the seventeenth and eighteenth centuries.

We will begin our journey of river exploration, in this Part One of the book, at the far western end of Lake Superior, near the city of Duluth. This is the smallest of the book's three major parts, but it is very special.

Two rivers—the Nemadji and the St. Louis—enter the big lake to make up the headwaters of the mighty Great Lakes and the St. Lawrence River. These two streams flow through Minnesota lands for most of their entire course, but in its final estuary the St. Louis is the border between Minnesota and Wisconsin. The estuary is an international seaport, serving ships from foreign ports around the world, the largest and busiest freshwater port in the world.

But upstream, in a network of wild rivers, hiking trails, state park and state forest camping, we find some of the best in Minnesota.

Happy river trails!

Chapter 1

HEADWATERS

The Rivers:
St. Louis, Nemadji,
Blackhoof, Whiteface

AT THE FAR WESTERN END of Lake Superior, the St. Louis River holds the premier status as the headwater stream of the Great Lakes/St. Lawrence River System. The St. Louis and its tributaries also occupy the western end of the North Shore watershed, mostly in the southwestern corner of St. Louis County.

The Estuary of the St. Louis has been greatly modified into a large freshwater shipping port, but we will consider this river and its tributaries mainly for their recreational opportunities farther upstream. The river gives us many opportunities, all those treasures we can enjoy in the riverine outdoors for which Minnesota is eminently famous.

A sister stream to the St. Louis, the Nemadji River, also empties into Lake Superior just south of the St. Louis. Although small and little known, the Nemadji offers much in the way of river recreation. The Nemadji and the St. Louis make up a pair that together really constitute the headwaters of Lake Superior, but they differ greatly in size, water quality, and biology. Most often the Nemadji, much the lesser, is left behind in considering the significance of the two rivers. Technically, the Nemadji might be assigned to the south shore of Lake Superior, as it enters the big lake in Wisconsin. However, upstream from its mouth, most of the upper watershed of the Nemadji lies in Minnesota's Carlton County.

And so we in Minnesota claim the recreational resources of the main St. Louis, the Nemadji, and their tributaries, with their wealth of fishing, excellent river canoeing, hunting, and other outdoor pleasures, and recognition as the Great Lakes head-waters.

*   *   *

TWO MAIN BRANCHES OF THE NEMADJI are the North and South forks, the North Fork being the main one. The Blackhoof River, the major tributary of the North Fork, is located entirely in Minnesota.

The character of the Nemadji's watershed is also the result of its glacial history. As the Pleistocene Epoch's glaciers melted back northward over a period of some ten thousand years, they often left huge pools of meltwater, temporarily held in place by moraines and other high land features. So it was in the Superior Basin. The largest pool of meltwater was given the name of Glacial Lake Duluth (after the city), a huge expanse of fresh water much larger than today's Lake Superior, which even now remains as the world's largest freshwater expanse. With further melting of the glaciers, a series of lower pools successively occupied the basin, leading eventually to today's Lake Superior. At the upper, or western end of Glacial Lake Duluth, a smaller, connecting basin existed for a while at a higher water level, once known as Glacial Lake Nemadji. But when continued glacial melting lowered the larger Lake Duluth, the Nemadji basin was left dry, its streams and rivers now flowing eastward to Lake Superior.

The water in Glacial Lake Duluth carried enormous quantities of suspended red mud, clay and silt, resulting from scouring of sedimentary rock and chemical reactions in the eastern part of the glacial pool. So much of this suspended sediment settled out in the Namadji basin that today as much as 450 feet of it remains under the surface. Consequently, the Nemadji's waters today often run thick with red sediment, and high steep banks continue to erode with the slumping red clay.

Certainly, the Nemadji can be canoed, and although the passing scenery is worth the trip, the water is often muddy with red clay, and the stream edges dangerous with soft mud. Greg Breining's excellent *Paddling Minnesota* includes information about canoeing the Nemadji. Two accesses are available, from the crossing of the North Fork by Minnesota Highway 23 to a take-out in Wisconsin, a paddle distance of thirteen miles.

Courtesy of University of Minnesota Press

The Nemadji River is subject to a great deal of erosion that causes the steep banks to slide into the river and muddy the water.

In pre-settlement times, prior to logging and agriculture, the Nemadji's waters probably ran somewhat clearer, and native brook trout occupied its tumbling waters. Some still do. Some small tributaries of the South Fork hold brook trout, such as the Net and Little Net rivers, and State Line, Silver, Anderson, and Clear creeks. Additional fishing opportunities exist in some other small streams tributary to the North Fork of the Nemadji.

A delightful small park embraces the Net River near the town of Holyoke, where both brook and brown trout can be found. The park includes a lovely waterfall, enhancing a lunch stop or some fishing.

Downstream from the waterfalls on the Net River, a young angler fishes near water rapidly flowing over a series of ledges.

A larger sport fishing interest in the Nemadji watershed lies in the annual spawning run of steelhead, or migratory rainbow trout, in their passage up the Nemadji to our next river of interest, the Blackhoof, the major tributary of the North Fork.

As Native Americans viewed the two headwater rivers from the waters of Lake Superior they applied their own term, *Nemadji*— or *left*—to the one on their left side.

*   *   *

THE BLACKHOOF RIVER, the major tributary of the Nemadji, winds down from the northwestern part of its watershed to empty into the North Fork a short distance up from that stream's crossing by Minnesota Highway 23. Total length of the Blackhoof is about twenty-five miles; although the stream in the upper five or six miles is sluggish and warm, without trout, the lower river flows through a deeply incised valley with timbered uplands and many coldwater springs and tributaries to produce summer-cool water for both browns and brookies.

*A hidden angler in the Blackhoof River hoping to hook
a large lake-run brown trout in the fall.*

Brook trout were probably native to many streams in the Nemadji Basin; they still exist in small streams and in the middle reaches of the Blackhoof. In lower reaches, however, brown trout predominate in year-round populations, reaching a good size. Although most brown specimens appear to be stream-bred, migratory browns swim up all the way from Lake Superior, through the Nemadji, to spawn in the Blackhoof in the fall. Many of these have reached four to five pounds, having attained their growth in the big lake.

The most popular trout fishing in the Blackhoof, however, may be for steelhead. These migratory rainbows ascend from Lake Superior in springtime through the Nemadji to spawn in the clearer waters of the Blackhoof. Some of these will also be in the four to five-pound size. Many small rainbows, progeny of the steelhead, stay in the river for about two years before migrating back to Superior for their adult growth. Juvenile rainbows are found in abundance through most of the river but may not be kept by anglers. Regulations stipulate that only clipped rainbows (adipose fin removed and healed) sixteen inches or longer may be taken by angling, that is, as adult steelhead.

The Blackhoof watershed includes a new, large Wildlife Management Area (WMA), over 6,500 acres. The lowermost five miles of river is thus open for public hunting along its shores. White-tailed deer abound here, but for the small game hunter, ruffed grouse and woodcock are the main quarry. Autumn in the mixed conifer-hardwood forest, including many maples with their autumn reds and golds, is a panoply of color—augmenting the joy of a day spent with dog and gun along a rippling trout stream. Development of this WMA in 1988 was a major addition to the public lands of Minnesota, protected and open for hunting, trout fishing, and other woodland opportunities such as hiking, birding, morel hunting, and nut and berry gathering.

The name Blackhoof is the translation of an Ojibwe name, possibly from the hooves of caribou or moose that roamed the region in pre-settlement times.

For PRIM maps that cover the Nemadji River and its tributaries, see maps DULUTH and SANDSTONE.

*   *   *

As THE LONGEST AND FARTHEST west of western Lake Superior's tributaries, the St. Louis River richly deserves its establishment as the major headwater river of the Great Lakes. Its glacial history is dynamic, its course variable. The St. Louis once flowed westward toward the Mississippi's course, but changes in glacial lake levels gradually allowed it to flow to the Superior Basin, its final form as one of Lake Superior's major tributaries.

The St. Louis begins in Seven Beaver Lake, in the far northeastern corner of its watershed, and from there it flows nearly 200 miles to its mouth between Duluth, Minnesota, and Superior, Wisconsin. Its major tributaries in the St. Louis's upper reaches include the Partridge River, Embarrass River, and the East and West Two rivers; farther downstream, the Whiteface and Cloquet rivers are major tributaries from the east. (The Cloquet, one of Minnesota's finest canoeing and fishing streams, is described in detail in the next chapter.)

A profound gap in the explorer/fur trader business in the eighteenth century was to find a way to travel from the Great Lakes watershed to the Mississippi watershed. The solution was the Savanna River, East and West. The old trail was some six miles long, and although part of the trail can be hiked by park visitors, the exact location of the full six miles remains uncertain. The two streams and the old portage are today memorialized in Savanna Portage State Park. This park boasts 61 drive-in campsites, 6 backpack sites and one camper cabin.

The St. Louis does some winding, and at the far westernmost river bend, the East Savanna River enters, a small stream that connects to the West Savanna River in the Mississippi watershed by a swampy waterway that today is hardly visible in places.

These two rivers are too small and swampy for canoeing or fishing, but several park lakes provide angling for warmwater fish (northern pike, crappies, others) and one for trout (brook and rainbow). Only electric motors can be operated in addition to the traditional canoe and rowboat on these park lakes.

For more details: www.dnr.state.mn.us/state_parks/savanna _portage.

East Savanna River which empties into the St. Louis River.

*   *   *

THE ST. LOUIS PRESENTS a great diversity in riverscape for fishing and canoeing. The main fishing is for northern pike and walleyes throughout its length, but smallmouth bass and channel catfish are also common in some reaches.

The uppermost canoe access is on Round Lake, downstream as a small creek from Seven Beaver Lake. For the first approximately forty miles down from Round Lake the river is a wilderness ride, but for the next 100 miles there are many accesses and opportunities for canoe camping, but no developed campgrounds. Here the St. Louis is a placid river with only small rapids.

Because almost all of the St. Louis's length remains well above the level of Lake Superior, the last few miles are steep. Much of the river's bed is of hard, broken slate, so this final stretch became one of the most spectacular scenes of wild rapids, cascades, and waterfalls among Minnesota's rivers.

The St. Louis is one of Minnesota's designated canoe routes, described in detail in the state's river guide at the website: www.dnr.state.mn.us/canoeing/stlouisriver.

Two special guidebooks for canoeing in Minnesota give us much needed information in planning our river trips: Greg's classic volume, *Paddling Minnesota* and, more recently, *Paddling Northern Minnesota* by Lynne Smith Diebel. (Later on, I will refer you frequently to *Paddling Southern Minnesota,* by Lynne Diebel and husband Robert.) Diebel's books give you many details such as camping facilities, river characteristics, outfitters, and interesting sidebar stories on history, riparian vegetation, birding, and other subjects. Breining's book and Diebel's first volume on northern Minnesota include the St. Louis and Whiteface. Their guidebooks for the Cloquet River, next chapter, also give you similar information.

*   *   *

THE RAPID FALL OF THE ST. LOUIS in its lower sections meant that it was ideal for building dams. And as the city of Duluth increased and modernized, it needed more electricity. Consequently, some now view the St. Louis primarily as a power generator.

In the late 1800s, hydropower dams were built to produce electricity for the Duluth and Cloquet area. Today, five hydropower dams back up the St. Louis's waters in the rugged lower section: Knife Falls, Cloquet, Scanlon, Thomson, and Fond du Lac. The largest, Thomson Dam, diverts water from the river, runs it through its electric-generating turbines, and then returns it to the river channel farther downstream. Jay Cooke State Park includes the often-dewatered section.

Water levels in this lower section fluctuate wildly, depending on the vagaries of snow and rainfall. Consequently, five more dams were constructed in the upper watershed on several tributary streams to alternately store and release water and provide stable water flows in the lower area of the main river. One of these, Orchard-Island, impounds the main Cloquet River, creating Island Lake, which now divides the Cloquet into its two quite different sections (see Chapter 2). There are two on the Beaver River, tributary of the Cloquet, creating Wild Rice and

Fish Lake reservoirs, one on Boulder Creek, also a tributary of the Cloquet, called Boulder Dam. And one more dam up the Whiteface River, a major tributary of the St. Louis, creates the large Whiteface Reservoir. All reservoirs now are lined with homes and recreational cottages, sometimes creating controversy over the fluctuating water levels.

In our early history, the turbulent lower gorge presented a major obstacle to explorers and fur traders attempting to reach farther into the hinterland of North America. But today the gorge is celebrated in Jay Cooke State Park, where a swaying footbridge over the roaring rapids continues to invite photographers and thrill-seeking tourists.

But Jay Cooke has much more to offer than the Swinging Bridge. At nearly 9,000 acres of rugged topography, it's one of Minnesota's largest and most inviting parks. Fifty miles of hiking trails get you into some back country for any degree of adventure that you might want, from easy to difficult, many along the wild river. Bicycle trails, from mountain biking to paved trails, horseback trails, many miles of skiing and snowshoeing in the winter—all here. Camping opportunities include some walk-ins to get you away from the crowd, backpack sites located in some magnificent scenery, two remote group camps, and a camper cabin available year-round, as well as many of the usual drive-in sites. All topped off with two picnic areas along the river.

Some of the wildest water in the world is a two-mile stretch of the St. Louis between the dam holding back Thomson Reservoir and Jay Cooke State Park in the lower part of the river. It's an international Olympic site, with kayaks and open canoes. Their riders from many nations attend the slalom races staged here. The events require additional water released from the dam for the occasion. Rapids are rated up to Class V. Hiking trails take you right along the banks of this wildest of riverscapes. Below the Swinging Bridge is a mile with Class VI rapids, un-runnable. But the foot trails along this part of the river give you some views you shouldn't miss.

Courtesy of University of Minnesota Press

The St. Louis River starts to drop down toward Lake Superior
where raging water tumbles and roars under your feet.
Don't worry. A swaying foot-bridge hangs from one
riverbank to the other and will take you safely back.

The river's name comes from an early explorer, who honored Louis IX, King of France, who led the Seventh Crusade in 1248.

For more on Jay Cooke State Park, see: www.dnr.state.mn.us/ state_parks/jay_cooke.

* * *

A MAJOR TRIBUTARY OF THE ST. LOUIS is the Whiteface River. The main stem of the river starts below the Whiteface Reservoir dam, and flows about sixty miles to its mouth in the St. Louis. The reservoir holds back the waters of the North and South branches of the Whiteface, both very small streams and not navigable by canoe. Of the two branches, the South Branch is the largest and most accessible by forest road.

Fishes present in the South Branch include only suckers and several species of minnows, but it functions mainly as a spawning stream for northern pike. Although not now a designated trout stream, a few brook trout are present in upper reaches of the Whiteface.

There are boat accesses at the north and south ends of the reservoir for anglers' access to the lake. Canoeists wishing to float the river, however, can put in below the dam.

Downstream, the Whiteface flows for sixty miles to its mouth in the St. Louis, a wilderness experience through some dense coniferous forests. Both Breining's *Paddling Minnesota* and Diebel's *Paddling Northern Minnesota* include details of canoeing the Whiteface. In addition, a river guide and map for the Whiteface are available in the state canoe guide for the St. Louis.

Fishing for coolwater species includes smallmouth bass, northern pike, and walleyes, particularly in lower reaches. The major portion of the fish population, however, comprises suckers of several species.

The name Whiteface is a translation from the Ojibwe, no doubt resulting from the Indians' encounter with white European explorers. Not surprisingly, a small tributary is the Paleface River, a variant, nearby.

The Whiteface awaits more exploration.

*   *   *

IN NUMEROUS WAYS, the St. Louis River and its tributaries offer so much for recreation of many kinds. Its popularity is increasing, and more and more Minnesotans are beginning to bring their love and concern to its stewardship.

For PRIM maps on the St. Louis and its tributaries, see maps DULUTH, TWO HARBORS, HIBBING, and VERMILLION LAKE.

We are extremely fortunate to have these recreational opportunities in their great diversity, on this headwater stream of the North American Great Lakes.

**CONSERVATION NOTE
NUMBER 1**

HELLO SEDIMENT

SEDIMENT IS THE MAJOR POLLUTANT contributing to damage of the health and vitality of a river—both in quantity and economic impact.

Whereas some sediment on the bottom of a stream is normal (essential for some organisms), it is *excess* sediment, resulting from disturbance of surface soil by human activity in the surrounding land that causes the problem. Most common are cultivation, logging, mining, roads, and recreational motorized trails.

We categorize sediment into two major groups: suspended sediment (SS) and deposited sediment (DS). The two are not independent and can interchange depending on water flow.

SS and DS act differently in the stream's biological community. At high levels SS clogs gills of fish and aquatic insects; DS can embed fish eggs and invertebrates. Embededness by DS is the most damaging.

Science defines a range of particle sizes that decrease from boulders to stones, to gravel, to sand, to silt, and to clay. However, clay is not simply ground up sand, but rather a precipitated chemical combination of iron and aluminum oxides.

The finer the particle, the more damaging it is to fish and invertebrates.

In the Conservation Notes found in future chapters, I will discuss some sediment sources and measures for control.

Chapter 2

CLOQUET RIVER

THE CLOQUET RIVER ranks as one of Minnesota's most treasured streams. Its beginnings are in Cloquet Lake, a small, remote body of water in the far northeastern corner of its watershed, in eastern St. Louis County. The river runs for a total of about one hundred miles to its mouth in the St. Louis River, much of it in Cloquet Valley State Forest. Many small waterfalls and cascades surrounded by conifer forests make this a stream of classic northwoods scenery—and in places, one of the most productive smallmouth bass fisheries in Minnesota. You can find the Cloquet River on PRIM maps DULUTH and TWO HARBORS.

Water quality is excellent, in both chemical and biological conditions, as is also the invertebrate population that provides food for fish, and, particularly, the crayfish, the smallmouth's favorite meal. The water is generally clear in upstream reaches, but like most northern forest streams, some bog color is present, more so in lower reaches. Essentially no pollution affects this lovely stream.

*　　　　　*　　　　　*

WE CAN DIVIDE THE CLOQUET into three distinct reaches. The uppermost runs from Cloquet Lake down to Indian Lake, which is small and shallow. There are no designated campsites or accesses, but several county and forest roads cross the river, which could give wading anglers access to the river and several trout stream tributaries.

The second notable segment runs from Indian Lake down to Island Lake, the so-called "upper reach." The Island Lake dam impounds the river, one of several water-storage reservoirs in the St. Louis watershed, but the only one on the Cloquet. For the canoeist running the river from Indian Lake to the St. Louis, the reservoir must be either crossed (several miles of open water) or portaged.

*The upper reach of the Cloquet River provides
much beautiful river scenery and numerous rapids.*

At the upper end of this upper reach, the usual canoe access is at the state forest Indian Lake Campground. For about thirty-five miles, this segment is remote, a wilderness run with many rapids and portages. Breining, in his *Paddling Minnesota* gives good directions for handling the boulders, ledges, and chutes. Lynne Smith Diebel, in her *Paddling Northern Minnesota*, divides the Cloquet into six sectors, each a daily trip, with more detail of accesses, distances, rapids and portages, and the character of the surrounding forest.

Below Island Lake, the "lower reach", about thirty miles, is less wild. The countryside is more settled, with some farms and cottages visible along the banks. Largely a pool-and-rapids reach, it is noted for excellent fishing for smallmouth bass and northern pike.

The Minnesota Department of Natural Resources (DNR) publishes a series of excellent, pocket-size canoe maps for thirty streams and rivers in Minnesota, free for the asking. You should take one in your pocket or packsack on any one of our main canoe streams, including the Cloquet.

See also the DNR's website for the Cloquet canoe route: www.dnr.state.mn.us/canoeing/cloquetriver. Or call the DNR Information Center at 651-296-6157 to request a copy of the Cloquet River map.

∗   ∗   ∗

A DIVERSE COMMUNITY OF FISHES is distributed throughout the length of the Cloquet River. However, as with most warmwater streams, the great majority occur in the sucker and redhorse family. With bait, you'll catch plenty, but they won't bother you if you're using artificials. Fishing in the upper reach may be somewhat disappointing, not many smallmouths, but there are walleyes, northerns, and channel cats. Better you pay attention to the rapids anyway.

Fishing is more productive in the lower stretch where canoeing is easier, and here you will enjoy some of the best smallmouth angling in Minnesota. Furthermore, while fishing for smallies you might very well hook up a large brown trout, especially during the *Hexagenia* hatch, with matching flies, in early July. Tim Holschlag in his fine book, *Smallmouth Fly Fishing*, recommends some of his best reaches and smallmouth flies, either from canoe or by wading. Take your time along this reach and keep your line wet.

Numerous small brook trout streams are tributary to the Cloquet. From Cloquet Lake to Indian Lake, in order, are: Cloudy Spring Creek, Whyte Creek, Kinney Creek, Sullivan Creek, Trappers Creek, and Murphy Creek, all in Lake County. These may be difficult to get to, and bushwhacking will be necessary. But those brookies are so beautiful! Another is Indian Creek, tributary to Indian Lake; you could give this a try before going on down the river. No tributary streams are designated as trout water between Indian Lake and Island Lake, although a couple of trout streams enter the reservoir—Carey and Marshall creeks. From Island Lake to the St. Louis River, however, are several nice little trout streams, relatively easy to get to: Lava (or Lavi), Hellwig, Chalberg, Cemetery, and Bear Trap creeks, all in St. Louis County. The TWO HARBORS, HIBBING, and DULUTH PRIM maps cover these trout streams, as well as the entirety of the Cloquet River.

*   *   *

PUBLIC HUNTING IS ALLOWED throughout state and county lands within the administrative borders of the Cloquet Valley State Forest, mainly for deer and ruffed grouse. If you're a woodcock fan, try some wet areas along the river. Most land in the upper reach is county property, open for hunting, but much of the lower river is in private ownership. There are no officially designated Wildlife Management Areas along the Cloquet River, but the large size of the state forest provides an immense region open for public hunting.

*   *   *

THE CLOQUET WAS UNDER STUDY for inclusion in the Minnesota Wild and Scenic River system when political conditions changed in the late 1970s. The Cloquet project was dropped, and no further additions have been made to the state's Wild and Scenic system. The Cloquet is greatly deserving of some kind of special protection.

The name Cloquet was probably given to the river after an early French trader, who sought the fur of the beaver.

.

**CONSERVATION NOTE
NUMBER 2**

SEDIMENT PREVENTION

OBVIOUSLY, THE BEST MEANS of controlling sediment is to keep runoff water from leaving the site of its origin.

Row-crop cultivation produces the greatest amounts of sediment by erosion of topsoil. Some of the oldest means of preventing runoff from farm fields include contour plowing and strip cropping to prevent runoff, and grassed waterways to allow flow of water off the field without eroding the soil.

More recent techniques fall under the general term of "conservation tillage". These all include abandoning the traditional deep plowing with the old moldboard plow, and instead using techniques that disturb the soil only shallowly.

These include slitting or punching openings in the soil to receive the seed or shallow furrows to receive seed followed by closing the furrow. In all cases, leaving last year's residue results in less disturbance.

Other control measures have been developed to reduce soil-carrying runoff in logging, mainly to avoid erosion on new roads and skid trails.

Any activity that disturbs the soil surface of floodplains—crop cultivation, gravel mining, motorized trails, or development of any kind—should be avoided entirely.

Chapter 3

THE LOWER SHORE

The Rivers:
French, Knife, Gooseberry, Split Rock, Beaver, Baptism, Manitou, Caribou

THE STREAMS AND RIVERS along Minnesota's portion of Lake Superior's northern coast are diverse, rugged, and lovely to look at.

In periods after heavy rains or snowmelt, they can be awesome, intimidating, and dangerous. But the very words, North Shore, elicit feelings of adventure, respite, and retreat. Here you can also time-travel to the pristine conditions of four hundred years ago when watery avenues led to the northern coast of Lake Superior and into the North American interior, rich with beaver.

In Minnesota, the words are always capitalized—*North Shore* —even when spoken!

The streams entering Lake Superior along the North Shore can be divided into two sections, differing in the ways in which they respond to drought and flood. In what we will term the Lower North Shore, many streams head up in springs and rivulets, even intermittently—that is, without lakes, ponds, or marshes—either as headwater trickles or scattered springs. Thus, in drought, there are no natural reservoirs to provide sustaining reserves of water; in flood, there are few places to temporarily retain excess water. In contrast, most streams in the Upper Shore have lakes and wetlands that provide reserves of water during drought or, in heavy precipitation or snowmelt, holding basins to retain floodwater.

Consequently, water flow in the upper section will be more stable and reliable in both conditions, and thus better suited, environmentally, for fish such as trout.

But in both sections, rivers are glorious in the beauty of their surroundings, and they provide the angler or hiker a memorable experience.

In this chapter we take up the Lower North Shore, almost all in Lake County. In this section, we choose the Knife, Gooseberry, Split Rock, Beaver, Baptism, Manitou, and Caribou rivers. All of these have their attractive and unique features, and altogether they take us about halfway up the Minnesota coast. There are other streams here, smaller but still important. (We leave a few things in this book for adventurous explorers to find for themselves!)

First, there are few opportunities for canoeing in the North Shore rivers. In their main stem, most are tumbling and fast, with many cascades and falls. In fact, it is the abundance of their waterfalls, some high, that hold us in such thrall. Most streams are short, twenty miles or less in their main stem, and high waterfalls remain as impassable obstacles to canoes, as well as to migrating fish. (More later on fish.)

By the way, the Department of Natural Resources (DNR) has developed a coastal canoe route along the North Shore, with fine maps showing points and bays, towns along the way, and harbors for retreat in a storm. This addition to our canoe and kayak resource, of course, is not a river, but holds promise for adventurous paddlers. Breining, in *Paddling Minnesota*, covers part of it, recommending a kayak over a canoe, and remarks about the stunning shore scenes when viewed from the lake side. Diebel, in her *Paddling Northern Minnesota*, describes this water trail in four sections, all the way from the Gooseberry River to Grand Marais, in great detail. Further development of the route continues by the DNR.

The big lake is subject to unexpected violent storms, and recourse to a protected shore is essential. For a canoeist or kayaker contemplating this trip, Greg Breining's exciting account of his paddle around the big lake, *Wild Shore: Exploring Lake Superior by Kayak,* is must reading.

In addition to the streams included here, there are more for your exploration: the Lester, French, and Poplar rivers, Kimball and Kadunce creeks, and the Reservation River, are just a few examples. Shawn Perich's *The North Shore: A Four-season Guide to Minnesota's Favorite Destination* contains a wealth of North Shore information on rivers and lots more. Eve and Gary Wallinga's wonderful book **Waterfalls of Minnesota's North Shore: A Guide for Sightseers, Hikers & Romantics** will lead you easily to most of them.

*   *   *

THE KNIFE RIVER IS BEST KNOWN for its spawning run of migratory rainbows, or steelhead, coming out of Lake Superior in springtime. This season, fishing for these big, strong, leaping acrobats can be among the most rewarding on the North Shore. Most steelhead caught from Lake Superior streams run about four to five pounds, magnificent specimens and hard fighters on a line. The record steelhead on the North Shore is a whopping seventeen-pound, six-ounce beauty caught in the Knife in 1974.

The steelhead is known for its ability to leap small waterfalls and cascades. So without high barrier falls, the Knife's distance attained by fish migrating upstream from Lake Superior is the longest on the North Shore, nearly twenty-five miles. Even if you don't fish, try a hiking trail that follows the stream on the west bank; you might be lucky and view a large, silvery rainbow leap a waterfall. Respect the Fish Sanctuary in the lower reach.

Small waterfall upstream on the North Shore's Knife River.
These falls do not impede the steelhead, a good "leaper",
from passage on its spawning run upstream.
(Photo courtesy of Minnesota Department of Natural Resources.)

The Knife is a very rocky river, with sharp edges of exposed lava. The Ojibwe had a name for those sharp edges which was translated into the English word *knife*.

Bob Linsenman's great book, *Best Streams for Great Lakes Steelhead,* includes the Knife on Minnesota's North Shore (and several on Ontario's shore).

*   *   *

THE GOOSEBERRY RIVER IS OFTEN CONSIDERED the gateway to the North Shore. Gooseberry Falls State Park is exceptional, with a greatly expanded visitor center constructed a few years ago; at least a short visit is a must. But by taking the easily traversed developed trails, you will get a quick, complete, first taste of the kind of stream flow, waterfalls, and general riverscapes to expect of North Shore streams.

Three major falls grace the Gooseberry at the park, with more falls accessible by trails leading up into the woods and others leading down to the rocky coast. For a bit longer trek, hike up to the fifth falls, cross over a bridge and, for a different perspective, hike back down on the other side.

The Gooseberry is one of those streams on the Lower Shore that have little in the way of lakes or other reservoirs in headwater reaches. In drought, the river flow is low and water temperatures become too high for stream trout. Some migrants from Lake Superior attempt an upstream journey, but the falls prevent any significant runs. Some brook trout can be found in cool upstream tributaries, but the fishing is not exceptional. On the other hand, the river and its falls in the park are extraordinary.

Gooseberry's name has two possible origins. One is from the Ojibwe name for *river-of-gooseberries*, abundant in the region. Another stems from explorer des Grosseilliers (French for gooseberry, say *grow-say-yay*) who brought a fortune in beaver pelts from the North Shore region to English merchants, which in 1670 launched Hudson's Bay Company. Early maps of the 1700s show a "Rivier des Grosseilliers." At one time gooseberry bushes, which serve as secondary hosts to the white pine blister rust, were targets of eradication attempts in our state forests. All attempts failed.

See the DNR website for state parks: www.dnr.state.mn.us/ state_parks/gooseberry_falls.

*   *   *

MOST OF THE SPLIT ROCK RIVER within the Split Rock Lighthouse State Park, including the stream's estuary in Lake Superior. The stream begins to the north in a series of small tributaries. About three miles upstream from its mouth, two major branches, the West Branch and the East Branch, join to form the main stem. The Split Rock River then drops about four hundred feet in a series of wild cascades and one high waterfall. Below the falls the Split Rock flows through a wide, flat valley to the lake. This last reach is available to migrating steelhead, which, along with the river's estuary and lake shallows, is a popular fishing spot for these large fish. Upstream, the two branches have fair populations of wild brook trout, especially the West Branch, a bit the larger of the two.

The lighthouse, however, is the major feature of the state park, having long been important in the history of Lake Superior navigation. Unnecessary today with electronic navigation, it is now administered by the Minnesota Historical Society. With its huge light, it sits atop a 124-foot-high cliff of an ancient rock formation. The extensive visitor center includes an excellent movie production of the lighthouse's operation during 1909 through 1969, a must for the Lake Superior history buff. For much of this time, with no roads, the only access to the lighthouse was by water. For these sixty years, the light and fog signal warned passing ships away from the rocky shoals known as "the most dangerous piece of water in the world." Modern warning systems have replaced the light, but once a year on November 10, the lighthouse throws its huge beacon out upon the lake. The occasion memorializes the Edmund Fitzgerald disaster on that date in 1975, when the big ship met one of Lake

Superior's legendary November storms and went down with all hands.

Near the shore, the park includes fifteen miles of trails and many campsites. In addition to the usual picnic area and drive-in campground, other sites include cart-in and backpack sites, and a kayak site for those using the Lake Superior sea route. All of these are along the Superior shore. About two miles of the Superior Hiking Trail follows the river up to its waterfall and rapids reach (and back). Other park trails follow along the lake shores and also connect to the new Gitchie Gami Bike Trail.

The Split Rock River loop of the Superior Hiking Trail, leading to the falls of the Split Rock, is tough going in places, but worth it.

The name comes from a crack in the cliff, visible from the lake side, which appears to be a large split. Don't worry. It's not likely to split further while you're there.

See the DNR website for more details:dnr.state.mn.us_parks/ split_rock_lighthouse.

                    *   *   *

THE BEAVER RIVER CONTAINS some marvelous scenes of river and watershed. The view of the wide, sweeping valley of its estuary, before the river escapes into Lake Superior, is extraordinary.

The Beaver is one of the most productive streams for steelhead fishing along the shore, although migrating rainbows can ascend no farther than the high falls on the north side of the highway. The fishery is thus supported by stocking of juveniles in upper reaches. As with other river headwaters in interior areas, many opportunities for brook trout angling are available in these small streams. The lower part of the river comprises the estuary with some of the best spawning habitat for steelhead. Land along the lower east side is accessible but private; be respectful of the privilege.

There are no state park or state forest campgrounds on the Beaver River, but the main stem and its branches can be accessed from several inland crossings by county and forest highway roads.

The Beaver River figured prominently in an environmental controversy and hearing on Reserve Mining Company's plan to cover part of the river's watershed with a huge taconite tailings dump in the 1970s. The loss of precipitation in the river's watershed would have reduced the flow of the river significantly and affected the success of steelhead spawning in the lower river. The conclusion of the hearing was to require the company to build its tailings disposal inland at the location of the mining, but then both the District Court in Duluth and the Minnesota Supreme Court found in favor of the company—not a good day of stewardship for Minnesota. Reserve Mining later abandoned its taconite operation before the tailings pond was completed, but the threat remains.

The Beaver flows through the town of Beaver Bay, the first white settlement to be established along the North Shore, in 1856. Outside the town is the gravesite of John Beargrease, an Ojibwe Indian who for twenty years (1879–1899), through snow and storm, by dogsled and rowboat, with his brothers carried the mail along the eighty-five miles of road-less route between Two Harbors and Grand Marais.

A look upstream from the highway gives us the scene of a high, fan-shaped waterfall that can never be misidentified as anything other than the Beaver River.

No doubt the river's name derives from the fur trapping days of centuries ago, when the beaver was abundant in the river watershed.

*   *   *

THE VALLEY OF THE BAPTISM RIVER must rank as one of the most scenic riverscapes along the North Shore. Tumbling and cascading, with high falls and rough rapids, the river drops 700 feet in elevation in only two miles.

The Baptism's waterfall is located a medium walk upstream from the campground, and at the top, a walking bridge that can take you back on the Superior Hiking Trail.

Partly located in the former Baptism River State Park, the same reach of river is in the more recently enlarged and renamed Tettegouche State Park. A good hike upstream leads to seventy-foot High Falls, the highest waterfall entirely within Minnesota, a location of extraordinary beauty. (Higher falls on the Pigeon River are shared with Canada.) A footbridge crosses the river at the top of the falls, from which one of the most splendid views along the North Shore meets the eye. Or, for another view, clamber down a stairway to the base of the falls.

Camping opportunities in the park include a regular drive-in campground along the river, about halfway to High Falls. Several walk-in and cart-in campsites are available nearby in quiet, more remote surroundings.

Many backpack and cart-in campsites are located throughout the park, a few along the river and some on the big lake. Rental cabins are available in the park's interior on several lakes nestled among semi-mountainous terrain, accessible by hiking trails— non-motorized boats and canoes only. Numerous scenic lookouts are located in this interior area.

Among many miles of trails, in addition to the trail to High Falls, are those leading to other spectacular views along the river as well as Superior's rocky shore and the mouth of the Baptism. The Superior Hiking Trail winds through the park, crossing the river on the High Falls footbridge.

Upstream, two state forest campgrounds are located on the river, Eckbeck Campground just outside the park to the north, and Finland Campground near the town of Finland on the East Branch; other Finland State Forest campgrounds are nearby but not on the river.

Another high point on the Baptism is forty-foot-high Illgen Falls, part way down the river's course. A modern, well-appointed cabin may be rented overlooking the falls, a luxury development that seems out of place, however, detracting from an otherwise wilderness surrounding. Just call it high-tech camping.

The Baptism's estuary is a favorite stretch of river for fishing migratory steelhead during their spring spawning run. Spawning fish ascend to Cascade Falls, about a mile upstream from the mouth, near the drive-in campground. Many small headwater tributaries of the Baptism hold brook trout.

The river's name derives probably from an early French name, Riviere au Bapteme ("River at the Baptism"; after capsizing a canoe?). Tettegouche comes from a "Tettegouche Club" of Duluth. In 1979, the area was acquired by state legislation establishing the present park, including river sections in former Baptism River State Park.

Greg Breining's account of the Baptism River's three-mile canoe route, in *Paddling Minnesota*, reads as if he's done it. I wouldn't be surprised. It's full of rapids and falls (III, IV, V, VI, and un-runnable), only for the *very* expert. There are nice trails for viewing, however, as Breining comments, "...if you tire of portaging and being scared to death."

See: www.dnr.state.mn.us/state_parks/tettegouche.

*   *   *

THE MANITOU RIVER IS ANOTHER North Shore river with outstanding scenic views. Most of the lower river is embodied in the George Crosby Manitou State Park, but it does not include the river mouth in Lake Superior. In the park, the river cascades and falls 600 feet in elevation through five miles of spectacular canyon. At the Lake Superior shore, a high falls pours its water almost directly into the lake. A bare quarter-mile of river is available to upstream migrating steelhead for spawning. However, the mouth of the river is private and closed to public use, thus closed for fishing except by watercraft coming in from Lake Superior.

Scenic riverscapes abound in the park sections of the steep gorge, where the river drops sharply in falls and cascades. Hiking trails parallel the stream, similarly steep. Gorgeous views!

George Crosby Manitou is designated as a Natural State Park, with minimum development. Camping is remote, accessible by hiking and backpack, thus preserving the outstanding features of the river in a quiet surrounding, broken only by sounds of the river and enveloping forest. Sixteen backpack campsites are available by foot trail, ranging in length from a quarter mile to five miles, located along the river canyon. An additional three sites are located on nearby Bensen Lake, managed for stream trout, canoe or boat carry-in—no motors. Several campsites are located on remote trails. Stream fishing is for brook trout in upstream reaches, including pools of the gorge.

Manitou is from a ghost legend of the Ojibwe, possibly from the mists that rise from the many rapids and falls. The Manitou is a prime treasure of the North Shore, worthy of its legendary source.

Mr. Crosby, a wealthy mining magnate, prominent in developing northern Minnesota iron mines, donated over 3,000 acres to the state for a park. This area has since been doubled with further additions and established as George Crosby Manitou State Park in 1955.

See: www.dnr.state.mn.us/state_parks/george_crosby_manitou.

*   *   *

THE CARIBOU RIVER, A RELATIVELY SMALL STREAM, enters Lake Superior a short ways north of the Manitou. A small wayside park marks the crossing of the highway. No state park here, but an unmarked trail along the river leads upstream to one of the magnificent waterfalls among the North Shore rivers.

Just before reaching the falls you may have to jump or wade across the stream—it depends on the water level. Alternatively, you can climb up to the upper reach of the stream to view the falls at the top. It's breath-taking. And you will be amazed at how such a small stream can produce this huge fall of water.

Lake County Road 8 crosses the Caribou farther upstream, where there's some pretty fair brook trout fishing.

Many geographic sites carry the names of the local flora and fauna. Some of the most common are Pine, Cedar, Spruce, Willow, Bear, Moose, Deer, Beaver, and Trout, for creeks, lakes, and rivers. In pre-settlement days, the woodland caribou roamed the northern regions that became Minnesota, giving way to moose as logging and civilization moved northward. The moose then gave way to the white-tailed deer, although a moose or a moose family can still be encountered at any time and place on the North Shore. So a river named after the caribou is not surprising.

Caribou River and its high falls, reached by a short hike,
half a mile from a Wayside on the highway.

Almost all of the North Shore river watersheds are included on the TWO HARBORS PRIM map. If you travel the North Shore for pleasure this is the map you want.

CONSERVATION NOTE
NUMBER 3

SEDIMENT INTERDICTION

IF SEDIMENT CANNOT BE RETAINED ON SITE, several means can be employed to interdict its passage toward a stream.

Buffers on or along the streambanks are commonly employed. Native grass and brush are best, providing good filtering. Trees alone may add little or no filtering, although they add to the stabilization of streambanks. Re-sloping of an eroding streambank is necessary prior to planting grass and brush.

Also effective is the "sand trap," consisting of a dam and reservoir, located upstream from a selected stream reach. The reservoir allows sediment to deposit out in the slower flow, and the basin can be further dug out to increase available volume for sediment deposition.

Small sand traps installed in tributaries and intermittent streams will reduce the input of sediment into the main stream.

An alternate system is the "diversion loop," a dug-out channel parallel to the stream with a dam at the lower end and a weir at the side of the natural channel at the upper end, allowing silt-laden water to pass over the weir at high levels. The reservoir at the lower end of the loop collects sediment, while clearer water returns to the stream.

Of course, all basins need to be dredged out periodically.

Chapter 4

THE UPPER SHORE

The Rivers:
Cross, Temperance, Cascade, Devil Track, Brule, Pigeon and Kadunce Creek

IF BY NOW YOU HAVE MADE YOUR WAY through Chapter 3, you will have noticed that the outstanding feature of the rivers along this northern Superior coast is the profusion of spectacular waterfalls. Almost every stream is so blessed—right beside the road, inland a short way (or long), or near the big lake's shore.

In most rivers, several more falls can be found farther upstream, plus many locations where roaring cataracts add to the overall plunge of about eight hundred feet from the highland moraine that parallels Lake Superior, down to the level of the lake. For waterfall buffs, a hike or drive inland from the highway will yield additional falls and whitewater rapids.

Don't forget the waterfalls in winter. Then you will be able to see their snowy splendor frozen in time and space. State parks are generally open in winter, with open trails leading to good viewing spots.

Chapter 4 includes rivers on what we will call the Upper North Shore, all in Cook County, right up to the border with Canada. We'll start with the Cross River with its lacy waterfall that seems almost to spill right through your car window—and continue on to the rest of Minnesota's North Shore rivers, each with its unique character of rapids, cascades, and waterfalls. The historic Pigeon, border river with Canada, will finish up the Minnesota portion of the North Shore. We'll also elaborate more on fishing and hiking and other adventures.

You will enjoy the new book: *Waterfalls of Minnesota's North Shore,* by Eve & Gary Wallinga. The trails leading to the more remote, inland falls are especially welcome. They open up a whole new opportunity for exploration.

*   *   *

WHERE THE NORTH SHORE DRIVE (Highway 61) passes over the Cross River, you can stop at the Cross River State Wayside, where a falls tumbles down a rocky slope to run under the bridge. (It is tempting to play around on this lacelike surface, but it's dangerous. Keep your kids in tow!) There are plenty more waterfalls and cascades upstream, with many hiking trails, some connecting with the Superior Hiking Trail, some leading to connect with trails on the Temperance River.

Try finding your way on small roads and foot trails that will lead along the stream to some of the most delicious river scenes and small falls along the North Shore. These inland trails include several shelters and backpack campsites. Brook trout fishing can be pretty good in these upper pools, too.

Some rough water on the Cross River, inland a ways.
The plunge pool in front holds some nice brook trout.

The Cross River with its extremely rugged lower reach was notorious in the old logging days for smashing up logs driven down from upstream. Many splash dams were constructed to hold back water until enough was dammed up to create large ponds. Then when the dam was opened, the rush of water carried the logs down to Lake Superior. Even so, when log marks were stamped onto the ends of logs (to identify the owners) they would be indistinguishable from the beating they took, necessitating stamping the marks on the sides of logs and even cutting them a foot longer to begin with.

Log drives were impossible on many other North Shore rivers, and consequently narrow gauge railroads were employed to bring the big pines out safely. The railroad grades were often constructed very poorly, because their use was only temporary. However, some of these old grades are still visible here and there, and they make good hunting trails.

Stretches of the Cross below the highway are well used by upstream migrating pink salmon, although this is as far as they can go. The pinks, or humpbacks, ascend many North Shore streams, usually in early September. This species of Pacific salmon was once thought to be the one least likely to adapt to a totally freshwater habitat. However, some pinks were accidentally introduced in a Canadian stream in 1955; they increased their population in only a few years. The life history of pink salmon is on an almost strict two-year cycle, and at first, spawning runs occurred only in odd years. Even-year runs soon developed, however, so the migrations occur now in all years. Smaller than its relatives the coho and chinook, adult pinks measure around fourteen or fifteen inches.

At first, pinks were considered a great nuisance, but innovative anglers soon developed lures and techniques to catch them and now pursue them avidly. Pink salmon deteriorate rapidly when they enter streams, but they are delicious eating when fresh from the cold waters of Lake Superior.

The Cross heads up in a group of several lakes, and consequently river flow is much more stable in both water discharge and temperature than other streams farther south. From these lakes, the Cross flows about twenty miles in its main stem, and drops over six major waterfalls. They cry out for exploration.

At the mouth of the river, accessible by a short trail from the wayside, stands a granite monument in the shape of a cross. The monument commemorates a historic crossing of Lake Superior by Jesuit priest Frederic Baraga, who in 1846 made a perilous trip in a small boat from the Wisconsin shore to tend to his Indian flock. He fastened a small wooden cross on a tree stump to give thanks for his safe crossing, which was later replaced by the present rock cross. Cross River took its name from the historic wooden structure.

While traffic zooms past a small waterfall on the Cross River near the community of Tofte, you can take a little trail leading to the river's mouth where stands Father Baraga's monument.

*   *   *

THE TEMPERANCE RIVER, IN ITS CRAGGY, lava-strewn gorge contains some of the most awe-inspiring river scenes on the

North Shore of Minnesota at, in Temperance River State Park. A short walk up along the gorge is awesome under any condition, but in high water it is earth-shaking. The old lava rock, broken but little eroded, melds the river into the enveloping forest in surroundings of pristine images remindful of the violence of its volcanic history. Spalling of lava leaves vertical walls that hide the stream and give the impression that much of the river flows under-ground. (Two deaths in 2008 reminded us of the danger.) Keep small children closely in hand!

In addition to the trails along the gorge are many others that lead farther into the Superior National Forest, connecting to the Cross River and the Superior Hiking Trail.

Park campgrounds are located on both sides of the river, picnic sites are plentiful along Lake Superior's shore, and short trails lead down to the river's mouth. Like other state parks nowadays, Temperance includes some cart-in campsites away from the crowd for greater solitude.

The Temperance estuary is a favorite place for fishing for those species that spawn in the river. Progeny put on their growth out in the big lake, and return to spawn when mature. Such is the case with steelhead in the spring and pink salmon in the fall.

Stream fishing for brook and brown trout is available on the Temperance upstream. A Superior National Forest campground is located on the river about twelve miles up from the park. Take the historic Sawbill Trail (Cook County Road 2), which runs along the river for many miles, and several national forest roads in the area cross or are near the river affording stream fishing in scenic river surroundings.

In early days of the park's development, the small area that it encompassed almost led to a conclusion that it was too small to warrant state park status. Fortunately, subsequent acquisitions of contiguous property were made to firmly establish the Temperance River as a full-fledged state park. Temperance River is still small compared with other state parks, but its unique character makes it one of the North Shore's best. It shouldn't be missed.

The river's name, Temperance, comes from the tongue-in-cheek legend that, unlike many other North Shore streams, it has no bar at its entry into Lake Superior. Like most legends, however, a bar—sand and gravel deposits at the mouth of a stream—does indeed form under conditions of wind, waves, and shore currents. The legend makes a good story anyway. For more details see: www.dnr.state.mn.us/state_parks/temperance_river.

Estuary of the Temperance River. Here, the "bar" is plainly visible, spoiling the old legend. A good story, though.

*   *   *

Pink salmon in excellent condition and ready for spawning.
This one is about 14-15 inches; in the ocean an
adult pink might.be about 17 or 18 inches.

Stanley Smith

Diseased pink salmon, taken out of the swift water of a river.

Courtesy of University of Minnesota Press

*The Poplar River— found between the Cascade and Temperance Rivers.
The estuary and lower reach of the Poplar River are given over to a
private motel/recreation establishment, but farther upstream the
Poplar runs rough and wild through a deep valley.*

NAMING OF THE CASCADE RIVER is probably the most appropriate of streams on the North Shore, if not of the whole state. Natural cascades abound; the river drops over nine hundred feet in its last three miles. Many spectacular falls and cascades can be found inland. However, only a very short way from its entry into Lake Superior, the river drops through a rugged canyon of ancient lava ledges in a dazzling array of thundering cascades— dropping 120 feet in the final quarter mile. Within this well-named Cascade River State Park, a steep trail with stunning views winds up along the gorge to a footbridge across the chasm, and then back down to its estuary on the other side. Don't miss it.

Cascade is a large state park, with many campsites extending along the Superior shore for more than ten miles. Campgrounds include many drive-in sites, as well as backpack sites inland and along the Superior shore for those who prefer solitude broken only by the sounds of wind and waves. At least one campsite for canoes and kayaks on the Lake Superior canoe route is located on the shore. Because of the cascades and gorge, no park campsites are located right on the river. An abundance of picnic sites are also available along the shore.

About ten miles north of the park is a small national forest campground on the river, which is also very small at this point. It's fairly remote and unused, a good get-away-from-it-all retreat. Some good brook trout fishing here; try it.

Hiking trails are plentiful in the Cascade Park. A network of many miles extends inland to the north, as well as along the shore leading to other, small streams. The major trail along the river, however, extends for several miles upstream, above the gorge, as part of the Superior Hiking Trail. It winds along the river, past more falls and rushing rapids, some of the most spectacular river scenes available by hiking trail in the North Shore region. Vegetation along upper reaches includes some outstanding examples of old growth white cedar, rare in these days after great changes. Upper rapids of the Cascade are also accessible from the Pike Lake Road about two miles north of the state park.

An out-of-the-way-"hidden" waterfall on the Cascade River.
Take a two-rut road up above Cascade River State Park. Hint:
the deep pool at the bottom of the falls no doubt holds some big trout.

History buffs will be interested in the early development of the Civilian Conservation Corps (CCC) camp at the river in 1934. CCC crews constructed the campgrounds, some trails, and the historic Highway Overlook Wall of native lava stone. The CCC work led to the Cascade River Wayside in the mid-1930s, precursor to the state park of today, established in the 1950s.

The Cascade's estuary is short, and consequently the river available to upstream migrating trout and salmon—and to anglers who seek them—is limited. However, stream accesses farther upstream provide fishing for brook trout, and fishing from Lake Superior's shore can sometimes be very good for all trout and salmon species and are available along the many miles of park shoreline. Early spring and late fall are most productive. But check your regulations.

From the lower cascades and gorge, the river's name origin is obvious.

See also: www.dnr.state.mn.us/state_parks/cascade_river.

*   *   *

THE HISTORIC GUNFLINT TRAIL winds north from the town of Grand Marais for many miles through the Superior National Forest, leading to many lakes and the Boundary Waters Canoe Area Wilderness (BWCAW). But it also crosses many small streams. A maze of national forest roads intersects the Gunflint and leads to more small streams.

No major rivers here, but these little watercourses often provide some fishing for the beautiful brook trout. They are small but lovely to look at, in some places abundant, and delicious for breakfast or dinner—especially in a cast iron frying pan over a little campfire.

Hint: carry a pocket thermometer and check the temperature of the water; if it's between 50 and 60 degrees on a hot day, you're in luck. Break out your tackle.

*   *   *

THE DEVIL TRACK RIVER IS ONE OF THE MOST unusual streams on the North Shore. It heads up in Devil Track Lake, which provides good stability to the river. From the lake outlet downstream it seems to be a slow, meandering stream going nowhere, but soon it drops down from its high elevation through a spectacular, narrow canyon, bordered by high cliffs of a type of lava rock that break off in vertical plates. These broken plates make up most of the river bottoms in riffles and rapids.

From State Highway 61, the hiker on foot attempting to walk and wade upstream through this canyon will find the way blocked by high waterfalls and deep pools, with no way around them. But these falls are some of the most spectacular on the shore. This lower reach of the Devil Track is private property, and legal access can only be obtained directly from the highway right-of-way. Some alternative upstream accesses can be reached from county roads by a hike downstream for viewing from above. Rock-climbing is another alternative, but only for the expert. Finally, try winter, when hiking with snowshoes upstream on the snow and ice is sometimes possible. Other streams in the same area have similar narrow gorges.

Fortunately, the lowermost high falls is over a mile upstream from the river mouth in Lake Superior, so that this reach of stream is readily available to migrating steelhead on their spawning run—and also to anglers in pursuit of this splendid fish. The Devil Track is one of the most productive in natural reproduction; in summer the river is replete with young rainbows. Regulations prohibit taking these young steelheads from their juvenile stream. The lower, at reaches of the Devil Track include a Fish Sanctuary in which fishing is permitted only during specified times; again, check your regulations.

Brook trout are present throughout the river, though in low abundance. But headwater tributaries, especially Swamp River above its entrance into Devil Track Lake, provide the best fishing for this beautiful trout. Stream fishing is accessible above the gorge from the Gunflint Trail crossing.

Kadunce Creek, along with many other streams nearby,
can only be visited by traversing the frozen rivers in winter.

No campgrounds or hiking trails are present on the river, but an excellent Superior National Forest campground is located on Devil Track Lake, providing nearby camping in the upper river area.

This mystery name suggests something supernatural, from the Ojibwe meaning spirit-that-walks-on-ice.

Moccasin tracks on the frozen river?

*   *   *

BETWEEN THE DEVIL TRACK AND THE BRULE RIVERS you can find Kadunce Creek, a small stream with some of the same characteristics as the larger rivers. Like all streams emptying into Minnesota's North Shore, the Kadunce tumbles down from the high moraines, creating some narrow canyons and deep pools at the bottom, which then serve as obstacles in the steelhead's spawning run. The fish congregate in these pools—which then makes good fishing!

*   *   *

THE BRULE RIVER IN MINNESOTA is sometimes confused with the Bois Brule in Wisconsin. So, in some localities, the Minnesota Brule is called the Arrowhead River, but mostly it's still the Brule here. It's one of the most fascinating streams on the North Shore with violent rapids, waterfalls, and one spot where half the river falls into a hole in the ground—and disappears!

Breining includes the Brule in *Paddling Minnesota*, but warns us that it is strictly for the expert, using such words as *screamer* and *fatal* (referring to some particular rapids). (If I were you, I'd keep my feet on solid ground and enjoy the scenery.)

The lower seven miles of the Brule is included in Judge C.R. Magney State Park, not a large park, but among the top few for its breathtaking riverscapes. The park is the location of a depression-era state work camp in the 1930s, and remnants of concrete structures remain.

High wall on the Brule, common in this part of the North Shore.

A modest drive-in campground is located near the river below all the fury and noise, but a nearby trail takes you across a footbridge and up along the east side of the river for plenty of action. About a mile of hiking and climbing gets you up to what is termed the Devil's Kettle, where the river splits around a large block of rock and one half drops down into a kettle-hole into legendary no-one-knows-where. Of course, all that water must come back into the main stream below, but it doesn't seem to be mapped out. After viewing this aberration, turn around for a spectacular image of a deep, narrow canyon, much like those of the Temperance and Devil Track, only bigger. From the Devil's Kettle the Superior Hiking Trail continues on up the river for several miles to turn off and continue east.

From the campground and parking, other hiking trails take you up on the west side of the river to join with the Superior Hiking Trail coming in from the south and then farther upstream to magnificent views of the stream and valley.

Steelhead run in the spring and manage to ascend some of the seemingly impossible falls and rapids to upstream spawning sites, also up and into a small tributary, Gauthier Creek. (Angling regulations are restrictive in the Fish Sanctuary on Gauthier Creek; check your rule book carefully.) Steelheads make it farther up the Brule until stopped by the truly impossible High Falls, a little more than a mile above Superior.

The Brule's estuary is especially good for steelhead, open on the west side; land on the east side is private, so be respectful.

Upstream stretches of the Brule can be reached at a crossing by county road where brook trout inhabit these upper waters. Brule tributary Mons Creek and nearby Flute Reed River can also be sampled for brookies.

The name of the park honors Judge Clarence R. Magney, former Minnesota Supreme Court justice, who was instrumental in establishing many state parks, especially along the North Shore. The name of the river means fire or burning (French), possibly from an early forest fire in the region. Wisconsin's Bois Brule River is even closer to a forest fire, bois meaning wood or forest. (Note to anglers fishing the Bois Brule in Wisconsin: pronounce Bois as *Bwah*, not *Boys*. And if you want, pronounce Brule as *Broo-lay*. In French, this may have meant a *forest fire*.)

For more on the state park see: www.dnr.state.mn.us/state
_parks/judge_cr_magney.

*   *   *

UPSTREAM FROM THE MOUTH of the Pigeon River in Lake Superior, the lower twenty miles is a reach of tumultuous rapids, narrow canyons roaring with swift water, and one very high waterfall. Impassable to any watercraft, the 20-mile segment had long
been bypassed by the Ojibwe on a shorter footpath, nine miles
long, avoiding the winding course of river obstacles. Early French
explorers quickly adopted that. The nine-mile portage was difficult, but it made possible a water route to the interior of North
America and the great Northwest.

Today, we visitors may enjoy not only some magnificent
river views, but also make some of the most significant elements
of our country's history come alive.

Within the new Grand Portage State Park, a hiking trail
parallels the river leading to Big Falls, at 120 feet the highest on
the Minnesota North Shore. (Of course, it is shared with Canada,
on the other side.) Other hiking trails lead farther in the state
park for several miles, including up to the extraordinarily beautiful Middle Falls. (You can drive up to Middle Falls on the Canadian side for the best view, but now you'll need a passport.)

At the upper end of the nine-mile Grand Portage, a landing
on the river was called Fort Charlotte. Here trappers (called
Northmen) from the interior changed their loads of beaver pelts
from canoes to their backs. On foot, each Northman carried two
ninety-pound packs over the arduous nine-mile portage.

A short way upstream from Fort Charlotte, lovely Partridge
Falls tumbles down through thick woods, the last of the Pigeon's
major obstacles to entry into the interior of lakes and portages
now incorporated into the Boundary Waters Canoe Area Wilderness.

Big Falls on the Pigeon River.

The upper trails of the state park connect by primitive road to the Border Route Trail for hiking along some of the upper

Pigeon's headwater lakes. This trail leads into the Pigeon River State Forest and the boundary waters, arriving ultimately at the upper end of the Gunflint Trail.

As the border between Minnesota and Ontario, waters of the Pigeon River also serve for a long way as the international border between the United States and Canada. Although crossing through the Grand Portage Indian Reservation, the old trail, today as Grand Portage National Monument, memorializes this significant portion of American history. The setting of the border is a fascinating story, one of perilous adventure and international intrigue where furs from the Northwest wilderness were exchanged for axes, tea kettles, pots and pans, and beads and baubles once a year. For the voyageurs it was an annual time of revelry, for the traders it was the exchange for loads of beaver pelts that were destined for the hats of Europe. It was the route of the Pigeon River that made the fur trade possible.

Reconstructed Great Hall at the Grand Portage National Monument.

The name of the river derives from the Ojibwe, who, as might be expected, observed great numbers of wild pigeons in the area.

For more on the national monument: www.nps.gov/grpo. Also, jump ahead, if you wish, to further description of the voyageurs and their route through the boundary lakes in Chapter 20.

Almost all of the Upper Shore watersheds are included on the GRAND MARAIS PRIM map, with a tiny bit of the Cross River on the TWO HARBORS map.

*   *   *

IF THE NORTH SHORE IN MINNESOTA has sparked your adventurous spirit, someday spend some time on the Canadian part. It differs, first, in its much greater length, three to four times as long as Minnesota's part. It's also wilder, more spacious with sweeping views, the shore more diverse with bays, peninsulas, and islands, and some truly wilderness canoe and hiking routes. There are some huge wilderness parks and, of course, more spectacular waterfalls.

CONSERVATION NOTE
NUMBER 4

SEDIMENT REMOVAL

WHEN ALL OTHER PROCEDURES FAIL, and excess sediment remains in the stream, several other procedures can be tried for its removal.

First, check the input of sediment at its origin. If that has been stopped permanently, natural flow may remove accumulated sediment from the stream. (Take care of what happens to it downstream.)

For a selected reach of stream, the sand trap (described in the previous Conservation Note) may be used to prevent further deposition while allowing natural flow to remove the sediment in a selected reach downstream, periodically dredging out the reservoir.

Another possibility to remove sediment is to release the water from a reservoir to create a one-time pulse sufficient in quantity and force to flush the sediment downstream. Called a *flush-flow*, this procedure has been used in large rivers to remove accumulated sediment.

Various machines have been tested to suck up deposited sediment with some success, employed specifically to clean gravel beds used by spawning trout and salmon.

A new procedure making use of natural flow has had much better success with actual removal.

See: www.streamsidesystems.com.

(But always remember: The best solution to any sediment problem is to remove the upstream source.)

Part Two

THE
MISSISSIPPI

Father of Waters

THE RIVERS
OF MINNESOTA

Recreation · Conservation

INTRODUCTION TO PART TWO
THE MISSISSIPPI

THE MISSISSIPPI, RIVER OF LEGEND, provider for Native Americans, pathway for exploration of the continent's vast interior modern-day commerce that provides food for the world, gives us a treasure chest of outdoor adventure.

Native Americans in our Minnesota region had a name for it: Mee-zee-see-pee (among others). Southern tribes along this greatest of North American streams had similar variations, but they all meant the same—Father of Waters. Not the longest or largest river in the world, but by far the river and its watershed are the largest and most important in North America.

From upper trickles in the eastern Appalachian chain, to the north woods of Minnesota, to the high Rockies in the West, their waters mix near St. Louis, Missouri, to continue on downstream to join the warmth of the Gulf of Mexico.

It's always difficult to measure the length of a river, especially one that has been tampered with as much as the Mississippi. But the Minnesota Department of Natural Resources (DNR) gives us the figure of 680 miles, from Lake Itasca to the Iowa border, much of which we share with Wisconsin. That's probably the best number we have.

The Mississippi's watershed includes the major part of the United States. As guardians of the Mississippi's source in Minnesota's Lake Itasca, and all along its course south to the Iowa border, we hold a high responsibility for the quality and character of this Father of Waters.

*   *   *

THE UPPER MISSISSIPPI is much different now than in prehistory, or even in the days of Huckleberry Finn. Two centuries ago, the Mississippi's currents enabled timber cutting that almost brought about the extirpation of the upper Great Lakes' vast pine forests as those flowing waters floated down the forests' production. In so doing they also provided lumber to build some of the nation's major cities. The creation of the navigation system, today comprising twenty-nine locks and dams, brought about the most dramatic changes in the physical river, its biological character, and its recreational use by the public.

Towboats, with their massive engines, move thousands of barges each year filled with fuel, agricultural produce, and manufactured goods, constantly up and down the river (in Minnesota, only during ice-free seasons). The resulting river traffic creates huge disturbances of the river bottom and its surroundings. With this development, uses of the river for recreation changed, some good, some bad, some new for the Mississippi. But overall, recreation opportunity on the Mississippi increased greatly. The whole navigation system itself became an object of tourists' attraction with thousands of visits to the dams and locks per year.

The United States Army Corps of Engineers divides the river into three sections: the Headwaters, from Lake Itasca to the Twin Cities of Minneapolis and St. Paul; the Upper Mississippi, from St. Paul to St. Louis; and the Lower River, from St. Louis to the Gulf of Mexico. The navigation system is installed only in the Upper River where much of the drop in the river's elevation occurs. An outstanding book on the Upper River is *Immortal River:*

The Upper Mississippi in Ancient and Modern Times, by Calvin R. Fremling, of Winona State University, Minnesota.

Recreational pursuits are common in the Headwaters and the Upper River; the Lower River—broad, slow, and devoted to commercial use—is generally of lesser recreational interest.

In this book, we will be concerned with the Headwaters (entirely in Minnesota) and part of the Upper River (much of which we share with neighboring Wisconsin). For the mainstem of Mississippi, we make four separate chapters, including a chapter on streams in the metropolitan Twin Cities. Furthermore, because some of the Mississippi's tributaries are special rivers in their own right, offering outstanding recreational opportunities, we devote separate chapters to each of them.

*   *   *

THERE IS STILL MORE TO THE MISSISSIPPI basin in Minnesota. Two major rivers are tributary to Old Miss—the wild St. Croix and the muddy Minnesota. Both are vastly different than the old man Mississippi, and both have unique tributaries of their own, offering a huge variety of recreational opportunities. Both the St. Croix and the Minnesota have separate chapters, as do some of their own tributaries.

In the Headwaters section, the Pleistocene Epoch left nine large glacial lakes in Minnesota draining into the new Mississippi. Thousands of years later, after human occupation, steamboat navigation was developed on the Mississippi. But water levels in the Upper River (St. Paul to St. Louis) were found unreliable (as Mark Twain has amply pointed out), and it was felt that the northern lakes had the potential of storing water during spring runoff and releasing more during droughts, stabilizing levels way downstream, from St. Paul to St. Louis, as aids to navigation.

Dams were built at the outlet of six of the northern lakes in the early 1900s. For part of the year, lake levels were stabilized and thus were attractive for cottages and homes, which soon lined the shores. Later, public pressure to leave stable lake levels continuously became intense, and the navigation problems downstream were solved through other means. The large lakes and their dams remain, mainly under control of the Corps of Engineers, which also maintains public campgrounds near some of the lake outlets. These sites also provide access for the beginnings of canoe trips.

The St. Croix enters the Mississippi near the southern part of the metropolitan area, adding greatly to the Mississippi's flow. Rising in Wisconsin, the St. Croix soon becomes the border between the two states. Unique in the abundance of its recreational opportunities and its long course with little development, the St. Croix was incorporated into the initial national Wild and Scenic River System. This protected section is now heavily used for canoeing, fishing, and, in its lower section, boating. Also contributing to the recreation potential in the watershed are the St. Croix's tributaries, two of Minnesota's outstanding canoe and kayak streams, the Kettle and the Snake, entering the St. Croix on their way to the Mississippi. We devote another separate chapter for these two lovely rivers.

The Minnesota River, for which the state was named, was created more than 10,000 years ago as the outlet of Glacial Lake Agassiz, the world's largest known freshwater lake ever to have spread its wide waters in North American history. Two placid streams wend their way southward from the state's lake and moraine country, the Pomme de Terre and the Chippewa, joining the Minnesota from the north. And, from the southwestern plains flow four more tributaries to the Minnesota, draining some of the richest agricultural land in North America (and causing some problems), but unique with recreational opportunities in their own right—the Lac qui Parle, Redwood, Yellow Medicine, and Cottonwood Rivers. From Iowa enters the Blue Earth— some good canoeing here too.

In the Twin Cities we'll spend a chapter on a group of metropolitan streams that bring river access to many residents.

Then we take up that part of the Upper Mississippi from St. Paul to Iowa, including some real jewels of rivers and streams.

A few miles downstream from St. Paul lies a large body of water (25,000 acres) resembling a wide spot in the Mississippi River (Le Seuer and Todd counties) which of course it is. It was big enough to be called a lake, Lake Pepin, and flowing into it from the Wisconsin side was the large Chippewa River. At first we wondered why such a wide and deep water body (sixty feet deep) would form just right there. The answer was soon to be revealed.

As the glaciers melted about 10,000 years ago, a good-sized river formed in central Wisconsin and ran toward the Mississippi. Several counties through which this river ran had their main subsurface composed of an extremely sandy nature, so much so that the natural flow of this river carried with it a huge load of sand. Remember Aldo Leopold's *A Sand County Almanac*? Because the flow of the Mississippi was slower than that of the Chippewa's, the sand dropped out, eventually forming a dam of sorts in the Mississippi. Thus Lake Pepin was formed by the elevated water behind the dam. Accumulation of sand continues today, necessitating dredging operations and forming sand islands.

In southeastern Minnesota's part of the Driftless Area flow outstanding smallmouth bass and trout streams, unmatched anywhere in Minnesota for top-notch fishing. These take up two more separate chapters, one on the Whitewater River with its huge Wildlife Management Area, and one on the watershed of the Root River, with its plethora of lovely, highly productive trout and smallmouth streams.

*　　　　　*　　　　　*

WITH THE EXCEPTION OF THE STREAMS AND RIVERS in southeastern Minnesota, most of the streams in the greater Mississippi watershed are so-called "warmwater" streams, which means, among other things, that the fish species are going to be very different and in a much greater diversity. Those species in warmwater rivers considered sport fish (that is, more desirable by anglers) include typical river fishes such as northern pike, small-mouth bass, and catfish. Here and there, however, especially in dammed-up reservoirs, we find mainly lake-living fishes, such as walleyes, largemouth bass, and several species of panfish.

Of course, don't get the idea that fishing is the main recreation here. The Mississippi and its hundreds of tributaries offer unlimited other river-oriented types of recreation, such as canoeing and kayaking on the state's most exciting rivers, hiking and camping along rivers, and many activities that can be pursued through the beauty of changing seasons from the banks of our rivers. Most warmwater streams freeze over in winter and are the most striking in their dazzling coats of white.

State parks and recreation areas, historic sites, designated canoe and boating routes, campgrounds, and thousands of miles of hiking trails await exploration along the Mississippi and its tributary rivers. Some very large wildlife management areas and national wildlife refuges, open to hunting, are also open for many other recreational uses.

Take advantage of these opportunities. Savor them, big river and small. And, most of all, enjoy and protect.

*   *   *

TODAY OUR TREATMENT of the metropolitan Mississippi writes a new history. We have made great progress in appreciating and restoring riverfronts, creating aesthetic parks, and developing science and historical museums. Entertainment and elegant shopping facilities line the banks instead of the backsides of warehouses. We enjoy more boat and canoe accesses and holiday steamboat rides. Pollution is only partly but significantly cleaned up. And more attention is being paid by natural resource agencies to restoring damaged ecosystems, and to healthy fish populations and fish species that are threatened and needing of help. It's a new day on the metro Mississippi. Furthermore, the fishing's good.

And, as the mighty Miss leaves Lake Pepin on its long journey to the Gulf, we should not forget an example of one of the nation's greatest resources for river recreation, the Upper Mississippi River National Wildlife and Fish Refuge. In Minnesota, the refuge runs eighty-five miles from Lake Pepin to the Iowa border. But its full length continues south of Minnesota, through parts of Iowa, Wisconsin, and Illinois for a grand total of 268 miles.

The refuge is rich in outdoor opportunity on the Mississippi corridor, with its backwaters, islands, oxbows, beaver ponds, and forested bottomlands open for camping, canoeing and boating, birding, and fishing and hunting.

*   *   *

RECREATIONAL OPPORTUNITIES ABOUND on Minnesota's portion of the Mississippi. We have divided this long stretch of river into many portions for description and discussion. In *Paddling Minnesota,* Greg Breining divides the river into nine sections; Lynne Smith Diebel divides her *Paddling Northern Minnesota* also into nine sections, a day's trip each, down to the city of Aitkin. *Paddling Southern Minnesota,* authored by Lynne and her river companion, husband, and photographer, offer us three daily sections—-through the Beaver Islands near St. Cloud and down for a day's trip; the metropolitan area; and part of the Mississippi River National Wildlife and Fish Refuge in the south. The state DNR's canoe guide number fourteen covers Itasca to Iowa. Both Breining and the Diebels pay special attention to the metropolitan section of the Mississippi.

To describe in detail the entire river from Lake Itasca to the Iowa border would take up the rest of this book, or an entire volume of hundreds of pages. In fact, hundreds of books have been published on the Mississippi River, as a whole or in part, most of these include the Minnesota portion. So, we will hit a few high points that just should not be missed.

These include: the unique, intimate headwater section from Lake Itasca to the city of Bemidji; the several state parks all along the main river; the two major tributaries, the St. Croix and

Minnesota; lesser tributaries Crow Wing, Snake and Kettle, Rum, Whitewater, and Root Rivers.

These are some of Minnesota's choicest: parts of the Mississippi chapters that are in the state's Wild and Scenic Rivers system; some special historic sites on rivers that preserve elements of Minnesota's past; the river as it courses through the Twin Cities with its several delightful small urban streams and the Mississippi National River and Recreation Area; the huge Whitewater Wildlife Management Area farther south; trout and smallmouth streams in the unglaciated Driftless Area; and the Upper Mississippi River National Wildlife and Fish Refuge. (We'll divulge a few secret fishing holes and some gems of little canoe streams.)

You can trace the Mississippi's route on the DNR's Public Recreation Information Maps (PRIM) all the way from Lake Itasca to Iowa. See PRIM maps LAKE ITASCA, BEMIDJI, GRAND RAPIDS, AITKIN, PINE RIVER, BRAINERD, SAINT CLOUD, LITCHFIELD, METRO NORTH, METRO SOUTH, ROCHESTER, and CALEDONIA, to the Iowa border.

As guardian of the true head of the nation's greatest and longest river, the state of Minnesota holds a huge responsibility for the river's quality and character. So far, we have stood up to that responsibility fairly well, but we must further ensure that when the Mississippi's waters leave our state, we have done all we can to maintain those qualities with a high level of stewardship.

Keep your craft, paddles, fishing tackle, and hunting and camping gear in good condition.

We'll see you on the water.

Chapter 5

MISSISSIPPI RIVER—
ITASCA TO BRAINERD

The Rivers:
Mississippi, Leech Lake River,
West Savanna, Pine

THE MISSISSIPPI RIVER IN MINNESOTA, all 680 miles of it and its uncounted tributaries, make up a treasure trove of outdoor recreation. Canoeing, fishing, hunting, biking, and camping, hiking trails galore, and all the other activities that we can enjoy in unspoiled natural environments—like birding, photography and painting, amateur nature study, admiring wild flowers—all are here along the big river in great profusion.

So, we break the Mississippi into four sectors—actually, four chapters. First, this Chapter 5 starts at the headwater Lake Itasca, and runs down to the city of Brainerd. Secondly, Chapter 6 continues on to the Twin Cities. Third, Chapter 7 covers the metropolitan Mississippi and other streams in the city area. And fourth, Chapter 8 takes us through the lower Mississippi and southern Minnesota into the Driftless Area, with its limestone bluff country and its myriad trout and smallmouth bass streams.

Of course, much of the lower part is shared with neighboring Wisconsin, but no matter, we're friendly. (Except maybe during football season.)

In this first section, three state parks grace the main river or its tributaries, as well as an untold number of county and city parks. Maps from the Department of Natural Resources (DNR) of the Mississippi's designated canoe route are wonderfully detailed. Furthermore, Greg Breining's *Paddling Minnesota*, Lynne Smith Diebel's *Paddling Northern Minnesota* and *Paddling Southern Minnesota* (by Lynne and Robert), and Mickey Johnson's *Flyfisher's Guide to Minnesota* are replete with tips on canoeing and fishing, and both are chock full of good information on other outdoor recreation along the Mississippi. Molly MacGregor's *Mississippi Headwaters Guide Book* gives us a greatly detailed trip from Lake Itasca over the river's first 400 miles, marvelously illustrated with detailed maps, many photographs, and beautiful wildlife paintings in color.

In chapters beyond these first four, we'll take up recreational possibilities along the two major tributaries of the Mississippi, the St. Croix and Minnesota, and some of their own tributaries.

Explore the whole of the Mississippi watershed, if you can. It would only take a couple hundred years or so.

*   *   *

FROM ITASCA, IN A LITTLE BIT of Clearwater County, the Mississippi winds through several more counties in north central Minnesota on its way to Brainerd: Beltrami, Cass, Itasca, Aitkin, and Crow Wing counties.

To many of us, this is the choicest part of the Mississippi River. From the little trickle that runs out of Lake Itasca to the midpoint of Minnesota, it grows from a creek to a real river. Here it's full of wonderful scenery, good fishing, miles upon miles of super canoeing, and lots of opportunity for observing wildlife.

*   *   *

THE ACTUAL BEGINNING OF THE MISSISSIPPI, like the start of almost any stream, is difficult to decide upon. For the Mississippi, it has been a matter of sometimes heated controversy, with the proposed initial point ranging from Lake Itasca to that lake's small tributaries, up farther to a couple of small lakes— to a raindrop falling from a pine needle somewhere farther back in the woods. In *Minn of the Mississippi* by Holling Clancy Holling, it makes a difference from which end of a crow sitting on top of the pine tree a rain drop falls to start a flow toward the Gulf of Mexico on the Atlantic Ocean.

The Mississippi River at the outlet of Lake Itasca. An artificial riffle of stones makes it easy for visitors to tell their friends: "I walked across the Mississippi!" A child opts for walking on a flat stream bottom, probably a good choice.

Most of us today, consider Lake Itasca and its immediate basin to be the functional beginning, the collection bowl whose waters make up the start of an actual stream. So the outlet of this lake, through a busy little rock-strewn riffle, is where we first call it the *Mississippi River*. From nearly fifteen hundred feet above the ocean, it runs 2,500 miles to the Gulf of Mexico.

To commemorate the site as the source of this greatest of North American rivers, Itasca State Park was established in 1891, the first and, now with a half-million visitors annually, one of the most popular in Minnesota. The focal point of the park is where the lake outlet flows through the small "rapids" formed of good-sized, flat stones. Here, many visitors enjoy walking across the mighty Mississippi. (It's said that rangers come out every Monday morning to rearrange the stones.)

In addition to the source of the Mississippi, Itasca State Park offers many more attractions. The entry road, lined with towering native red pine, first gives you an introduction to the historical significance of this park. Preachers Grove, a remnant, still standing, of the virgin pine is a stunning reminder of the vast forest that once covered this land. Three interpretive centers invite your visits.

Two huge campgrounds (over 200 sites) are available for drive-in camping year round; backpack and cart-in sites can be enjoyed for more privacy. A sixteen-mile, one-way circle drive through autumn-colored maple woods and many miles of hiking trail wind through the park. A seventeen-mile bike path around the park is outstanding, passing by record-high white and red pines, historic sites, and a profusion of spring wild flowers. You can even take a yacht cruise around Lake Itasca. (The fishing's good, too.)

If you need indoor accommodations, historic Douglas Lodge offers rustic single rooms, spacious suites, and a luxurious dining room lined with windows to keep you conscious of the splendors outside. Or you can choose among an assortment of rustic or housekeeping cabins and a remote cabin on Ozawindib Lake (named after the Ojibwe Indian who guided Henry Rowe Schoolcraft to the river's source), a mile or so from the rest. Take your choice.

As an educator, I must make mention of the University of Minnesota's summer forestry and biological station in the park, in which many forestry, fisheries, wildlife, and ecology students learn in the field the basic principles of outdoor science and management. Located on the transition zone between eastern woodlands and western prairie, and their waters and wetlands, these programs provide a practical, hands-on introduction to the major natural resources of Minnesota.

*   *   *

FROM ITS ROCKY OUTLET of Lake Itasca, the infant Mississippi flows north for a ways as a small, mostly wooded stream for about sixty miles to the city of Bemidji. Some canoeists start right at Lake Itasca's outlet, but shallow water would make a canoe beginning much better a couple of miles farther downstream.

This trip is a fascinating, intimate canoe journey. Molly MacGregor's *Mississippi Headwaters Guide* describes this section wonderfully. Numerous accesses and canoe campsites are scattered along the way, with some short portages around beaver dams and one old logging dam, as well as marshes that may tax your sense of direction. However, the marshes are great for birding.

*   *   *

IF YOU OPT FOR CANOEING these first 350 miles to Brainerd, you will of course want to break them up. This trip will take you many days and nights. Maybe several annual vacations.

The river is greatly diverse, generally flat but with good currents, some big lakes, a number of small ones, some dams, many landings and campsites for short trips. Three main canoe guides are available to you: Greg Breining's *Paddling Minnesota*, Lynne Smith Diebel's *Paddling Northern Minnesota*, and the first four DNR river maps (of a total of fourteen for all of the Mississippi in Minnesota). They differ somewhat in detail, so you would profit from having all three for your planning. You will end up with a huge set of indelible memories, the intensity and loveliness of which on this great river you will never forget.

After you have treated yourself to the headwater reach below Lake Itasca, expect the river in its continuation northward to soon enter large Lake Bemidji, by way first of tiny Lake Irving, only 600 acres. So a canoe paddle across Lake Bemidji would entail a long canoe ride in big water to the river's exit. But Lake Bemidji State Park on the north end could very well interest you for a non-riverine diversion.

A young Mississippi River wanders through a marshy segment down from its origin in Lake Itasca, beginning a 2,500-mile journey to the Gulf of Mexico (660 in Minnesota).

Downstream from Bemidji, the Mississippi takes a big loop toward the south, to continue its wandering route toward the Gulf. For the rest of the Mississippi's journey to the city of Brainerd, you will find a tremendous diversity. Plan on experiencing as much of the following as you can.

You may wish to avoid the big lakes altogether, as Diebel describes her route, but they tell a fascinating story about the

Minnesota's Mississippi River history. In the past, these lakes served to stabilize water levels for navigation downstream from the Twin Cities, controlled by federal dams that now benefit recreational interests on the lakes. The Army Corps of Engineers maintains recreation areas at the outlets of the lakes, below which canoe landings provide put-in access to the Mississippi and several of its tributaries. These include large picnic and camping areas below the dam on Lake Winnibigoshish (Winni to most of its users); below huge Leech Lake below the Federal Dam on Leech Lake River; on the Mississippi below the dam backing up Pokegama Lake, near Grand Rapids; on Big Sandy Lake, near the dam on Sandy River, tributary to the Mississippi; on Cross Lake near the dam on the Pine River, near the village of Cross Lake; at the dam on Gull Lake, backing up Gull River, a tributary to the Crow Wing River near its mouth in the Mississippi. Below the last of the big lakes the Mississippi regains its character as a genuine river.

From a large bay on the east side of Leech Lake, the Boy River runs about twenty-five miles designated as a National Canoe Route within the Chippewa National Forest. It's slow, shallow, and weedy, something different in the way of a canoe paddle.

Near Grand Rapids, don't miss Schoolcraft State Park on the river. It's relatively small as state parks go, but quiet and secluded on the river. Schoolcraft includes a lovely grove of native pines with Minnesota's oldest white pine at three hundred years. Drive-in camping, one separated canoe campsite, and a group camp are available. A two-mile trail winds through shaded pine forest. The park is open year-round. Fishing is reputed to be good, on the Mississippi.

Much of the Mississippi for the rest of its course to Brainerd is greatly meandering, replete with many oxbow lakes and marshes (great for birding). Some major tributaries enter here, including Leech Lake River. You can pass through the Mud Goose Wildlife Management Area (WMA). At 18,000 acres (28 square miles) it's one of Minnesota's largest WMAs. Located in

Hill River State Forest, it includes large areas of wetland managed mostly for waterfowl. Two campgrounds are included.

Just upstream a few miles from Aitkin the Rice River enters the Mississippi from the east. Farther east the Rice River flows down through part of the Rice Lake National Wildlife Refuge. The greater part of the refuge contains some of the best birding opportunity in Minnesota, mainly waterfowl and shorebirds. The river heads up in this lake, large and shallow, the centerpiece of the refuge with much wild rice and a favorite breeding and stopover for migrating waterfowl. Hunting opportunity in the refuge is open in selected areas for deer and small game, but not in Rice Lake. A bit of canoeing is available in the river, including fishing for northern pike and walleye, and fishing is also allowed in nearby Mandy Lake. The refuge also includes a smaller area near the town of Sandstone where hunting for deer and small game is also permitted. This Sandstone Unit includes a short reach of the Kettle River, tributary to the St. Croix.

The Pine River, through much of its length a small, intimate stream, is covered by Breining's *Paddling Minnesota* in two sections, as does also the DNR's designated canoe route maps, and Diebel's *Paddling Northern Minnesota* into three one-day sections, with more detail of the surroundings along the way. The Pine flows through the Whitefish Chain of Lakes—which will probably be avoided by river paddlers—Upper and Lower Whitefish and Cross lakes. The upper section of the Pine runs from Lake Hattie to Upper Whitefish Lake, a small, clear-running stream surrounded by dense hardwood forest, with only a few small rapids. It's a pleasant, secluded float of about fifteen miles; Greg Breining calls it an "unheralded gem."

*   *   *

PRIM maps start at Lake Itasca and follow the river down to Brainerd: LAKE ITASCA, BEMIDJI, GRAND RAPIDS, AITKIN, PINE RIVER, BRAINERD, SAINT CLOUD, and LITCHFIELD.

*   *   *

THE SMALLMOUTH, OR "SMALLIE" in the angler's lexicon, is reputed to be "ounce for ounce and inch for inch" the strongest, hardest-fighting of our freshwater fishes. Although this conclusion may be debated, there is no doubt that most anglers consider it the superior game fish species, especially on a fly rod (with apologies to devotees of the rainbow trout). The amazing strength of the smallie combined with its repeated aerial leaps, seems always incredible after the fish is brought to hand—it shrinks in size upon entering a landing net.

Throughout its major range, the smallmouth is king of Mississippi River fishing. Of course, other fishes are present in large sizes, and offer good sport and eating, such as northern pike (some very large), muskellunge (huge), walleyes, and others, and may compete with the smallmouth, but according to many anglers, never to equal. In his statewide *Flyfisher's Guide to Minnesota*, Mickey Johnson gives special advice and directions to canoe accesses, wading possibilities, and fishing methods for smallmouths throughout their range in the Mississippi. Tim Holschlag, warmwater fishing guru, pays great tribute to the smallie in his two books, *Stream Smallmouth Fishing* and *Smallmouth Fly Fishing,* and tells you how and where to catch them.

For screaming reels and aching arms, give the Mississippi a try for the smallmouth bass. This Itasca-to-Brainerd section of the river is particularly noted for it. They are abundant all the way to Brainerd, where we'll begin our next chapter.

CONSERVATION NOTE
NUMBER 5

STREAMBANK EROSION

THE ERODING STREAMBANK is probably the worst offender as a cause of sedimentation. Common in almost any creek or river, we're so used to them when we fish, paddle, or hike, we often pass one by—as just a normal part of the landscape.

Eroding banks are often small and not important. But many in concert can easily add tons of soil to our usually clear waters.

Such a streambank can appear perfectly natural. After all, that's the way a stream writhes back and forth across the valley floor. If you straighten a stream channel, it tends to meander back again.

The problem is that all too often human activity too close to the stream increases the degree of erosion or actually creates another eroding streambank. Major offenders include row crops, roads, lawns, and cows.

For restoration, first remove the cause. A steep bank should be sloped back in two steps. The lower slope holds minor spates. Major flooding will run over the second slope. A narrow terrace between the two will serve admirably as an angler's path. All surfaces should be treated with tough grass.

Make the job effective against high water, and at the same time make it look like nobody's done anything at all.

Chapter 6

MISSISSIPPI RIVER— BRAINERD TO TWIN CITIES

The Rivers:
Mississippi, Platte, Sauk, Elk & St. Francis, Crow

HERE THE MIGHTY MISSISSIPPI begins to earn its sobriquet—Old Man River. The stretch from Brainerd to St. Paul and Minneapolis is the part of this great river most familiar to us folks heading north on weekends to our lake or river cabins. Many bridges are crossed, probably with little thought to the discoveries awaiting beyond the visible river bends.

Diversity of stream and riparian area is high in this stretch from Brainerd to the Twin Cities, 135 miles, and many are the reasons to dally for some side explorations.

The diversity is partially treated by dividing the entire stretch into three major sections, as in the Department of Natural Resources (DNR) canoe guide and also by Greg Breining in his *Paddling Minnesota*. From Brainerd in Crow Wing County, the river comes down through Morrison County, then for quite a ways runs as the border between Stearns and Benton counties, then between Wright and Sherburne, and finally into Hennepin and Ramsey, the two major counties of the Twin Cities.

The Mississippi National River & Recreation Area winds its way through most of Minneapolis with its plethora of parks and other recreational sites. The Minnesota River includes the Minnesota Valley State Recreation Area and the Minnesota Valley National Wildlife Refuge and Recreation Area.

Several dams were built in the years before public concerns had developed over the impact that dams have on the ecology of rivers. We now bemoan the loss of rapids and falls that remain drowned beneath the impounded waters; early explorers waxed eloquent over their beauty.

Besides the Mississippi itself, several major tributaries contribute to the recreational resources in this section. The Crow Wing River, one of Minnesota's best, a designated canoe stream, enters the Mississippi ten miles south of Brainerd; the Platte, an excellent canoe stream by itself; the Sauk, a long stretch of mixed river and lakes; the Elk and its tributary the St. Francis, which flows through much of the Sherburne National Wildlife Refuge; the Crow River, the North Fork of which is a component of the Minnesota Wild and Scenic Rivers system; and the Rum, outlet of huge Mille Lacs, also a Wild and Scenic River with outstanding smallmouth bass fishing. See Chapter 8.

*   *   *

FROM BRAINERD, THE MISSISSIPPI no longer is a small, intimate stream, but wider, bounded by mixed forest and open prairie, and, for a ways, containing numerous small islands. Breining reports great fishing here.

Just ten miles downstream from Brainerd, Crow Wing State Park is located at the junction of the Crow Wing River on the east side of the Mississippi. The park includes four miles of the Mississippi. As the Crow Wing approaches the Mississippi, the river splits and surrounds the large Crow Wing Island; its shape resembles a bird wing, and thus the local Indians, much appreciative of the ubiquitous crow, considered the island to be in the shape of a *crow wing*. Crow Wing and Mississippi rivers are both open for canoeing, with quiet water on both sides of the "wing."

The park boasts about 60 drive-in campsites, one camper cabin, two picnic grounds, and boat and canoe ramps. It also offers many fascinating features for the outdoor enthusiast: fishing in the Mississippi, hiking along nearly twenty miles of scenic trails, including some along the big river, and some that give the hiker an important view of the woodland/prairie transition by winding through both types.

History buffs will be interested in the area, a past greatly significant in the settling of our western plains, as well as in the history of the state. The park commemorates the connection between the northern Red River settlements, which was made by Scots and Irish through Hudson Bay, and the Twin Cities area, settled by Scandinavian immigrants coming up the Mississippi.

This connection was made possible by the Red River oxcarts that traveled laboriously between the northern Red River and St. Paul. The carts were constructed with wooden wheels and bearings; they squealed, and it was said they could be heard miles away. At the Crow Wing junction, preparations for the carts' arrival could be made at leisure, for it would be a long time between hearing the squeals and their arrival. The carts carried furs and farm produce from the Red River settlements to St. Paul, and supplies back north. A reconstructed fur-trading post and other prominent sites are located in the park. Logging was another important economic industry, and the two rivers served as an important location for handling the big pine logs.

Not now do we hear the squeal of the oxcarts, nor the rumble of river log drives, but oxcart ruts still remain.

See: www.dnr.state.mn.us/state_parks/crow_wing.

For a fuller description of the Crow Wing River, see Chapter 7, next. It's special, and it deserves a separate chapter.

On the long float down the Mississippi, a variety of riverscapes
is always around the next bend. Autumn is best.

BELOW CROW WING STATE PARK the west bank of the Mississippi is occupied by Camp Ripley Military Reservation (keep
out!), although there is access on the east side called Fort Ripley
Landing, about midway. At the end of the reservation, Camp
Ripley Junction offers campsites and canoe access. The river then
leads into the city of Little Falls with its reservoir and hydroelectric power dam.

Practically in the city of Little Falls is Charles A. Lindbergh
State Park, on the west bank of the Mississippi. It commemorates
the home of former Congressman Charles A. Lindbergh, Sr., and
the boyhood of Charles A. Lindbergh, Jr., famed aviator who
made the first solo flight across the Atlantic in 1927. The old Red
River oxcart trail passed nearby, served by a trading post located
along the trail on the east side of the river.

The park offers much more than its historic significance.
Pike Creek (canoeable) wanders through the park for a couple of
miles to empty into the Mississippi, where a canoe access is

available on the river. A large campground offers ample drive-in camping, and hiking trails wind through the area of forest and prairie.

For more information, see: www.dnr.state.mn.us/state_parks/ charles_A_Lindbergh.

*   *   *

THE REACH DOWNSTREAM from Little Falls includes the cities of Sauk Rapids and St. Cloud, with dams at both cities. However, many canoe landings, riverside campsites, and county parks with river access are scattered along the river.

The stretch of river from St. Cloud to Anoka, fifty-eight miles, is a designated portion of the state's Wild and Scenic Rivers system. From St. Cloud to the town of Clearwater, about a quarter of the way to Anoka, or fifteen miles, the river is designated as "scenic" and from Clearwater to Anoka as "recreational." Initial designation was made in 1976, and further management is proposed.

Just below St. Cloud is an archipelago called the Beaver Islands, one of the more fascinating areas on the Mississippi. Intimate channels, backwaters, and beaver ponds offer canoeists an opportunity for exploration and a slow-paced, scenic break from the big river. Lynne and Robert Diebel in *Paddling Southern Minnesota* also wax eloquent about the Beaver Islands, and give more details. They last about two miles, giving a view of the Mississippi unlike the wide waters of most of the river in this area. No rapids here, but strong currents, they say. This recommended section is the Diebels' first trip of three on the Mississippi in their Southern book. After the Beaver Islands, it's a section categorized as "Scenic" in the National Wild and Scenic system. They describe more islands, various landmarks and alternate landings and finally the end of this segment at the mouth of the Clearwater River (Sherburne County).

The Diebels complete their treatment of the Mississippi with two more suggested trips, one in the Twin Cities urban area (our

Chapter 9), and the last one on downstream near the city of Winona (our Chapter 10). We'll see them again.

*   *   *

FISHING FOR THE THREE MAJOR PREDATORS, walleyes, small-mouth bass, and northern pike, is good in the river and in the reservoirs behind the dams. Some muskies are here too. Channel catfish, not present above St. Anthony Falls in pre-settlement times, have been introduced in the river above Minneapolis and are increasing in popularity. In his excellent *Flyfisher's Guide to Minnesota*, Mickey Johnson expounds effusively on the fishing in this portion of the Mississippi—all the way from St. Cloud to Anoka—with much counsel on fishing techniques and details of river access.

*   *   *

SOUTH OF LITTLE FALLS the Mississippi receives the Platte River, a small but interesting stream in its lower reaches. The Platte heads up in Platte Lake, southern Crow Wing County, and flows for some forty miles or more as a small creek through an agricultural area. Flowing through Rice Lake, however, the Platte is the centerpiece of the Crane Meadows National Wildlife Refuge, at 1,825 acres. The refuge embraces and protects much wetland and is rich with marshland wildlife, and yes, including large numbers of sandhill cranes.

After passing through Rice Lake, the Platte becomes canoe-able, with an access below the lake, at least in medium to high water. Below Rice Lake the stream wanders through the refuge, mostly marshy. Breining, in his *Paddling Minnesota*, recommends a put-in at a Royalton city park. In this lowest reach, especially in the last few miles, the Platte is larger and swifter. The Diebels in their *Paddling Southern Minnesota* also include this section of the Platte with more detailed treatment.

The Platte River also boasts excellent fishing. The fish fauna comprises the common game fish in the Mississippi, namely, smallmouth bass, northern pike, and walleye.

The Platte is a little used gem of a river, well worth a pleasant day's outing—and a valuable element of our state's rich river resources.

*   *   *

THE SAUK RIVER STARTS AS THE OUTLET of large Lake Osakis in southwestern Todd County and begins its long journey of 100 miles to the Mississippi. First it's a small creek that enters Sauk Lake, a narrow body of water about eight miles long, north to south. The river enters the lake at its northern end and exits from the southern end in the town of Sauk Centre. As a consequence of the impassable small stream above the lake and the eight miles of open water of the lake, the best start of a canoe trip is below the dam located at the lake's southern end. It is here that Breining's *Paddling Minnesota* begins a description of his suggested main canoe route.

Sauk Centre, by the way, was the community upon which Sinclair Lewis based his controversial book, *Main Street*, the population of which he characterized as small-minded hypocrites.

Sauk River, upstream from Guernsey Lake.

Below the dam at Sauk Centre the Sauk is a pleasant, calm canoe paddle. Through the upper part of this reach, to the town of Melrose, the Sauk passes through much low ground and marsh, including several Wildlife Management Areas (WMAs) open to public hunting. A high dam is located at Melrose, below which riverside scenery changes to higher ground that is forested along the banks. Overall, however, the Sauk flows in agricultural lands and, unfortunately, is badly polluted. Several organizations and agencies are addressing this problem.

Below the town of Richmond, the paddler is faced with a maze (literally) of clearwater lakes, called Chain of Lakes (just one of several such "chains" along rivers in Minnesota). Several public accesses are available among the lakes, as are some private resorts and campgrounds. The fishing's good, and you could spend many days in exploration—but the six to eight miles of still water straight through are not *river*. The chain ends at the town of Cold Spring and another dam. But from there to near St. Cloud, the Sauk picks up some speed. For the paddler, Breining suggests a take-out at Pine View Park in the town of Waite Park, a suburb of St. Cloud, avoiding the final run of rapids to Old Man River.

Overall, the Sauk would be one of Minnesota's choice recreational rivers—if only the pollution could be diminished or eliminated. As it is, body contact is not recommended. The landscape of the Sauk's watershed is almost all agricultural, including thousands of feedlots with their dense concentration of animals and the huge amounts of manure generated. Encouraging, however, is the list of organizations addressing the problem: the Sauk River Watershed District, Clearwater River Watershed District, Stearns County Environmental Services, Stearns County Soil and Water Conservation District, Minnesota Pollution Control Agency, Minnesota Erosion Control Association, and the cities of Eden Valley, Melrose, and Sauk Centre. Even so, much creativity to overcome political resistance will be required to reach a state of good stewardship.

*   *   *

SOME RIVER MILES NORTHWEST OF ANOKA, the Elk River enters the Mississippi. The Elk heads up in northern Benton County near the community of North Benton and flows as a small stream southward to Elk Lake in Sherburne County, from which its character as a real river begins. The best canoe trip, described by Breining in his *Paddling Minnesota,* is the lower reach of six miles. He describes the Elk here as a "quiet, woodland river," sliding past marshes and forested hills and bluffs, a pleasant day's float or fishing trip. In the clear water of the Elk, fishing is good.

A couple of miles north of Big Lake, the Elk's principal tributary, the St. Francis River, flows almost unobtrusively into the Elk, but enlarging the latter significantly. The St. Francis comes down from the Sherburne National Wildlife Refuge, one of the prime recreational and educational areas in Minnesota, much of it enjoyed from this little river.

Headwaters of the St. Francis River irrigate a wide,
spreading wetland in the Sherburne National Wildlife Refuge.

A treasure chest of recreational opportunities abounds in the refuge. The emphasis is on wildlife, and many options greet visitors. Past use of the land was in settlement and agriculture, and consequently much effort has been placed in restoring native habitats to their special diversity, including oak savanna and wetlands, along with some of the original hardwood forest termed the "Big Woods." With its location on the prairie and forest transition, wildlife habitats are greatly diverse, and a main objective of this refuge is to maintain that diversity. Each of these types was home to native animal species, including migratory birds that utilize the aquatic resources of the St. Francis River and associated wetlands. Specifically, emphasis is now placed on restoring that diversity and managing public use to maximize the best use of the resources to inform and educate visitors in the ecology of wildlife, all without disturbing the natural systems.

The St. Francis enters the refuge from the north near the border between Sherburne and Benton counties. After wandering throughout most of the refuge, through forest, prairie, and especially large wetlands, the river leaves the refuge near the town of Orrock. Several points provide access to the river for fishing and canoe landings; total river miles available for canoeing equal about eight or ten miles. However, in the refuge at least, the St. Francis is a small river, and canoeing would be possible only in the higher waters of spring.

Many species of warmwater fish occupy the waters of the St. Francis. The most notable sport species with widespread distribution is the northern pike. Several panfishes such as bluegills, yellow perch, and pumpkinseed sunfish, are common, but smallmouth bass, although present, are in low numbers. Most common are carp and many smaller fishes like darters and minnows. Best fishing for northern pike is in the early season.

A special Wildlife Drive of seven miles offers wildlife viewing of various habitats from your car. Two hiking trails of several miles each are established to offer scenic views as well as providing the visitor a more intimate experience with different types of vegetation and wildlife habitat. In addition, most of the rest of the refuge is open to hiking, skiing, and snowshoeing in fall and winter. As with all national refuges, no camping is available.

Some hunting is permitted in designated areas under state, federal, and special refuge regulations. Hunted species include white-tailed deer, most migratory birds, grouse and woodcock, and other small game, under limited regulations.

In all, 475 National Wildlife Refuges have been established throughout the United States, resulting from the efforts of President Theodore Roosevelt who initiated the system a hundred years ago. In total, these protect a huge resource for wildlife and their environments. But equally important are the refuges' objectives in acquainting all citizens with the need for protection of our remaining heritage in natural resources. The refuges are large enough to provide living space for the needs of certain species, and still offer healthy, informative opportunities for us to enter and view these environments, without disturbance to the birds and mammals living there. These intimate experiences can further our knowledge and understanding and, ultimately, a deeper sense of appreciation and stewardship.

Sand Dunes State Forest is located just to the south of the national refuge. This state forest is one of those that include many recreational facilities, although not much is associated with the St. Francis River. However, its proximity to the national wildlife refuge adds significantly to opportunities to enjoy the river.

The state forest is divided into two parts that we can call the northwest and southeast. The two almost touch, but in between is a small portion of the national refuge; also, the St. Francis River flows through this gap. A canoe access is located at this point, giving the paddler a put-in from which a float downriver is possible. About another fifteen miles of river brings you to the junction with the Elk. Good fishing, especially for smallmouth bass, in this stretch, and easy paddling.

For folks interested in a longer visit to the refuge, an ample campground and picnic area is available in the state forest, located in the northwest portion. Also here is the Uncas Dunes

Scientific and Natural Area (SNA) with good hiking trails all around it (a small portion of the SNA is also in the southeast part), and there are many miles of hiking trails throughout the forest in both parts.

Between the national refuge and the state forest, you can spend a whole vacation here and never run out of lots of ways to enjoy some of Minnesota's finest natural resources. (Just don't forget about the river.)

*   *   *

ONLY ABOUT FIVE MILES below the entrance of the Elk, the Crow River enters the Mississippi from the west. About twenty-five miles upstream from the mouth in the Mississippi, the Crow splits into the North Fork and the South Fork. These two branches share much in common, such as the level of flow and length of the streams, but the characters of the two streams differ greatly. Much more attention has been given to the North Fork.

For example, a large segment of it is included in Minnesota's Wild and Scenic River System; for another, it's included in the DNR list of designated canoeing rivers. Consequently, the North Fork is much more functional as a recreational river than the South.

The upper North Fork flows as a small stream, generally not canoeable, to enter large Lake Koronis near the town of Paynesville. From a dam at the lake outlet, the North Fork runs a hundred miles to the mouth of the South Fork, after which the main stem runs another twenty-five to its confluence with the Mississippi at Dayton, a total paddling distance of about 125 miles. Breining's *Paddling Minnesota*, the Diebels' *Paddling Southern Minnesota*, and the state designated canoe route map, together provide excellent and complete information to the prospective canoeist and kayaker.

Much of the North Fork, as well as the main stem below the junction with the South Fork, are muddy most of the time, with the products of agriculture, eroded silt and soil from cultivated fields. Although waters are clearer in upper sections, all parts of the Crow River system are coming under extreme pressure from expanding residential development extending westward from the Twin Cities. Wastewater from sewer systems and lawn fertilizers, although treated, still contain large quantities of organic matter and nutrients, consuming the dissolved oxygen upon which fish and other aquatic animals depend. The Minnesota Pollution Control Agency has placed all major portions of the Crow River system into an "impaired waters" classification. Stringent measures will be required to implement good conservation plans for continued development to improve and protect the Crow River's many potentially good qualities.

Apart from the river many Wildlife Management Areas open for hunting have been established throughout the watershed, for waterfowl and upland game.

Many choices for short day trips are available throughout the hundred-mile lower reach of the North Fork. An abundance of parks offers drive-in camping, canoe landings, and other recreational activities such as hiking and visiting historic sites. From the junction of the two forks to the Mississippi on the Crow's main stem, two associated parks in the Three Rivers Park Reserve system, Lake Rebecca and Crow-Hassan, are large and offer many recreational opportunities.

You can find the Mississippi River and its major tributaries from Brainerd down to Anoka in this chapter on the PRIM maps that generally follow the river: BRAINERD, LITCHFIELD, SAINT CLOUD, NORTH METRO, AND SOUTH METRO.

*   *   *

SOON AFTER THE MISSISSIPPI RIVER leaves Anoka it enters the slack water above Coon Rapids Dam; so we end this chapter at Anoka. After Chapters 7 and 8 on two of Minnesota's finest canoe streams—the Crow Wing and the Rum, we will move ahead to the Twin Cities' urban area that includes the junction of the Mississippi and Minnesota rivers in Chapter 9.

See you there!

CONSERVATION NOTE
NUMBER 6

FOREST MANAGEMENT

WITH 58 STATE FORESTS IN MINNESOTA comprising near five million acres (ten per cent of the state's total) it should not come as a surprise to anyone that we have an enormous land area open to the public for outdoor recreation.

Those five million acres contain or give access to most of our streams and rivers.

A hundred years ago, the main procedure in harvesting the great white pine forests of central Minnesota was "cut and run," leaving the land desolated. Furthermore, the massive river drives scoured the bottoms and riparian edges of rivers, destroying fish habitat and creating eroding banks that left huge deposits of sediment. The native grayling was extirpated.

With the environmental revolution of the 1970s and the shift toward forest recreation, harvesting practices improved. Clear-cutting was reduced or ceased; log-skidding operations were revised to prevent gullies. The old log drives are long over.

Much greater attention is paid to riparian zones on rivers, with setbacks and buffers. More procedures complement direct protection—such as wetlands care, better roads, and fewer trail crossings.

Today's forestry is a far cry from the old lumberjack days.

Chapter 7

CROW WING RIVER

With eleven numbered lakes making up the Crow Wing River's headwaters like a giant string of pearls, its geography must certainly be unique among the rivers of the world. One would think they would be numbered from the uppermost down, but no, the uppermost is the Eleventh Crow Wing Lake, and the First Crow Wing Lake is located about twenty-five miles downstream from the Eleventh, with the Second through the Tenth in between along the string. Probably the result of an early fur trader making his way upstream and counting his way up.

All eleven lakes lie in eastern Hubbard County, and most of the rest of the river flows southward through the length of Wadena County, while the remainder makes up the border between Cass and Todd counties and in its final run between Cass and Morrison, a total of 115 miles.

All eleven lakes and the river itself are unusually clear— not so in most waters these days. Consequently, the river is clear, too. Furthermore the lakes tend to hold back high water and provide water in drought. For these reasons, the Crow Wing's water levels remain remarkably stable.

*   *   *

THE CROW WING is one of the state's designated canoe routes, one of our very best. Although it is possible to navigate through all the lakes (with the possible exception of the Eleventh) and the short stretches of the river between, most river paddlers will probably opt for accessing the Crow Wing downstream somewhere.

The Crow Wing is one of Minnesota's premier streams for family paddling enjoyment. Essentially no rapids on this stream, but currents are moderately fast, so the forest scenery slips behind quickly. But near its confluence with the Mississippi the river becomes quieter and more lake-like.

The state's canoe guide includes all lakes in its map; but because most stream sections between lakes are short and provide little actual stream paddling, Breining, in his *Paddling Minnesota*, suggests putting in between the Seventh and Sixth or, preferably, below the First where the Crow Wing establishes its true riverine character. However, a short stretch of river is available just between the Fifth and Fourth, for a pleasant run of six miles. Diebel in her *Paddling Northern Minnesota* also recommends this reach, but taking out at a road landing after four miles.

Breining in his *Paddling Minnesota* breaks up the Crow Wing River into five sections. His last section, way downstream, runs mainly through the reservoirs behind two large dams, a final twenty miles. In between, the main Crow Wing flows for sixty-five miles, three sections in Breining's book, all river, and probably the most interesting for the paddler.

Diebel's treatment is much different, fewer lakes and shorter, but with more details on accesses and camping. Furthermore, each section is a day's trip. Diebel's suggested paddle totals about fifty miles, including the initial four miles of small stream paddling with plenty of camping possibilities along the way.

The state canoe map, covering all lakes and the entire river, is more detailed with accesses, campsites, roads, nearby lakes, and Wildlife Management Areas. Total length of 115 miles includes the section of rivers and lakes, about twenty-five miles, and then another ninety miles of lovely river. Take a week, camp out, do some fishing.

The upper half of the riverine ninety miles is wild, with little civilization visible. The banks are lined with a forest of jack pine, oaks, and other hardwoods. Many accesses and riverside campsites are available, so choices exist for shorter trips or for a variety of scenery. Not far below the lakes the Crow Wing courses through Huntersville State Forest in Wadena County that includes several campgrounds, with access.

Between the Second and First lakes, the large Crow Wing Chain Wildlife Management Area surrounds the three miles of river between these two lakes, where deer and grouse are the major hunted species. The wildlife area extends along the river for about five more miles below the First lake, within which is located Wadena County's Tree Farm Landing with canoe camping. Just below the wildlife area, the Crow Wing flows through parts of Huntersville State Forest, also open for hunting. A well-appointed Huntersville State Forest Campground offers both drive-in and walk-in camping. Many other canoe landings are located in the state forest, providing a choice of short trips.

Find the Crow Wing on PRIM maps PINE RIVER and BRAINERD.

The Crow Wing's name, like so many names in Minnesota, comes from the Native Americans, who saw an island in the river's mouth in the Mississippi as the wing of a raven, a larger cousin of the common crow. Raven Wing River wouldn't be a bad name, either.

*   *   *

SOME GOOD-SIZED TRIBUTARIES enter the Crow Wing. About a mile below the First lake, the Shell River enters from the west. A good part of the Shell offers some nice scenery and easy paddling. Two runs are possible: An upper, longer one from Lower Twin Lake runs to the Shell's mouth in the Crow Wing, for ten miles. The lower, shorter run runs four miles from the Shell City Campground to the Shell River's mouth. Diebel describes the ten-mile trip for a day, and gives good directions in her *Paddling Northern Minnesota* for the Shell River possibilities. The Shell is also included in the state's Department of Natural Resources (DNR) canoe map for the Crow Wing.

The name derives from the great abundance of large mussel shells readily visible on the stream bottom.

Farther up the Shell, the Fish Hook River enters as a tributary, and tributary to the Fish Hook is the Straight River, a trout stream with a great reputation for large brown trout, perhaps the best in the state.

The Straight lies in east-central Becker County, crossed by US Highway 71 where the Straight is not much for trout but holds large numbers of minnows, such as creek chubs and shiners. Upstream in the best trout water these minnows are still present and make good forage for the big browns. Incidentally, the large browns also feed recklessly on emerging *Hexagenia* mayflies in season (the "Hex hatch"). Besides that, the Straight is a lovely small river on which to spend an hour or so at dusk of a warm summer evening.

Farther upstream, the Straight exits Straight Lake to which a small trout stream is tributary, Straight Lake Creek, with those beautiful little brook trout.

The Straight River in Becker County.

Way downstream on the Crow Wing, the Gull River empties through the Sylvan Lake reservoir, the lowermost impoundment in the Crow Wing. But way up in the headwater region of the Gull River's watershed, a little trout stream, Stony Brook, runs into Upper Gull Lake. It's one of Mickey Johnson's favorite trout streams, and he includes a good description of it in his *Flyfisher's Guide to Minnesota*. It's noted for good-sized brook trout, and it's lovely.

*   *   *

TWO LARGE HYDROPOWER DAMS impede the Crow Wing's waters in the lower few miles above the river mouth. Most canoeists will probably take out at the landing in the town of Motley, avoiding the lower stretch with the two dams and large reservoirs.

Fishing is reported excellent in the chain of eleven lakes, but not so good in the river. However, northern pike are fairly abundant in the river, constituting the most prominent game species, especially in the Huntersville State Forest area. Walleye, rock bass, and smallmouth make up the rest of the sport fish species in the main river. However, as is usual in most warmwater streams, suckers and redhorse predominate in the fish fauna, and in their early life stages they provide the principal forage for the fish-eating northern pike and walleye.

For most of the river shallow water is the norm with few pools and depths rarely over three feet. Consequently, with such little cover, fish abundance is on the low side. Although invertebrate abundance on the river bottom is relatively low, the Crow Wing is rich with crayfish, good food for several species of fish, primarily the smallmouth bass and rock bass, best in the lower river below the dams. The Fifth Crow Wing Lake occasionally gives up some huge brown trout, apparently originating in some small tributary trout streams. The impoundments backed up by the two hydropower dams at the river's lower end support mainly lake species, such as largemouth bass, walleye, and panfish, reportedly with good angling success. Below the lowermost dam; however, a four-mile stretch of the river before it enters the Mississippi can be very good for smallmouth bass according to Mickey Johnson in his *Flyfisher's Guide to Minnesota.*

This section also sports an unusual mayfly emergence (or "hatch") in mid-summer—the "white fly"—when all fish go into a feeding frenzy. Almost all mayflies have a long immature stage under water and two short flying stages in air, but only in the second flying stage are they sexually mature. In the life cycle of the white fly, however, the female is mature in the first flying stage and the male in the second—a true oddity of nature. Of course, the fishing can be spectacular at such times.

*   *   *

THE CROW WING, with its eleven headwater lakes, all its special tributaries, its marvelous canoeing opportunities, and its fishing, offers some of the best recreational experience in the state of Minnesota.

Although much of the river and watershed is currently in public ownership, much is not. The river deserves complete protection, either in the state Wild and Scenic Rivers System or in some other kind of system that would guarantee the river's natural qualities untarnished and available for future river lovers. The Crow Wing truly is one of Minnesota's most treasured resources.

CONSERVATION NOTE
NUMBER 7

SPACE AND FOOD

THROUGHOUT THE HISTORY OF STREAM "IMPROVEMENT" in America many projects involved the installation of concrete blocks, sawn lumber, hog wire, sheet metal, and iron spikes. Some of it is still there.

All of it was for the purpose of adding more space for trout—bank covers and pools. The expectation, of course, was more trout. Did anyone consider that to grow more fish, more food had to be available?

The right habitat makes up what we call the "carrying capacity" for fish: the maximum fish population that a stream can sustain according to the limits of its space and food.

Some years ago I did a little personal study of the literature to see if production increased by adding structures.

Out of about a hundred reports on "stream improvement," I found only three cases. These were small, headwater streams with mostly riffles (with an abundance of invertebrates) and few pools. Adding space with more pools increased the carrying capacity because an abundance of food was already present.

Maybe it's my age, but I get as much pleasure out of wandering down a lovely trout stream as I do from the number of fish I catch. I love a stream free of the signs of human tampering, a stream pretty much how the glaciers left it and subsequent climate maintains it.

Chapter 8

THE RUM — SPIRIT RIVER

FROM AN AIRPLANE OR A WHIRLING SATELLITE the course of the Rum River will appear in a dogleg shape, or call it a zig-zag, with two "zigs" and a "zag."

Heading in huge Mille Lacs (or Mille Lacs Lake, if you pre-fer), in Mille Lacs County, the Rum zigs almost directly south, then zags to the northeast, and finally zigs back south again. The three sections differ from each other, which of course adds to the diversity of this splendid river. The diversity also offers us three different paddling experiences and good fishing-times-three.

From the shores of Mille Lacs, the river enters Mille Lacs Kathio State Park, a National Historic Landmark commemor-ating the history of Native American occupation and the early conflict between the resident Dakota (Sioux) and the more ag-gressive Ojibwe (Chippewa) in the mid-1700s. History buffs will enjoy this part of an always-fascinating Minnesota history, with many displays, artifacts, and stories from those early times. Park guests will find much to enjoy in the Visitor Center and in the Mille Lacs Indian Museum, this latter administered by the Minne-sota Historical Society.

In the uppermost stretch of river, the Rum flows through three small lakes, Ogechie, Shakopee, and Onamia. All three are reputed to offer good fishing. The principal target of lake anglers is the walleye, but largemouth bass, sunfishes, and yellow perch are present, too. Yellow perch are particularly abundant and delicious on the table. Two of these lakes, Ogechie and Shakopee, are located within the state park's borders, accessible by canoe from the park's landings. You could spend a pleasant few days here sampling the lakes' fishing, while camping at the state park.

Mille Lacs Kathio also offers abundant drive-in camping, some modern sites with all facilities, and others, more rustic that are shaded and secluded. A few walk-in sites are more private and wooded, for tents only. There are also a horse camp and two group campgrounds, one along the Rum; five camper cabins are available near the river below the Shakopee Lake outlet dam, by reservation. A total of thirty-five miles of hiking trails can take you through forest, to two lakes, to beaver ponds, and along the river.

For more information on Mille Lacs Kathio State Park, see: www.dnr.state.mn.us/state_parks/mille_lacs_kathio.

*   *   *

BELOW THE THREE LAKES, the Rum takes on its true riverine character. Continuing south in the first zig still in Mille Lacs County, the river then zags over east into Isanti County, and finally zigs back south through Anoka County to its mouth in the Mississippi. The first zig south follows closely the route of US 169 to the town of Princeton, about fifty miles. This portion of the river may appeal the most to river enthusiasts: it's small and intimate, with broken water and good currents, attractive fishing holes, and clear water.

But now the Rum makes an abrupt turn northeastward, for the zag of about forty miles, during which the river character changes dramatically. Currents are slower, meandering is constant, the surrounding forest is close on both sides, and trees and branches hover menacingly overhead and, often it seems, fall into the water. But this section has a character of wildness and solitude, leaving highways and civilization behind. And the fishing's good. Some call it the "jungle."

The Rum River in the "jungle" stretch, where the river slows down and angles back north.

The Rum changes again near the town of Cambridge. Here it continues its southward passage in the final zig, another fifty miles to the Mississippi. For about half of this portion the river picks up its current again, with broken water of small rapids, and some of the best fishing. From the town of St. Francis, however, the Rum is wider with open skies, the vistas broad, a scenic route. In this final stretch, the river meets civilization, with many accesses and many parks, all quiet water, more of an urban river.

Three Anoka County parks greet you in these last miles before the Rum meets the big river. These are the Rum River County parks, North, Central, and South. All three include park-type recreational facilities, picnic grounds, and canoe access to the river. Rum River North County Park is small, located at St. Francis. Rum River Central Regional Park, located in Andover, is much larger, has many more facilities, including camping and hiking trails, with several miles in the park's own land and access to many more miles of the Rum. Rum River South County Park is located in the city of Anoka, a small urban park. Access is available to the Rum, only a short distance above its junction with the Mississippi.

*   *   *

THE RUM IS ONE OF MINNESOTA'S favorite canoe streams, especially for families, beginners, and intermediate paddlers. The first eight miles upon exiting from Mille Lacs make up a lake-and-stream paddle, through the three lakes and intervening stream sections. There's a small dam at the lower end of each lake, each requiring a short portage.

Good fishing in the Rum River's "jungle" reach.

The state DNR canoe guide and Breining's *Paddling Minnesota* include the lakes segment and then start the main river canoe trip below the dam on Lake Onamia. Lynne and Robert Diebel in their *Paddling Southern Minnesota* also start the Rum River trip below Lake Onamia dam, dividing the rest into six segments, representing six daily trips. Their treatment is rich with many details—accesses and landings, campgrounds, rapids and riffles, obstacles, water levels, and many other directions and tips that will make your trip enjoyable. They warn intensely about the deadfalls and downed trees in the section we call here the zag (the "jungle"), oft times heavily blocked. The DNR map gives good details too, including additional features like the large nearby Mille Lacs Wildlife Management Area, the Rum River State Forest, and Sherburne National Wildlife Refuge.

There's only one rapids of significance, called Bradbury Rapids, Class II, about five miles below the Onamia dam, requiring some special caution. (If you want to avoid Bradbury, you can access the river about ten miles down at a landing and canoe campsite.) Canoeing through the rest of the river is relatively smooth with some Class I rapids, mostly in the upper zig sector.

After Bradbury Rapids, the trip proceeds through what will probably appeal to most canoeists, a distance of some forty-five miles to Princeton, where the river starts to zag to the east. This rather long stretch from Lake Onamia to Princeton requires either camping or breaking into shorter sections, easily done with the several accesses and campsites along the way, especially in Lynne and Robert Diebel's *Paddling Southern Minnesota*. Water is attractively very clear, the result of the big lake's source water. Dams at Milaca and Princeton require portaging. Whatever the choice, this section of the Rum is special, with scenery and good fishing, a diverse riverine topography with riffles and pools and lots of opportunity for stops, wetting your line, camping, and exploration.

The zag section beginning at Princeton is a totally different stream of about forty miles. Slow, meandering, and exceedingly green. You might think you're in the upper Amazon jungle. It's a fascinating piece of rare water, rich with fish habitat, and you could easily spend two or even three days on it. Just watch out for downed trees, or "sweepers"; you'll be able to get around most of them, but if a new one is really across the river, take care, and pull out and around. (As a state designated canoe stream, the DNR periodically removes anything dangerous, but there's always the chance that some new ones have fallen across.) The Diebels recommend skipping this section because of the likelihood of blockages and difficult portages.

At the end of this east-flowing section, the river makes another significant turn and heads south again in about five miles coming to the town of Cambridge.

The last zig, from Cambridge down, is about another forty miles. Something like the upper zig, the first twenty miles to the town of St. Francis, the river has a lot of broken water with small rapids, pools, riffles, and good fishing holes. You'll like it. From St. Francis down for a final twenty miles the Rum finally settles into a larger, slower, deeper river. Still, the scenery is great, even with more signs of civilization.

Because the Rum's water source is in Mille Lacs, the large lake acts as a buffer on the river's flow, and canoeists usually meet with reliable levels. There are lots of accesses, for picnics, fishing, camping, or just resting for a while.

For more information on the Rum's designated canoe route, see: www.dnr.state.mn.us/canoeing/rumriver.

*   *   *

THE RUM RIVER WAS ONE OF THE FIRST to be included in the state's Wild and Scenic Rivers system. This program was established by the Minnesota Legislature in 1978 to protect the natural and scenic values of the river, its adjacent lands, and selected tributaries. River sectors are classified in three categories: Wild, Scenic, and Recreational. The first of these, Wild, includes the more natural areas without the structures of civilization. The Scenic category may include some development, and the Recreational sectors may include even more. The Rum has some of all three.

The Wild category runs only along the two short stretches of river that connect the three lakes. The uppermost, about three miles between Lakes Ogechie and Shakopee, strangely, is rather highly developed with state park recreational facilities, including camp and picnic grounds and river access. The lower river sector, two miles between Shakopee Lake and Lake Onamia, remains untouched, aptly considered wild, and is well worth a pleasant hike on some of the park's foot trails.

Next is a sector classified as Recreational. From the outlet of Lake Onamia the river flows about twelve miles through about one-third of the upper zig, actually to the crossing of County Road 20. This sector includes the Bradbury Rapids. Then from County Road 20 to near Milaca, for about sixteen miles, the Rum is designated as Scenic, well deserved.

Below Milaca, the river is again designated as Recreational for the next twenty miles, to a bit north of Princeton. At this point, however, the river becomes Scenic once more. It begins to meander a lot and soon swings east to enter the zag and its dense, green jungle. On through the zag, down to Cambridge, and south through the lower zig for its last ninety miles it runs as Scenic— to its end in the city of Anoka, at the Rum River South County Park. Wild, Scenic, and Recreational indeed.

For more on the Rum as a Wild and Scenic river: www.dnr .state.mn.us/waters/watermgmt_section/wild _scenic/wsrivers.

*   *   *

THE RUM MUST BE RATED as one of the most productive smallmouth bass fishing rivers in Minnesota. Several reasons: It's a warmwater stream, and smallies like warm water, but not too warm; biologists classify it as a coolwater stream. The Rum has lots of good habitat with broken water and gravel/rock bottom substrate, and alternating pools-and-riffles. Not the least—and perhaps the greatest—factor is that the Rum is loaded with crayfish, the adult smallmouth's favorite and often only food.

In Tim Holschlag's fine book, *Smallmouth Fly Fishing*, he emphasizes a key factor: smallies (unlike trout) are on their best bite when the water temperature is highest, for example, in mid-day. With rod-bending runs and repeated leaps, they are regarded among the world's fightingest fish. It's amazing how much larger they seem when on the end of your line than when they lie quietly, and smaller in your landing net!

Northern pike and walleyes also make up part of the sport fish group, although less so than smallmouths. And, as is the case with all warmwater rivers, the Rum's fish fauna is dominated by several members of the bottom-feeding sucker family—in the Rum we have mostly the white sucker and four redhorse species, all in the sucker family. If you fish with bait, especially in the deeper, slow pools, you'll catch some suckers. A big redhorse will give you a fast, long run.

However, both of the zig sections of the Rum are excellent for smallmouth bass. These include the rocky stretch from Onamia down to Princeton and, secondly, from Cambridge through St. Francis and down. These two areas have gravel and rock bottoms. The east-flowing zag section, slow, deep, and overgrown, with soft bottom, holds the northern pike as the main predator fish. They leap too, a remarkable sport fish.

If you love to combine canoeing and fishing, don't pass up these diverse reaches of the Rum.

*   *   *

MANY HUNTING OPPORTUNITIES are offered in the Rum River region. Most prominent is the large Mille Lacs Wildlife Management Area (WMA). While the Rum River does not flow through this WMA, it's located nearby just to the east of Onamia and south. It is also just east of the river where Bradbury Brook enters the Rum, and is accessible by several county roads leading east from US 169. It is especially noted for grouse and woodcock hunting, but deer hunting is also popular. Mille Lacs WMA is a large area (39,000 acres, or 60 square miles), surrounded on all sides by many parking spots, leaving the interior open and wild with miles and miles of hunter trails.

Mille Lacs WMA offers opportunities not only for hunting but also for many other outdoor experiences. Solitude is the rule, for no motorized recreational vehicles, such as ATVs, are permitted in the wildlife area. The many miles of trails are open to public use for wildlife viewing, wonderful birding, photography and painting, wildflower appreciation in spring, and the splendor of autumn-colored woods—keeping in mind that hunting is the primary use in season. Even so, it's also a place to use your binoculars and just enjoy the natural environment of a misty morning, a sunny afternoon, or in the darkening mood of a summer evening.

Just south of the Mille Lacs WMA, the Rum River State Forest is also open to hunting. No camping here or any other developed recreation areas, but many snowmobile trails have been established, also open for hunting, hiking, and wildlife watching during snow-free seasons. The Rum River forest, however, is laced with ATV trails that can be avoided if you're careful. Nearby is the Sherburne National Wildlife Refuge, partially open for hunting; the St. Francis River runs through it (See Chapter 6).

More information and a map of the Mille Lacs WMA contact the DNR's Information Center at 651-296-6157, also for the excellent book, *Traveler's Guide to Wildlife in Minnesota*, by Carrol A, Henderson and ten others. It details Minnesota WMAs, Scientific and Natural Areas, park reserves, National Wildlife Refuges, and other areas pertinent to wildlife. Lots of maps and beautiful photos. You can order it from the Minnesota's Bookstore, at 660 Olive Street, phone 651-297-3000, or at any major bookstore. If you're interested in Minnesota's rich fauna of wildlife, as well as its rivers, this is your major reference. Try the PRIM maps MILLE LACS LAKE and MORA for the Rum.

*   *   *

DAKOTA INDIANS REGARDED MILLE LACS LAKE and the Rum River as having a Great Spirit. Their name was translated by white explorers to "rum," a common spirit of the day.

Or so the legend goes.

CONSERVATION NOTE
NUMBER 8

SPECIAL REGULATIONS

RESTRICTIONS ON THE TAKING OF FISH were among the first attempts at management for trout at least 75 years ago. The idea was to give the mature fish protection until they had spawned at least once.

Other regulations that kept the population at carrying capacity depended on progress in fish ecology, and that didn't come about until the 1960s.

More specific regulations for trout were proposed in the 1960s under Commissioner George Griffith, chairman of the former Michigan Conservation Commission (and founder of *Trout Unlimited*). Lowering the daily creel, raising minimum size limit, and others, including complete release of all fish caught, were just some.

In Michigan, the three trout research stations were ordered to experiment with some of the new proposed rules. As Biologist-in-Charge at the Pigeon River Trout Research Station, my assignment was to try two: a longer minimum length and a decreased daily creel. Neither seemed to have any effect.

Today, the catch-and-release regulation is widely employed where heavy use and the threat of overharvest exist.

One happy result is to allow winter trout fishing, strictly catch-and-release, of course.

Chapter 9

RIVERS IN YOUR BACKYARD

The Streams:
Mississippi, Minnesota, and St. Croix Rivers
Minnehaha and Rice Creeks
Vermillion River

RIVER RECREATION IN THE MIDDLE of our large cities and suburbs? But no, you don't have to drive long distances up north to a pine-covered wilderness.

This may seem oxymoronic. But just try the rivers and streams in the Twin Cities metro area! There are lots of them, rich with river recreation, and nearby.

A half-century ago, it was true that metropolitan reaches of our major rivers were bad. Many fish species were gone, the victims of toxic waste and low oxygen levels. The few caught by anglers smelled bad and were inedible.

But with the environmental movement that began in the 1970s conditions were changed for the better. Many fish are back and they taste good. Canoeing is refreshingly pleasant. And many people, city folks and suburbanites alike, are now taking advantage of this resource close to home.

We're concerned here with three major rivers—the Mississippi, Minnesota, and St. Croix, and some of their tributaries. All three of the major rivers now have their urban reaches designated in a national system protecting the river and at the same time providing huge resources for river recreation.

In the Mississippi region, with this greatest of all North American rivers, both the United States Fish and Wildlife Service (USFWS) and the Minnesota Department of Natural Resources (DNR) offer greatly increased public opportunities for river-based recreation in parks, and water access. The Minnesota now includes thousands of acres in a new metropolitan National Wildlife Refuge jointly administered by the USFWS and the Minnesota DNR. The lower St. Croix River, in the national Wild and Scenic Rivers System, attracts thousands of river users, even in more developed areas. Also part of the national Wild and Scenic Rivers System, the Mississippi enjoys both protection and open public access to a treasure chest of recreational opportunities in the Mississippi National River and Recreation Area.

Aside from these major rivers, small tributaries are getting more attention too. For example, we have more interest by canoeists and kayakers on Minnehaha Creek—places to paddle leisurely through residential areas and local parks, with plenty of accesses.

Minnehaha Creek is the outlet of Lake Minnetonka, a huge body of water with exceptionally complex shores surrounded by residential development. The creek begins below the small outlet dam, runs twenty-two miles, and drops over fifty-foot-high Minnehaha Falls, the object of Longfellow's long epic poem about a beautiful Indian maid.

A canoe or kayak paddle down Minnehaha Creek presents a sampling of the metropolitan landscape—a marsh and wetland to start, scattered homes and barns, a cluster of ordinary residences, elite homes approaching the style of mansions, and city bridges that roar overhead.

After a put-in below the dam, you drift slowly through a bird-filled marsh for a mile or two, and then through a long stretch of twenty miles with quick water, winding past some elegant homes and under many bridges, but also with many city parks along the way. There are rapids, yes, mostly small, which grow rapidly with high water. Minnehaha Falls ends the canoe course. Be sure to stop.

Lynne and Robert Diebel give us a much more detailed account of the paddle down Minnehaha Creek, including more on rapids and the creek's hundred bridges. They add a delightful sidebar about poet Longfellow's tale, a romance that bridged the Dakota and Ojibwe tribes.

From the Dakota, Minnehaha is "laughing water." They knew it well.

For more information, check the Minnehaha Creek Watershed District at www.minnehahacreek.org. The site includes current creek levels and flow rates for your guidance. In high water some spots can be dangerous. They publish a great map; ask for it at 952-471-0590.

                    *   *   *

THE VERMILLION RIVER, in southern St. Paul suburbia, offers two major segments with different recreational opportunities. One, an upper section now restored from a warm and muddy stream overwhelmed by agriculture, to a thriving trout stream cool and clear, with a growing self-sustaining brown trout fishery. Two, way downstream near its entry into the Mississippi, the Vermillion winds its way through river bottomlands, an exceptional wildlife area, open for hunting, that can be enjoyed with canoe or shotgun.

With recent land acquisition and financial grants, restoration work has resulted in an improved health of the upper stream and its productivity of trout and fish food organisms. A large volunteer effort by Trout Unlimited and other citizen organizations has contributed thousands of hours of manual labor, building fish cover, moving boulders, and planting native riparian vegetation. All are aimed to reduce flooding, to eliminate erosion of sediment from streambanks and cultivated fields, and to maintain the clear, cool water needed for trout and healthy river recreation.

This Vermillion River project is an outstanding example of modern environmental management, providing high quality river recreation in the middle of rapid development and a burgeoning residential population.

Downstream from the restored trout stream segment, the Vermillion drops a sheer twenty feet in a lovely waterfall. Located in the city of Hastings in a nicely developed park, the falls marks the change from upper agricultural plains to the bottomlands of the Mississippi Valley.

The Vermillion River (Dakota County). Not yet a crystal spring for brook trout, the Vermillion is in remarkably better condition than it used to be, including some nice brown trout.

Below the falls, a first mile of drops and whitewater attracts kayakers, but then the Vermillion River settles into a quiet passage across a spreading floodplain of the Mississippi. Wooded, marshy, braided, and island-studded, the Vermillion also receives several large sloughs (tributary backwaters). In their *Paddling Southern Minnesota*, the Diebels describe a canoe route of about seven miles through this area, abundant with wildlife, where birding is the big draw.

Beyond, the Vermillion flows twelve miles along the large Gores Pool Wildlife Management Area (Dakota and Goodhue counties), tucked in between the Vermillion and the Mississippi—extremely popular with hunters and wildlife watchers.

The name of the Vermillion River is a translation of a word from the Dakota who used nearby deposits of the reddish iron oxide for coloring.

*   *   *

IN THE NORTHERN SUBURBS OF MINNEAPOLIS, Rice Creek heads in a large (2,600 acres) and delightful Rice Creek Chain of Lakes Regional Park. The creek flows through the lake chain, protected in the park: George Watch, Marshan, Rice, and Baldwin.

Most of the lakes and interconnecting streams are marshy, with little fishing, but with excellent habitat for wildlife observation.

An egret and blue heron in the background can scarcely be seen in this image of Rice Creek.

Many choices in trip time are available. From exploring a single lake or a day-long expedition through them all, or whatever you have time for in between, will give you a wonderful outdoor experience just on the very edge of our metropolitan area. And it's always easy to paddle back upstream.

Below the Chain of Lakes, Rice Creek assumes the character of a natural, unobstructed stream on its further journey to the Mississippi. On its way south, it courses through Long Lake Regional Park and then heads west toward the Mississippi. Rice

Creek West Regional Trail follows the stream closely from Long Lake to its mouth. Breining, in his *Paddling Minnesota,* details a short section of about seven miles in the lower part, from US Highway 10, through Long Lake and on west to the Mississippi. The Diebels, in *Paddling Southern Minnesota,* include approximately the same stretch, also ending near the Mississippi.

Much of Rice Creek was ditched and straightened in the 1930s for flood control and wetland drainage for farming, not realizing at the time that such tampering only exacerbates erosion and flooding overall. A major project on Rice Creek recently restored the original channel for nearly a mile, changing the path of the stream back into its old meanders. Accumulated sediment in the old channels was removed, streambanks were sloped and modified to prevent future bank failure and erosion, and native grasses and shrubs were planted. A previously ditched wetland nearby was blocked and restored to its former water-retention capability. Eventually nature will take its course to reclaim the original appearance of the landscape of stream and riparian corridor, adding greatly to the watershed's recreational opportunity for hiking, paddling, and wildlife observation. The area will be managed in the Ramsey County Parks and Recreation system.

We must keep in mind that all streams, having developed alone for millennia, evolve natural meanders. This intrinsic system slows the current by allowing more water of precipitation to filter into the groundwater and maintaining good subsurface water levels instead of rushing it downstream to cause floods elsewhere. Furthermore, a straightened stream always tends to restore its natural meanders, eroding the banks and causing sedimentation and muddy water. We recently learned these principles, to our distress, in the Mississippi River floods a number of years ago, but the same principles apply to small streams too, like Rice Creek.

In spring, canoeing on this urban stream is an adventure, short but exciting. Paddlers will appreciate a more natural experience, and birders will see more birds!

The potential opportunities on Rice Creek are some of the closest and best in the Twin Cities metro area.

Like other Rice Creeks and Rice Lakes in Minnesota, the name probably comes from wild rice, much used by our Native Americans long ago.

*   *   *

MANY REGIONAL COUNTY PARKS have sprung up and grown in our urban area. Not all are on streams and rivers, of course, but many are. Regional parks are mostly large and offer all kinds of recreational facilities. However, the ones on rivers—some in the Three Rivers Park System (Hennepin County) and the Anoka County parks, as examples—boast many canoe landings, riverside trails, and campgrounds, rich resources for river-based recreation.

*   *   *

THE MISSISSIPPI RIVER, once exploited, degraded, polluted, and otherwise forgotten, has a new facelift. In the 1970s, the environmental decade, a new awareness arose to the latent aesthetic and recreational values of Old Man River. He is now ready to influence the quality of our lives.

Both citizen and official efforts for improving public recreation on the Mississippi have doubled and redoubled. National, state, and local governments, and many citizen environmental organizations have focused on this greatest of North American streams to recreate the natural value of its metropolitan river reaches.

The Mississippi National River and Recreation Area, a unit of the National Park Service, encompasses seventy miles of river. Through this distance—from the town of Ramsey in the northwest, southeastward through Minneapolis and St. Paul, to the mouth of the St. Croix River in the southeast—the Mississippi winds its way through and past scores of parks, waysides, historic sites, canoe and boat landings, playgrounds, picnic areas, and campgrounds, or sometimes just a picnic table here and there on a riverbank.

A towboat on the Mississippi with a load of barges. Actually, a towboat pushes its raft of barges, rather than towing or pulling them. Seems to be easier to manipulate.

Even a short list includes numerous major regional parks: Mississippi West Regional Park (near Dayton); Lake Rebecca Regional Park, Crow River (near Rockford); Coon Rapids Dam Regional Park (Coon Rapids); Anoka Riverfront Regional Park; North Mississippi Regional Park (Anoka County) and Central Mississippi Regional Park (Minneapolis); Mississippi Gorge Regional Park (between Minneapolis and St. Paul); Minnehaha Creek Regional Park and Minnehaha Falls (Minneapolis); and Battle Creek Regional Park (St. Paul). The Three Rivers Park District (formerly Hennepin County Park Reserve) includes Crow-Hassan Park Reserve and Lake Rebecca Park Reserve on the river. Others include Rice Creek Chain of Lakes Regional Park Reserve and Minnehaha Regional Trail. The Dakota County

Big Rivers Regional Trail takes you along a high hike with stunning views of the Mississippi and Minnesota River valleys.

If you should chance to paddle your way through the entire seventy miles, you would encounter the following: two locks and dams (and yes, you can "lock through" with a canoe) with public viewing areas; the mouths of the Crow, Rum, Minnesota, and St. Croix rivers; Fort Snelling State Park (DNR) and Historic Fort Snelling (Minnesota Historical Society); Grey Cloud Island; Historic Stone Arch Bridge; St. Anthony Falls; and a host of local parks. There are more for overnight camping, too.

For more, see: www.nps.gov/miss, or write to: MNRRA, 111 East Kellogg Blvd., Suite 105, St. Paul, MN 55101. Be sure to ask for a map!

Lock-and-dam on the Mississippi River. Downstream,
the river flows through the Upper Mississippi River
National Wildlife and Fish Refuge.

Whereas the Mississippi National River and Recreation Area is located administratively within the National Park Service, the State DNR also makes its own significant contributions. The

Minnesota Wild and Scenic Rivers System includes a long section of the river, from St. Cloud to Anoka, overlapping slightly with the national program. Down in the valley of the junction of the two rivers, the Mississippi and Minnesota, Fort Snelling State Park also makes important input to the area with its contribution of hiking, historic sites, and exploration. (Sorry, no camping here, a day-use park only.) The DNR's canoe maps, extremely useful, from Anoka to Fort Snelling to Hastings, add more stopover parks and canoe landings, as does Greg Breining's *Paddling Minnesota*.

The DNR booklet *Metro Area Rivers Guide* gives details of essential information about locking through the dams, navigational aids, regulations, and private dockings, and much more, particularly for the boater. All three major rivers are included. Available from the DNR Information Center, 651-296-6157.

A wonderful Mississippi River Visitor Center is located in the Science Museum of Minnesota, and nearby is the Headquarters of the National River and Recreation Area. For a full seventy-mile automobile ride, try the federally designated Great River Road, following closely the Mississippi River all the way.

Lynne and Robert Diebel, in *Paddling Southern Minnesota*, give us a short trip they call a fascinating perspective on the cities. It surely is. Starting at Boom Island Park (Plymouth Avenue Bridge) they take you through the St. Anthony Falls locks, past numerous metropolitan landmarks, high bridges overhead, surprising wooded bluffs and rocky outcrops, and past the mouth of Minnehaha Creek and its Hidden Falls Park. Finish up and take out at Fort Snelling State Park. This will give you an introduction to the urban Mississippi and whet your appetite for further explorations.

Love cities and the river? You could easily spend a summer-long vacation paddling, hiking, driving, camping, and exploring on the urban Mississippi.

Want to join others while enjoying, protecting, and learning about Old Man River in your neighborhood? Meet with the Friends of the Mississippi River and their many on-the-water activities. See www.fmr.org.

*   *   *

THE ST. CROIX RIVER, though a fair distance away from the Twin Cities, is still close enough to be considered part of the urban river recreation system. The character of the lower river lends itself to many day-use activities.

The St. Croix Boomsite Park, near Stillwater about twenty-five river miles above the river's mouth in the Mississippi, can be considered the start of most urban interest and activity. The stretch of river down from the Boomsite is essentially a long lake, Lake St. Croix, created long ago by a natural dam formed by sediment carried by the Mississippi and deposited at the mouth of the St. Croix. The Boomsite marks the spot on the river where, more than a century ago, logs floated down from northern forests, were collected in huge separated "booms" and sorted by log marks according to company ownership. For more information on the St, Croix River, see Chapter 13.

About nine miles upstream from the junction with the Mississippi is Afton State Park, relatively new. Although indeed on the river, Afton does not emphasize river use, but hiking trails offer the enjoyment of strolling through restored prairie and some of the most spectacular views of the sweeping St. Croix River valley. From towering river bluffs, steep ravines drop down to the river, through shaded, moist habitats.

Afton State Park is designed for quiet recreation. Twenty miles of trails wind through marvelously diverse environments, including the overlooks on the river, a small trout stream, shelters and rest areas. Summer biking and horse trails and winter skiing and snowshoeing offer visitors day-use pleasures at all times of the year.

There's no drive-in camping, but there are two dozen individual backpack campsites, one camper cabin, and one canoe campsite on the river. Two large group camps are included, one for tents and small trailers, vehicle accessible, and a separate one for tents only, carry-in.

For a quiet respite from the city only a few miles away, Afton State Park provides a magnificent experience of this nationally protected wild river, virtually in your backyard. For more information: www.dnr.state.mn.us_parks/afton.

One more major park, St. Croix Bluffs Regional Park, a large unit of the Washington County Parks Division, lies along the river shortly before it empties into the Mississippi. Along with all the amenities and facilities of a large state park, St. Croix Bluffs offers many hiking trails, including spectacular views of the river from high, wooded bluffs.

For the very last site on the St. Croix River, where it meets the Mississippi, find Point Douglas Park, a small site in the Washington County park system, where a long spit of sand projects eastward between the two rivers toward Wisconsin. Here you can see these two major rivers as they come together to mingle their respective waters for their continued journey south to the Gulf of Mexico and the Atlantic Ocean. On most days, you can watch the two streams of water, one muddy and the other clear, coming together but still retaining their own characters of difference for a ways farther downstream. This is a day-use park, offering picnic grounds and, in the St. Croix River, a fishing pier and swimming beach. Highway US10 continues across a bridge to Wisconsin.

*   *   *

IN TOTAL, THE SUM OF ALL—state and county—provides one of the richest recreational resources in the nation available to all in our metropolitan neighborhoods.

Of course, PRIM maps for METRO NORTH and METRO SOUTH cover the area.

Visit, use, and enjoy—and learn how to help protect these areas from inappropriate use and intrusions, as development increases and threatens the special rivers in our backyards.

CONSERVATION NOTE
NUMBER 9

STREAM "IMPROVEMENT"

MANAGEMENT PRACTICES that deal with fish habitat in streams have long been with us.

Such practice in American trout streams increased in the Great Depression days of make-work programs, notably the Civilian Conservation Corps (CCC).

Thousands of young men, unemployed, were put to work in forests across the country, including installing structures in trout streams and conducting creel censuses. (I remember one who, in army-type uniform and with clipboard and pencil, met me coming up from a Pine River pool with a small trout or two. I must have been about nine or ten. It may have been at that point when I had my first glimmer of what fisheries management was all about.)

Stream "improvement" in those days meant placing concrete blocks and sheet metal into streams for more pools.

Years later we learned more about the ecology of stream trout and their two major lifetime necessities. These two needs include *both* physical habitat, (the pools and cover for protection), and food to grow on, like aquatic insects.

This interrelationship between *space* and *food* will be the subject of our next Conservation Note.

Near Mankato, the small Minneopa Creek tumbles down to the Minnesota River. In its course the stream drops over two lovely waterfalls, located in Minneopa State Park.

Considered as the entrance to the North Shore, Gooseberry Falls State Park includes five named or numbered waterfalls. The first two are large and located just down from the highway, nearest to Lake Superior and almost out of sight, aptly called "Hidden Falls," pictured here.

The Lower Falls of the Snake in high water becomes a roaring cauldron of whitewater. Man and dog enjoy the sight and sound.

*Headwaters of Badger Creek, tiny here, are cold springwaters,
holding some small but lovely brook trout.*

After winding back and forth across the Minnesota-Iowa border, the Upper Iowa River flows south across the border and into some of the most spectacular riverscapes of towering limestone and sandstone cliffs, protected in Iowa's Natural Rivers System. A superbly scenic canoe trip.

In northern St. Louis County, the Vermilion River has it all. A huge lake for starters, lots of quiet river for good fishing, small rapids, larger rapids, one high falls, and death-defying as it enters the "Chasm", aptly named, just before it enters Crane Lake in the Boundary Waters.

Although small, the lower reach of Kadunce Creek receives good returns of adult steelhead, as well as providing an abundance of juveniles to Lake Superior, where they will grow and return later as adult spawners.

The St. Croix River was one of the original eight rivers to be named in the National Wild and Scenic River System, established in 1968. Nicknamed "instant wild rivers," eight streams across the country were designated to begin the system.

The Cedar River heads up in southern Minnesota, flows through the city of Austin, and later crosses the state border into Iowa. There it grows into one of Iowa's largest rivers, an excellent smallmouth bass stream.

The Zumbro River's streambanks are loaded with maples, so the river is a favorite for a family canoe outing in the fall. Watch out, though, for downed trees and other obstacles.

When the brown trout was introduced into American trout streams holding our native brook trout , some interbreeding was probably inevitable, because both species spawn in the fall at about the same time. The result was what we call "tiger trout."

Wayne Bartz

Minnesota is rich in river recreation, particularly trout and smallmouth bass fishing. More than a hundred designated trout streams grace the Driftless Area alone in the southeastern half-dozen counties. Some are so small you might have to crawl through tall grass; and for others, there is plenty of room for a long backcast. Don't forget to take old Rover along.

Chapter 10

DRIFTLESS AREA I

The Streams:
Mississippi, Cannon, Straight, & Zumbro Rivers, Hay Creek

WITH YOUR FIRST EXPERIENCE in the southeastern part of Minnesota, you might think you are in some southern state, and not in Minnesota at all. It's true in a sense; it *is* different. And it's full of marvelous recreational surprises.

The geological history of the watershed can be credited for this seeming anomaly. Hundreds of millions of years ago, a huge portion of what was later to be central North America lay under a salty sea. These waters contained large quantities of calcium carbonate, or lime. Under chemical and biological action, the lime precipitated out to fall to the ocean floor, later to be hardened into limestone. Other kinds of sedimentary rock, such as dolomite, sandstone, and shale were often included. Throughout much of the United States these sedimentary strata now exist beneath our feet as bedrock.

173

It so happened that a portion of this huge rock mass, now parts of Wisconsin, Minnesota, Iowa, and Illinois, became elevated into a plateau higher than surrounding regions. Not mountain-high, of course, but high enough that when the last of the Pleistocene glaciers came along a couple million years ago, the ice simply flowed around the plateau, leaving a large area recognized today as an unglaciated region of central North America. Consequently, the stones, gravel, sand, silt, and clay that glaciers usually dump upon the land when they melt—what geologists call *glacial drift*—do not occur in the unglaciated region, now known as the *Driftless Area.*

When the surrounding mile-high ice at last melted (only about ten to eight thousand years ago), huge volumes of meltwater flowed across the Driftless Area. Rushing down into the Mississippi Valley, the torrents eroded a host of ravines and streams that cut down through the limestone bedrock. The result was the creation of some of our most valued streams and rivers, tumbling down toward the big river in a profusion of deep, scenic valleys. Today, fed by many springs at the bottoms of limestone bluffs, emitting groundwaters remain relatively cool in summer, relatively warm in winter, favoring trout and smallmouth bass. And the chemicals dissolved from limestone bedrock greatly increase biological productivity.

Add the canoeing opportunities in these rushing waters, a summer climate more like that of the Ozark Mountains, camping and hiking in the blufflands and deep valleys and, of course, the Mississippi River with its diverse riparian areas available for fishing, hunting, floating, and exploring—and we have Minnesota's part of the Driftless Area, our heritage from the glaciers.

Approaching the Driftless Area, you will find the outlet of Lake Pepin. Lake Pepin, literally a wide spot in the Mississippi, was formed long ago when sediment, carried from central Wisconsin-land, was dumped in the river. The sandy sediment thus formed a dam, so to speak, in the big river and a huge lake formed behind it.

Today Lake Pepin is a very large fishing hole, for walleyes, of course.

*   *   *

MUCH OF SOUTHEASTERN MINNESOTA has been established as the Richard J. Dorer Memorial Hardwood State Forest, mostly in Goodhue, Wabasha, Olmsted, Winona, Fillmore, and Houston counties, north to south. Unlike other state forests, the Dorer Forest does not occur in a solid block; rather, it's a collection of stream valleys, often wooded and unsuitable for agriculture, that make up the state forest. Thus, many streams and their immediate riparian areas are protected for public use. Which is just fine for us, because these are the critical areas needing professional management and access for fishing, canoeing, and other recreational uses.

Richard J. Dorer was a wildlife supervisor in the old Department of Conservation (preceding today's Department of Natural Resources, DNR). Back in the 1930s, he looked ahead with great vision to the future of this area that had been damaged so severely. He worked diligently for the forest's establishment, and his name is worth remembering as we enjoy this beautiful area.

*   *   *

FROM ST. PAUL DOWNSTREAM TO ST. LOUIS, the big river is known in official circles as the Upper Mississippi. In the geologic past, the river below St. Louis was a huge embayment in the ocean, and now the Lower Mississippi is pretty quiet. But the Upper Mississippi was a stream of varied currents, tumbling rapids, a constantly weaving channel, oxbows and broad flood-plains, fallen trees, and snags. (Recall that Mark Twain and other river pilots always had a tough time navigating this stretch in their firewood-powered steamboats.)

The United States Army Corps of Engineers changed all that with their series of twenty-six locks and dams, starting back in the 1930s. Now the Upper Mississippi is a string of dams and impoundments, through which much of the nation's produce and fuel is barged easily up and down the river, even though having to contend with delays of the twenty-six locks. (See Calvin Fremling's definitive book, *Immortal River*, on the fascinating history of the Upper Mississippi, available everywhere.)

Nevertheless, the Mississippi still contains a huge playground of recreational opportunities. Through the 1920s and 1930s, after much urging by the Izaak Walton League and other conservation organizations, the federal government established the Upper Mississippi River National Wildlife and Fish Refuge, including the river and its floodplains. From about the city of Wabasha, Minnesota, and stretching for 268 miles along the river, the national refuge is open to the public as a huge resource of outdoor recreation. For canoeing and boating, camping on the many islands, fishing and hunting, the river and its riparian floodplains are available for exploration.

Mississippi River—island of dredge spoil, ideal for camping while doing some fishing.

The refuge, being as large as it was, needed some subdivisions for administration. It's now divided into four districts: Winona, Minnesota; La Crosse, Wisconsin; McGregor, Iowa; and Savanna, Illinois. Minnesota's portion: its own side of the river through the Winona and La Crosse districts, shared with Wisconsin on the other side, about ninety miles.

For more information on the refuge, see: www.fws.gov/midwest/uppermississippiriver. For more on the Army Corps's lock-and-dam system, see: www.mvr.usace.army.mil/Brochures/WhyAreLocksAndDamsImportantToYou.asp.

＊   ＊   ＊

IN PRE-SETTLEMENT DAYS, the streams tributary to the Mississippi in the Driftless Area contained large populations of native brook trout. Except for lake trout farther north, the brook trout was the only native member of the trout group in the region. Many are the recollections by early settlers of great quantities of these delicious fish, available for the dinner table. Not now, of course. All things change, and so have trout populations in the Driftless Area streams. A few populations of brook trout remain, mostly in remote valleys, in all probability still containing some of the genetic strain of the originals. Many years ago, stocking of brook trout from other parts of the country diluted the original strain.

Other changes took place too, the result of various fish management procedures. The one most profound in changing the trout resource was the introduction of brown trout in the late 1800s. The original idea was just to add a new feature to our fishing opportunities, and little did our fisheries folk know what a change that would make!

Brooks and browns both spawn in the fall and both eat about the same kind of foods, mostly aquatic insects and small crustaceans. Ecological conflicts were inevitable. But there the similarities stop. The brown turned out to be one tough custommer, tougher than the brookie, anyway.

The brown can stand slightly poorer conditions—a bit warmer water, siltier conditions, and not as dependent upon groundwater springs. Browns grow larger than brooks in small streams. The slightly poorer conditions that favor the brown also harbor more warmwater minnows, like the creek chub and shiners, good forage for the predacious brown. This food base often results in the brown's faster growth and larger sizes. It's also warier and usually more difficult to catch, so it survives better against heavy fishing pressure. (The brook trout is really pretty gullible.) And the larger brown can bully the smaller brook for prime locations for shelter, feeding, and spawning. Add to all that another factor only recently realized: the brown trout spawns a bit later in the fall (maybe only a few days), so it may superimpose its nest-building upon the brooks' and destroy their eggs. Tough.

Consequently, the brown has replaced the brook in much of the latter's suitable range, a fact bemoaned by admirers of North America's native brook trout.

There's another side, however. The greater survival of the brown means that it provides a huge recreational resource that is *self-sustaining*—reproduction is eminently successful. This factor assists greatly in maintaining a viable trout fishery, with bigger fish always possible, especially in Minnesota's Driftless Area.

Looking for a good trout stream? Minnesota's DNR publishes an excellent booklet, *Trout Angling Opportunities in Southern Minnesota*, detailing locations of nearly 150 streams, with maps, public accesses, and special regulations. Keep one handy in your trout vest. There are many hundreds of miles of excellent trout water in the Driftless Area. You can get a copy by calling the DNR Information Center at 651-296-6157.

Two major watersheds provide most of our trout waters: the Whitewater and the Root. These are described in more detail in the next two chapters. However, farther south along the Mississippi there are many more, including some that empty directly into the Mississippi. The following is just a sample:

Hay Creek, one of the most popular trout streams in Minnesota, empties into Old Miss near the city of Red Wing (Goodhue County). It heads up south of the city and flows northward, where excellent trout populations and its proximity to the Twin Cities make it especially attractive. Much of the stream is accessible through public easement. Special regulations are in force, so read the rules, some of which are aimed at increasing the size of the fish.

Located about halfway between Kellogg and Weaver, Snake Creek is a lovely little gem of a brook trout stream. The upper half flows through part of the Dorer State Forest where a great hiking trail winds its way. Wabasha County. (Actually, Hay Creek empties into the Zumbro, very near its own mouth in the Mississippi.)

Farther down, just a mile or so north of the mouth of the Whitewater, East Indian Creek joins the Mississippi through the Weaver Bottoms, a large, marshy floodplain along the big river. Much larger and longer than Snake Creek, almost the entire upper half of East Indian is bordered with public easement, about five or six miles. With both brown and brook trout, a joy to fish. Also Wabasha County.

Gilbert Creek, near Lake City, is known for both brook and brown trout. It is readily accessible from a county road that follows most of the stream. About a mile is bordered by public easement. Mostly in Wabasha County.

Garvin Brook heading above the town of Stockton flows north and joins Rolling Stone Creek (another trout stream) just before emptying into the Mississippi at the village of Minnesota City. The best part is upstream from Stockton, special regulations in force. Again, both brook and brown trout. Winona County.

Gilmore Creek, near Winona, perhaps the best of the small Mississippi tributaries, is a fascinating little stream tumbling down through a deep ravine with much pocket water. It's rich in brown trout. Winona County.

Down in the farthest southeast corner of Minnesota flows Crooked Creek, the largest and longest of the Mississippi direct trout tributaries. Along with a number of its own tributaries, including its South Fork, this watershed offers something between fifteen and twenty miles of trout water. This stream is one of only a few trout streams in the Driftless Area of Minnesota that receives some stocking of hatchery trout, including some rainbows. Houston County.

And there are many more.

*   *   *

STILL, TROUT ARE NOT the only prey for anglers, for the Driftless Area holds a wealth of excellent smallmouth streams. Mostly in the Cannon, Zumbro, and Root tributaries, the waters are a bit warmer than in trout streams, fishable by both canoe and wading. The North Branch is the most notable; some of the scenery in the deep valleys and below towering limestone bluffs is spectacular. And the fighting ability of the smallmouth is legendary. Good sources of excellent smallmouth information are Tim Holschlag's two fine books, *Smallmouth Fly Fishing* and *Stream Smallmouth Fishing*, available everywhere.

The Upper Mississippi River is famous for its fishing opportunities of all kinds. Angling in the main river, floodplain lakes, side channels, and beaver ponds requires experience and angling know-how, but experts find their special "honey holes" and so do very well, thank you. Among the sport fishes are smallmouth and largemouth bass, bluegills, and other sunfishes, crappies, walleye, northern pike, and channel catfish.

Backwater channel on the Mississippi.

But many other species occupy their particular habitats in this upper river: carp, buffalo fish, gar, American eels, paddlefish, drum, flathead catfish, and a host of small forage fishes that provide food for the large predators. Around two hundred species occupy the river and its associated waters, most you will never see.

The common carp, an exotic from central Europe and Asia, was first introduced into Minnesota in 1883 as a highly desirable fish. But it became so undesirable, widespread, and damaging to the habitat of other species that it has become known as a major mistake in the history of fisheries management. Some folks call it the "Rodney Dangerfield of fishes"—it gets no respect. On the other hand, the carp is greatly enjoyed by smoked fish gourmets. The paddlefish is a leftover from dinosaur days and is a threatened species; it has a huge mouth that looks dangerous, but it is vegetarian, and there are no teeth in it. The American eel, spawned in the Atlantic's Sargasso Sea (the Bermuda Triangle), migrates to the North American continent as tiny, glasslike larvae. Then, as adults, the females swim upstream to continue their growth in many inland rivers, including the Mississippi, later to drift back downstream again to meet their mates. The trip back to the Sargasso Sea to spawn completes the amazing round trip of four thousand miles across the open ocean.

The Upper Mississippi contains nutrient-rich water that has drained most of the United States. The resulting lush plankton and riparian vegetation feeds enormous invertebrate populations, in turn fed upon by a huge collection of fishes. The assortment of fishes occupies a great diversity of bottom types and underwater structure. All told, the Mississippi system was created over millions of years as one of the most productive ecosystems of the world. Tight lines.

*   *   *

MANY CANOE AND BOAT LANDINGS are located along the big river, although boats with reliable motors are preferred. (You may have to move quickly to avoid the towboats and barges that churn up and down the main channel—and are not maneuverable enough to avoid *you*!)

Canoeing the Mississippi is a far different experience from paddling a smaller stream leisurely down to a takeout landing. The river is big, variable in its unseen currents, and confusing in a maze of islands and braided channels.

Greg Breining, in his *Paddling Minnesota*, recommends making trips among the diverse backwaters, and then returning to your starting point. As examples, he suggests "the sloughs around Colvill Park downstream from Red Wing, the islands and sand spits between Wabasha and Weaver Bottoms, and the islands and back channels just upstream from Fountain City, Wisconsin."

Between Lock and Dams 5 and 5A, Lynne and Robert Diebel, in their *Paddling Southern Minnesota*, give us a brief view of the Driftless Area's Mississippi River, with its high rocky bluffs and wild, wooded shores. The current is negligible, because we're in Pool 5A, the impoundment above the lock and dam downstream. Then they guide us off the main river for a taste of the Upper Mississippi River National Wildlife and Fish Refuge where marked canoe routes lead through the fascinating sloughs and backwaters of the refuge, rich with bird life and good fishing. This is a marvelously complex system of back channels, islands, beaver dams, bottomland fields of aquatic plants, and both feathered and fur-bearing animals. Without a guide or the buoys marking the routes you'd be sure to get lost!

Available from the DNR Information Center, the *Mississippi River Guide: A Guide to boating on the Mississippi River between Hastings, Minnesota and the Iowa Border* is essential for motor boating. However, if you prefer your favorite Old Town, Grumman, or Kevlar, use the detailed canoeing guides from the DNR, printed in six separate maps, from Fort Snelling to the Iowa border. They are marvelously detailed with landings, parks, cities along the way, backwater lakes, islands and oxbows, and a host of other details you will want to know about. The Army Corps of Engineers also has detailed guides for boating the Upper Mississippi, especially for avoiding old rocky wing dams projecting out from the banks.

The river and its diverse habitats are also rich in bird life, both for waterfowl hunting and for the simple enjoyment in observation of water birds such as herons, pelicans, egrets, ospreys and eagles, and several species of shore birds.

You could spend years there.

*   *   *

HUNTING OPPORTUNITIES ABOUND in and along the Mississippi. The river's publicly owned wildlife areas are hunted mostly for waterfowl, since the watery floodplains are rich with the aquatic vegetation that sustains ducks and geese in their migrations. Many remote coves, sloughs, and beaver ponds remain isolated but beckon the adventurous who will seek them out. White-tailed deer are abundant in the bottomland forests and wetlands, some of them approach record size. Although almost the entire refuge is generally open for hunting, some sanctuaries are in place, to provide a few safe areas for migrating waterfowl in special locations.

Hunters can gain detailed information from the DNR's PRIM maps and their publication *Wildlife Lands, Southern Minnesota*. (Especially see WMAs in Fillmore, Goodhue, Houston, Olmsted, Wabasha, Waseca, and Winona counties.) The wonderful book, *Traveler's Guide to Wildlife in Minnesota*, also from the DNR, describes a bounty of special places, including WMAs (actually throughout Minnesota), recommended not only for hunting but also for the enjoyment of birding and other wildlife observation. The United States Fish and Wildlife Service makes available much information about the Upper Mississippi River National Wildlife and Fish Refuge.

See Chapter 11 on the Whitewater River and its associated Wildlife Management Area, coming up in the next chapter.

*   *   *

THE MISSISSIPPI'S TRIBUTARIES include some of the choicest recreational streams in the state. The number of fishing, canoeing and kayaking, and hiking/biking opportunities in the Driftless Area, in and along the rivers and valleys, are endless. All four major rivers—Cannon, Zumbro, Whitewater, and Root—are designated canoe streams that, with their high limestone bluffs and deep valleys include some of the state's most stunning scenery. Most streams hold good populations of brown trout, smallmouth bass, and other species, probably realized only fully when a biologist surveys their populations by electrofishing. Frequently, their tributaries also hold similar fish populations.

Watersheds of the four major rivers are greatly dissected. Aside from their broad similarities in topography of the land and chemistry of their waters, the local diversity is high. Each stream is unique.

Stream waters vary in temperature, which determines the fish species present. In uppermost reaches, small, cold headwaters may harbor brook trout exclusively. Middle reaches are a little warmer and larger with brown trout and a few more species such as certain minnows and suckers. A little warmer yet, often more turbid, are the smallmouth bass streams, with lots of other fishes like rock bass, minnows, and suckers. Finally, some typical warmwater streams hold typical warmwater species including carp, catfish, and freshwater drum. Some are quiet streams, maybe with a few little rapids. Cool trout streams often exhibit good pool-and-riffle topography, and some small trout streams are almost continuous, rippling riffles. However, you may find all types in a single river—-from headwater to the Mississippi.

We'll take up the four main rivers and their tributaries in some detail, north to south: Cannon, Zumbro, Whitewater, and Root. The Cannon and Zumbro have a few trout stream tributaries, but most waters in these two watersheds are warmer. Both offer excellent canoeing opportunities and some fine smallmouth bass fishing.

The Whitewater and Root watersheds offer mostly trout waters; we'll take up these in separate chapters. Both are known and loved by trout anglers throughout Minnesota. They are special.

*   *   *

THE CANNON RIVER, one of the first to be placed in Minnesota's Wild and Scenic Rivers System, is one of the premier canoe streams in Minnesota. Although the Cannon starts in agricultural counties of southern Minnesota, Le Sueur and Rice, in its lower reaches the bluffland scenery is superb, mostly in Goodhue County. (See PRIM map SOUTH METRO.)

Heading up in a series of lakes—impounded reservoirs, actually—the Cannon flows northeastward toward the Mississippi River. The river paddler is offered three major sections: a twenty-five mile stretch from the city of Faribault (below the upper lakes) to the upper reaches of Lake Byllesby (another reservoir) where you would probably want to take out; from below Byllesby and the city of Cannon Falls, another reach of twenty-five miles on the Cannon will take you to the Mississippi; and a third possibility is the tributary Straight River, which provides a canoeable reach of thirty miles northward to join the Cannon near Faribault.

*The Cannon River, a southern stream with good water,
some small rapids, and good fishing (although you never
know just what you will catch). It's lovely in its
early spring greenery, brilliant in the fall.*

The Cannon and Straight are included together in the DNR's designated canoe guide. Many details, such as dams and portages, several parks and canoe accesses, WMAs, and water level gauges are located along both streams. Some fine hiking trails are also located here, such as the Sakatah Singing Hills State Trail (along the upper lakes) and the marvelously scenic Cannon Valley Trail, Cannon Falls to the Mississippi.

Both Breining, in *Paddling Minnesota,* and the Diebels, in *Paddling Southern Minnesota,* offer excellent descriptions of the Cannon and Straight. Their first recommendation, from Faribault to Northfield, describes a pleasant float through hardwood forests that shield surrounding agricultural fields and wooded bluffs; this section goes through Rice County's Cannon River Wilderness Park, which includes trails and canoe campsites. The Diebels, however, warn of boulder fields in this park, impassable in low water.

Breining does not recommend a ten-mile stretch between Northfield and Lake Byllesby because of the dams, difficult access, and lack of canoe landings. The Diebels cover it, although not enthusiastically, quiet at first, then some exciting whitewater. The lower end leads into the Byllesby reservoir, which most of us would rather avoid.

The choicest section of the Cannon for paddlers, both agree, starts at the town of Cannon Falls, with a couple of choices for take-out. Access is good, and from Cannon Falls the river drops down through a deep Driftless Area valley, its most scenic section.

About thirteen miles down from Cannon Falls a small rapids now runs where an abandoned dam at Welch used to obstruct the stream. A private access and campground offers take-out access arranged ahead of time. The outfitter here puts in hundreds of tubers on a busy day, and you could take out your canoe or kayak here if you did not want to join the crowd. Besides, Diebel warns of many "strainers" (fallen limbs and branches) and some snags and deadfalls farther down. Take out on the Mississippi, landings either up or down.

The name of the Cannon River has nothing to do with Civil War artillery. French fur traders left their canoes for exploration at the mouth of the stream they called "Riviere aux Canots" ("River of Canoes"). As usual, we English speakers misunderstood the French, and "cannon" stuck.

The major tributary of the Cannon River is the Straight River in Rice County (not to be confused with the trout stream the

Straight River in Becker County, famous for its large brown trout, especially during its *Hexagenia* emergence.)

With a twisty channel course that swings back and forth—and here and there seems to double back on itself—the Straight is anything but "straight," and in some circles it is acknowledged as the main "Not-so-Straight River." Furthermore, labeling it as a tributary seems strange, as it's actually a bit larger than the Cannon.

The Straight runs about twenty-seven miles, flowing north first from Owatanna to Medford taking up eleven miles, and sixteen more to Faribault, where the Straight joins the Cannon. The river is full of sharp meanders, boulder fields, and small rapids that get larger with rising water. Both Breining and the Diebels warn of the difficulties upon higher levels after heavy rains.

In the first trip, about six miles into the beginning, Clinton Falls meets the river traveler with a steep drop on a sharp bend. The Diebels do not recommend this Day 1 trip except for the experienced canoeist, and the Diebels and Breining both strongly urge a portage for everybody. However there are plenty of landings and campsites for shorter floats.

Much of the Straight is small and intimate with tricky maneuvering required. The Diebels divide it into the two daily sections, eleven miles and sixteen miles, different from each other, although both have some rapids that could be dangerous in high water. Both Breining and the Diebels urge portaging around a twisting drop a few miles up from Owatonna called Clinton Falls.

Breining considers the Straight for *beginners*; the Deibels deliver some warnings and call it *exciting*. Of course, water levels make a difference.

Not much for fishing in the Straight, although past records indicate it was once a good smallmouth bass stream. Lots of carp now; maybe that's the reason. Anyway, you may have your hands busy with the paddle.

THE ZUMBRO RIVER has the reputation of having the most spectacular scenery in the Driftless Area. Limestone and sandstone cliffs over two hundred feet high seem to literally lean over the river, and some simply drop off right into the water.

The Zumbro's watershed is large, the largest in Minnesota's portion of the Driftless Area. It's also very complex. There's the South Fork, the Middle Fork, and the North Fork; the Middle Fork has both the North Branch and South Branch, and so on. The folks originally naming these streams, it seems, just ran out of imagination. So many tributaries come together in such diversity, you'll need a compass just to be sure you are still on the Zumbro.

Bear Creek, a small tributary of the Zumbro system located near Spring Valley. The ledges, as seen in this photo, provide good cover for smallmouth.

We will not deal with this complexity in details, because, although many stretches are sometimes canoeable and fishable, most upper reaches are small and navigable only in high water, some choked with downed trees and branches, some very slow and turbid, and not attractive for fishing or very productive of sport fish.

On the other hand, you will find some trout fishing on the Zumbro. On the North Fork, from the village of Forest Mills (southeast corner of Goodhue County) downstream about twelve miles, through the town of Mazeppa, to approximately the confluence with Mazeppa Creek, you must return all trout to the water—that is, practice catch-and-release fishing. By the way, Mazeppa Creek is a good trout stream, too.

However, for scenery and pleasant canoeing, and small-mouth fishing to boot, the main stem of the Zumbro is one of the many gems of the Driftless Area. While Breining's *Paddling Minnesota*, Diebels' *Paddling Southern Minnesota*, and the DNR's canoe maps all take you through some of the forks and branches, they give the best details of the main stem, all fifty miles of it, free of dams, most snags and deadfalls (and most signs of civilization), together with many accesses and ample campsites.

The Diebels divide their treatment into six daily trips and give you a wealth of information on the stream's character, its surroundings, and the many campsites and landings. The Diebels and Breining describe the North Fork and the South Fork which later come together to form the main stem. The South Fork runs through the city of Rochester and flows north. The Middle Fork is small until it picks up the North Branch of the Middle and later joins the South Fork. Confused?

All agree that the choice stretch is the Zumbro's main stem from Zumbro Falls (where the North and South forks meet) downstream to Millville for both canoeing and fishing, a reach of fifteen miles. Smallmouth bass are the main sport fish here with excellent rocky habitat and good pools. Access is good at both ends with a private campground at Zumbro Falls, canoe camping at Millville, and another canoe campsite in between.

The North Fork of the Zumbro, a trout stream,
runs through some wooded country.

Below Millville, the scenery of limestone bluffs continues—some of the best—but the fishing tapers off as the river broadens, shallows with sand bottom, and approaches the Mississippi through its bottomlands. The Diebels add a trip through the Zumbro bottoms prior to its entry into the Big River. This last includes an unusual campground on a hillside slope in the Kruger Recreation Area, honoring Willis Kruger who, with Richard Dorer, helped develop the memorial state forest now bearing Dorer's name. The Diebels also point out some use of the river for tubing and its banks for motorcycles, suggesting either spring or fall as the best times of the year. The main stem's dense hardwood forest is noted for its spectacular autumn colors, best in late autumn. See PRIM map ROCHESTER.

The naming of the Zumbro must be the most interesting in Minnesota. It comes from the French fur traders, as do many of Minnesota names. Their name was "Riviere des Embarras," meaning "river of embarrassments, or disappointments," that is, obstacles such as downed trees and snags. Their pronunciation sounded like "z" to the English, and somehow Zumbro emerged.

Stay tuned for the next two chapters on major trout streams of the Driftless Area, the Whitewater and the Root. Together, they mean *trout fishing* in Minnesota.

CONSERVATION NOTE
NUMBER 10

THE RIPARIAN ZONE

ALONG THE EDGES OF ALMOST ANY STREAM OR RIVER, the *riparian zone*— partly vegetated, usually moist and often flooded—was recognized only a few decades ago as a particularly valuable part of the stream ecosystem, a transition strip from land to water.

A protective shield to the stream, the riparian zone interdicts sediment, pesticides, and agricultural fertilizer, while natural vegetation reinforces the shield against the erosional forces of floodwaters.

Unrestricted access to cattle for drinking water is perhaps the most destructive of all. Effective techniques have been designed to give animals access without trampling the riparian zone, but they are too often ignored.

When we remove the natural vegetation to give us a clear view of a manicured lawn right down to the water's edge, we destroy the shield and allow access to poisons and sediment.

The riparian zone also collects leaf and woody debris that provide energy for bacteria and fungi, which in turn provide food for invertebrates.

When we restore an eroding bank, we should also revitalize that thin green line to its principal job of sustaining and protecting our streams and rivers. The stream ecosystem is not just that channel of water from streambank to streambank, but rather from ridgetop to ridgetop, that is, the whole watershed, including especially the riparian zone.

Chapter 11

DRIFTLESS AREA II

The Streams:
Whitewater River: Mainstem, North, South, and Middle Branches

A S YOU GET DOWN DEEPER into the Driftless Area, into the Whitewater and Root valleys, you'll be in some of the best trout fishing in the country. The Whitewater watershed is relatively small, most of it in Winona County. In contrast, that of the Root River is much larger, taking up all the southeastern corner of Minnesota.

In Whitewater, however, don't be fooled by the size of the watershed. It's the quality of the trout fishing opportunity that attracts more anglers than any other destination in the state, almost year-round. A major element in this popularity is that, today, the trout fishing is a center piece of the Whitewater Wildlife Management Area, a natural resource open to big and small game hunting, wildlife observation, hiking, birding, nut-, berry-, and morel-gathering—and stream fishing. All three main

branches of the Whitewater plus Beaver Creek are covered on the
PRIM map ROCHESTER.

*   *   *

HERE WE MUST DIGRESS A BIT to consider just how this huge area
came to be in the public domain, and why it remains open to
such high quality outdoor recreation.

A hundred years ago, the watershed boasted not only many
trout streams, but also the deep valleys bordered by wooded
hillsides and the towering limestone bluffs so characteristic of the
Driftless Area. In those days, the small floodplains, critical for
handling the high water of floods, remained undisturbed. It was
rugged country, but when earlier immigrants settled the area, they
found it productive. Fresh water suitable for their homes and
livestock was nearby, fertile soils mantled the floodplains, and
clear streams flowed abundant with brook trout. They cleared the
hillside forest for wood, grazed the barren slopes, and cultivated
the floodplains. The agrarian paradise was lost forever, it seemed.

In the 1930s came severe floods. Subsequent erosion took a
disastrous toll. Grazed hillsides turned into roaring gullies, and
the fertile soil of the floodplains, cultivated in rows that led toward the rivers, washed away downstream. Farms and whole villages were buried yards deep with silt and sand. The brook trout
were gone. The Whitewater watershed was turned into a wasteland sheared of its former productivity.

And then in strode Richard J. Dorer, with his dreams of the
future. As leader of the game division in the old Conservation
Department, his profession emphasized natural resources.

With his characteristic vision, he saw not a wasteland but a
restored paradise, vegetated hill slopes with new forests, floodplains with waving grasses and bottomland woodlands, rich
habitat for abundant wildlife of many species and, in place of
barren, muddy streams, the fresh, clear water that might again
hold trout. His efforts were diligent with the same verve and
dedication with which he created the future state forest today
holding his name in memory. Helping him now were modern

agriculturists, a cadre of wildlife and fisheries biologists, and all the resources of new conservation agencies. The once worthless land, having been reverted to public ownership, now in its new revival as the state-protected Whitewater Wildlife Management Area (WMA) stands open for all of us to enjoy.

At 28,000 acres (near forty-five square miles), Whitewater is among the largest WMAs in Minnesota. It's not a rectangular block, but like the state forest, these WMA lands follow the streams, including high limestone bluffs, surrounding bottomland forests, fertile floodplains, and hundreds of miles of clear-flowing streams. Three major tributaries (variously called branches or forks), Beaver Creek and a few smaller tributaries, and the main stem of the Whitewater River make up the river system.

The original designation as a wildlife area first emphasized hunting for small game such as ruffed grouse, fox squirrels, and cottontail rabbits; soon the big game was the white-tailed deer, now abundant.

About twenty years ago, following experimentation with different strains, the wild turkey was introduced into the Whitewater. It flourished, and today the population of turkeys has reached high levels. Turkey hunting throughout the Driftless Area now attracts more hunters than any other small-game species, even though current hunting regulations strictly limit numbers of hunters. It's hardly possible to drive through the WMA, or even go fishing, without seeing turkeys. This native bird of Minnesota now pleases not only hunters but also birders and other folks who just enjoy its simple observation, and take joy in knowing we have prevailed in saving a valuable natural resource. Furthermore, the turkey is slowly moving northward in its continuing increases in population and distribution, and may even someday announce its woodland presence through much of the state with its melodic gobble. It's a remarkable success story in wildlife management.

Trout fishing interest came slowly after restoration of the Whitewater watershed. First, the streams were heavily stocked with hatchery fish, but then we recognized that the newly acquired quality of the streams provided for successful natural reproduction, and stocking has been greatly reduced to favor wild fish. Later yet, wildlife observation and other outdoor pursuits gained in popularity. The state DNR holds many seminars and, especially, guided outdoor trips for a variety of outdoor experiences. The deer season in November now attracts many hunters, and some of those harvested are huge specimens. Ruffed grouse and now woodcock attract hunters in the early seasons, while squirrels and cottontails have a small, but dedicated following through fall and winter. And wildlife observation, birding, and hiking attract more and more persons who simply enjoy the expanse of varied habitats in those stream valleys for many kinds of outdoor recreation.

Of course, trout fishing is extremely popular in all the Whitewater branches. The brown trout-rich tributary, Beaver Creek, empties into the main stem, while tiny Trout Run Creek, cold, clear and alive with small brookies, after trickling over gravel riffles and pools, empties into the Middle Branch.

*   *   *

ALL MAJOR STREAMS IN THE DRIFTLESS AREA head up in the cultivated flatlands of south-central Minnesota, often turbid, over-fertilized, and warm. But flowing eastward they meet the steep valleys along the Mississippi, cutting into bedrock limestone and picking up necessary nutrients and cool groundwater from hillside springs and bottomland seeps. Protected now by wooded slopes of new forest and undisturbed floodplains, the rivers run cool and clear. During severe summer storms (characteristic of southern Minnesota), stream waters sometimes turn muddy, leaving bottom stones and gravels coated with sediment, but clear water soon returns. Management programs continue to reduce erosion in the watershed.

Unless too severely affected by storms, the stream bottoms harbor thriving populations of various aquatic insects and, conesquently, huge emergences, or hatches, of mayflies, caddisflies, and stoneflies—the bread and butter of trout foods. The experienced and knowledgeable trout angler, knowing when and where to meet these hatches, armed with accurate imitations of the adult flying insects, enjoys the ultimate experience of fishing for trout.

You say you don't have that knowledge and experience right now? You're still in luck. Availability of the necessary knowledge awaits. A huge armory of excellent books, videos, and magazines can give you knowledge of trout behavior and aquatic insect life history. (An example: *Midwest Fly Fishing*, which emphasizes regional stream destinations, fishing gear, entomology, and tips on techniques.) Check out your local bookshop and internet bookstores; you'll find hundreds of helpful and fascinating items. Ask the Department of Natural Resources (DNR) for their brochures and maps of trout streams, public access, and special regulations. Look up local chapters of fishing clubs and environmental groups, like Trout Unlimited, the Fly Fishing Federation, and Minnesota Waters (a new amalgamation of the Rivers Council of Minnesota and the Minnesota Lakes Association); you will find a host of helpful new friends and comrades on the water.

And now the experience. This is the best part. Take time to spend on the water. Become acquainted with Minnesota's part of the Driftless Area. With hip boots or waders and some beginning level of rod and other tackle—preferably with a companion—enjoy the adventure along with learning. You will find that by learning you will gain appreciation of this resource, so full of wonder and beauty, then a feeling of proprietorship, and finally a dedication to good stewardship.

Keep your boots and fly line wet, as often as you can.

*   *   *

THE WHITEWATER RIVER BEGINS in a series of widely distributed warm headwater streams. In three separated groups they gain flow and current speed as they begin to drop down into the Mississippi Valley. These become the North Branch, Middle Branch, and South Branch of the Whitewater River, and all three soon cool down and change to good trout habitat in the spreading Whitewater Wildlife Management Area.

*One of many sandstone/limestone cliffs in the Driftless Area,
like this one on the North Branch of the Whitewater River.*

The South, Middle, and North branches all contain the two common trout species, brook and brown, but it is the brown that predominates. Reproduction is highly successful, all sizes are abundant, and a few huge specimens (up to ten pounds or more) are occasionally taken. Brook trout are far less common, found only in a few small headwater trickles. And rainbows, while not reproducing, are occasionally encountered after having been stocked by the DNR; some survive to larger sizes (one to two pounds).

　　　*　　　　　　　　*　　　　　　　　*

THE THREE BRANCHES COME TOGETHER near the town of Elba, and from there the main stem flows for about fifteen miles to the Mississippi River. Because the main river is warmer than the three upper branches, it harbors several other species of fish, including catfish, carp, and a few smallmouth bass—and some large brown trout.

Early in the history of the Whitewater, this lower section was severely channelized, and was useless for fishing and unattractive for canoeing. A few years ago, however, about one and a half miles of straight channel were restored to the old, meandered course, and an additional winding channel was created, adding nearly three miles of meandering productive river.

A lovely small stream, Beaver Creek, enters the main stem of the Whitewater, about halfway down, very productive of brown trout, some very good size. It flows through the old village of Beaver, buried decades ago by sediment from the severe erosion of the '30s. On a hill overlooking the village is Beaver Cemetery where Richard J. Dorer lies in permanent rest in a plain pine coffin, at his own special request.

*   *   *

FOR CANOEING, IT'S THE MAIN STEM that is mainly suitable. Lynne and Robert Diebel, in their *Paddling Southern Minnesota*, give us directions and instruction on a ten-mile canoe run through the flatland course of this famous stream.

It's a great marsh for birding and waterfowl hunting. Wild turkeys roam the area, fair game but under strict regulations on seasons and locations. And if you bring along some tackle, a giant brown trout may make your day.

The Diebels point out the presence of many deadfalls and fallen trees, some artificially created rapids that you might want to avoid, and the fact that the lower six miles of deadfall obstacles may be bad enough to discourage your proceeding.

But they also point out the variety of birds in their spring migration, the scenery of distant hills, and the beauty of the river, which, they conclude, outweigh the "pesky details".

*   *   *

THE SOUTH BRANCH IS PROBABLY the most popular of the three branches. It has some of the best insect hatches from productive gravel riffles and fish-holding pools below the riffles, the classic, preferred mix of good trout stream habitat. The South Branch runs about twenty-five miles in the WMA; and while ample parking spots exist and popular angler paths lead along nearby stream banks, there remain many miles of stream that offer more remote solitude to the lone angler.

South Branch of the Whitewater, miles of pretty water. Lots of fish, probably the most popular in the state with trout fishers.

A couple of miles upstream from the junction of the three branches the Crystal Springs State Fish Hatchery lies astride the South Branch. Years ago the facility produced mainly brown trout for restoring trout fisheries in southeast Minnesota, resulting in today's extraordinary brown trout fishing throughout the area. Today, Crystal Springs produces brook trout fingerlings from wild stock in order to recreate sustainable populations where habitat is found to be suitable for this species. Also, the hatchery produces catchable-sized rainbows to provide temporary fishing in some areas of heavy fishing pressure. Tours are provided for visitors to observe this special operation.

Although the choice reaches of the South Branch lie within the wildlife area, fishable sections extend farther south into mainly private property. Even in the private areas, however, the DNR has arranged easements with landowners to allow fishing access; some of these have fenced corridors that protect the river from livestock. (Be sure to check for legal access.)

About midway in the South Branch course, lies a special area known as Kriedemacher Valley. Although for many years and several generations the Kriedemacher family has permitted public fishing, care should be exercised to respect the fences, livestock, and leased private camps in this special place.

The South Branch is the one of the three most susceptible to sedimentation. However, recovery always occurs and productivity always comes back with increased insect hatches and rising trout. The watershed needs work to eliminate sediment pollution.

The Middle Branch is the shortest of the three branches in the WMA, five miles in the wildlife area. Heading up in the southwestern part of the Whitewater watershed, the Middle Branch joins the North Branch also near Elba. It offers trout fishing just as productive as in the other branches.

Near one corner of the WMA is Whitewater State Park, one of the most popular parks in the state on the Middle Branch. At 2,800 acres the park is mid-sized among Minnesota's state parks. Included are campgrounds with more than a hundred drive-in sites, some walk-in, one camper cabin, and three group camps. Fifteen miles of hiking trails will take you along the river and up to 200-foot high bluffs that overlook the valley. Known widely as a trout angler's park, Whitewater's access to the Middle Branch is as intimate as it could be. About fifteen miles of the Middle Branch run through the park. And you can watch trout rising for emerging mayflies from your evening campfire.

The North Branch is the favorite of only a few anglers, so it's rarely crowded. The mouth of the stream is located right in the town of Elba; you have to wend your way through some residential area from which the road upstream continues along the river. After about four miles and passing a couple of concrete bridges, the road leaves the valley, but trails continue on upstream about twenty miles, still in the WMA, giving you miles more of excellent trout water, away from the madding crowd. (Unfortunately, this is also a favorite place for illegal ATV and motorcycle use. Be careful.)

A fly fisher tries her luck on the North Branch of the Whitewater.

About twenty-five winding miles of river upstream from the Whitewater Wildlife Management Area (WMA) on the North Branch, Carley State Park nestles quietly in the high blufflands, well separated from the wildlife area and its crowds. The North Branch is small here, but it still contains some fine trout water. The park is only a little over 200 acres (about five "forties") and rustic. Horseshoe pits are a main attraction; there are about twenty primitive campsites and no flush toilets. But the beauty of the surroundings and river is further enhanced by a profusion of overhanging white pines, high overhead, and five miles of trails that cross the stream frequently. Try it for a quiet camp in a rustic setting, no officialdom to bother you. If you're lucky, maybe a couple of brown trout for supper, fried over a real fire—and a lovely little trout stream rippling outside your tent at night.

*   *   *

THE NAME WHITEWATER, like so many others in Minnesota, originated from the Dakota Indians. Their name, Minneiska, means "white water," probably referring to the little rapids sprinkled throughout the three branches. The town of Minneiska is located nearby.

CONSERVATION NOTE
NUMBER 11

THE FLOODPLAIN

At MANY PLACES ALONG ALMOST ANY RIVER, stream flows rise above the banks occasionally and spread out over a floodplain. Actually part of the riparian zone, the floodplain shares the same function of protecting the stream.

Floodplains were created by floods that repeatedly deposited sediment. In its natural state, a floodplain thus serves as an important sediment trap, removing sand and silt from the river.

However, when floodplain surfaces are disturbed by cultivation, gravel mining, or roads and trails, or any other soil-disruptive activity, they become susceptible to erosion. Without the filtering by natural vegetation, the floodplain loses surface soil as flood waters return to the river.

Instead of a *sediment trap*, the floodplain becomes a *sediment source*.

Soil scientists in the U.S. Forest Service, after extensive research on the dynamics of both natural and disturbed floodplains, have concluded that all human activities having the potential of soil disturbance should be kept permanently off of floodplains.

Chapter 12

DRIFTLESS AREA III

The Streams:
South Branch Root River,
North Branch Root River,
Root River Main Stem,
Many Tributaries

THE LARGEST OF THE DRIFTLESS AREA watersheds in Minnesota is the Root River drainage, covering the entire southeastern corner.

Still, with its richly forested bluffs, high limestone cliffs, myriad trout and smallmouth bass streams, and a half-hundred miles of main stem canoe and kayak water, the Root provides more outdoor recreation per square mile than any other similar-sized watershed in Minnesota, and in greater diversity.

Add two state parks, nearly a hundred miles of spectacular hiking trail (forty miles along the river), and scores of public easements on the trout streams—the results of management to provide public access to the natural resources of this prime area.

Like the other major rivers of the Driftless Area, the Root's waters begin on the agricultural plateau of southern Minnesota and flow eastward toward the Mississippi. The mainstem watershed of the Root occupies all of Fillmore and Houston counties, while some of the smaller tributaries stretch up into Olmsted and Winona counties. Small, warmwater streams at first, these upper tributaries join to form many intermediate forks and branches, finally connecting to two major rivers, again named without much imagination: North Branch of the Root and South Branch of the Root. There is also a Middle Branch, which is small, warm, and generally unused for canoeing or fishing.

Varying in habitat, temperature, and productivity, each of the two large branches grows to achieve its unique character. The two finally join to form the main stem of the Root River, flowing for fifty more miles through some of the most spectacular river environment in Minnesota.

*   *   *

Main stem of the Root River, lined with high hills and wooded bluffs. Small rapids and deep holes for fishing. Plenty of accesses.

WHEN TWO SMALL STREAMS JOIN at different locations, it becomes difficult to tell which is the main one and which the tributary. And thus, which name should prevail? Custom rules, sometimes a long-standing tradition.

Custom tells us that the Root River begins with the North Branch. Several tributaries, born in the western plains, soon come together and flow east and south into the Driftless Area's deeper and steeper valleys.

In the town of Chatfield, the North Branch flows as a stream capable of canoeing. Greg Breining in *his Paddling Minnesota*, Lynne and Robert Diebel in their *Paddling Southern Minnesota,* and the DNR's canoe guide for the Root, all recommend a put-in here, preferably in the higher water of spring.

In about four miles the Middle Branch enters the North Branch to form a larger stream that then qualifies as the Root River. From this confluence down, about thirty more miles, the Root winds around in its deepening valley, affording intimate canoeing and some fine smallmouth fishing. From Chatfield to Lanesboro, a good two-day trip, the Root enlarges as it cuts deeper into its valley, and consequently the overhanging bluffs and limestone cliffs add an ever-increasing beauty to the valley scenery. This stretch, in its deep valley, qualifies as one of the most scenic river paddles in Minnesota, with great fishing to boot.

Several landings and campgrounds are available to the weary. About midway are Pilot Mounds Campsites, and farther down are Whispering Pines Campgrounds, both in the Richard J Dorer Memorial State Forest.

Near Lanesboro the river meets the South Branch, and from there on you're on the *real* main stem of the Root.

*   *   *

THE SOUTH BRANCH OF THE ROOT RIVER is one of the major trout streams in Minnesota. In its upper reaches it sometimes actually flows partly through Mystery Cave, a tourist attraction that is part of Forestville/Mystery Cave State Park. This is some of Minnesota's most exceptional trout fishing for perhaps twenty miles to the town of Preston. Because the river here is small and shallow, with a series of many riffle-and-pool habitats, it is not useful as a canoe route, but its trout fishing is superb.

Near Preston, the South Branch becomes a bit warmer and loses some of its trout productivity. Smallmouth bass increase in the fishery here and prosper on the greater forage, such as crayfish, minnows, and other small fishes. The greater supply of forage also results in some large brown trout. As you get closer to Lanesboro, the river, wider now, offers more paddle space to the canoeist. You may encounter some wading anglers here; it's not difficult to give them a wide berth and maybe a cheery greeting.

A primitive canoe landing is available in Preston, the first on the South Branch. For about fifteen miles the stream winds through open country with little touch to civilization. A power dam impedes your flow at Lanesboro, so you might want to end this one-day trip and avoid the city part of the river. (But by this time, your arm may be aching anyway from doing battle with those fighting smallmouths.) Here, the South Branch joins the main Root and together they proceed downstream. From Preston to Lanesboro, the South Branch is included in the state DNR's Root River canoe route.

The Diebels cover most of the Root River in five segments, a day's trip each, plus the South Branch. The first of these, about nine miles, is mostly quiet, no rapids, and the scenery, while nice, is simply suggestive of the delights to come. In the next two sectors, fifteen miles each, the Diebels exclaim mightily about the scenic riverscapes, high wooded bluffs and limestone cliffs, and some easy rapids. It is here also that smallmouth bass fishing begins in earnest, with lots of rocky cover and pools. Nearby is the town of Lanesboro, a popular spot in the Driftless Area.

Then beyond Lanesboro, Lynne and Robert Diebel describe many accesses, landings, and campsites. They wax eloquently about the scenic cliffs, through the towns of Whalen and Petersen, and then to Rushford for their last two segments, twenty miles. Beyond Rushford, the Root River drops away from its deep valley and spreads out to flow lazily to the Mississippi, a final thirty-five miles. Highway 16 and the Root River State Trail continue on to the big river.

*   *   *

Some of the best small trout streams in Minnesota enter the Root's North and South branches, the South Fork, and the main stem. As examples, Lynch Creek enters the North Branch, Badger Creek enters the South Fork, and Money Creek and Torkelson Creek enter the main Root. Tributary to the South Branch, above Preston, two of the most unusual trout streams enter the river within Forestville/Mystery Cave State Park—Canfield Creek and Forestville Creek. (Canfield is also known as South Branch Creek, and Forestville as North Branch Creek.) Both are highly productive of wild trout and both are extremely popular. What's unusual is that both begin in caves where rushing water pours out to create fully formed streams, and trout live right up to the cave openings.

The headwater cave, origin of Forestville Creek (North Branch Creek), provides excellent trout fishing right up to the cave opening.

Canfield Creek flows entirely in the park, accessible after some easy hiking, from its mouth to the cave. Although Forestville Creek flows through a section of the park, upper private sectors are available (along with parking and camping) on a private farm charging modest fees. These are some of the most productive trout streams in the state. Of course, this is not to say the catching is easy. Both are well suited to fly fishing, but you'll need experience on the water and knowledge of the insect hatches.

Forestville/Mystery Cave State Park is one of the most frequented parks in Minnesota. For the not-so-timid are tours with hardhat, and elbow and kneepads for crawling through some tight spots. (Of course, there are regular lighted tours for the rest of us.) Ample campgrounds are available: one on the bottom flats with the river alongside, others on high ground up above the river. An excellently managed park, Forestville offers campsites well screened by vegetation for privacy, as well as modern amenities. A group camp, many lecture and field trip programs, and horse trails add variety to Forestville.

Farther downstream where the main stem winds its way toward the Mississippi, two small gems enter the main Root from the south. Diamond Creek and Gribben Creek, with both brown and brook trout. These are very productive trout streams, but again the catching requires experience.

Farther downstream yet, the South Fork of the Root, (not to be confused with the larger South *Branch*) enters the main stem. Into the South Fork flows Beaver Creek, with two branches of its own, East Beaver and West Beaver. Beaver Creek Valley State Park is located on East Beaver Creek, a gem with a sparkling spring. Camping includes two dozen drive-in sites, a half dozen remote walk-in sites, and one camper cabin. The stream inside the park is remarkably clear and beautifully alive with small brookies. Westward over the watershed you will find its partner, the West Beaver Creek, another small but lovely trout stream.

Downstream from the cave origin of Canfield Creek, a shallow riffle with grasses and other aquatic plants adds to the productivity of the stream, as it provides cover and food for many aquatic insects.

Leaving the main watersheds a bit, several excellent trout streams flow directly into the Mississippi. Garvin and Gilmore creeks in the vicinity of the city of Winona, and Crooked and Winnebago creeks in the far southeast corner, are just a few.

Of course many more trout streams can be found in the Driftless Area that are not listed here. Many are scattered as tributaries throughout the lower sectors of the three major rivers, and some simply flow directly to the Mississippi. All are located and further described in the state DNR's new booklet *Trout Angling Opportunities in Southern Minnesota.*

Included in the booklet are new regulations on selected streams aimed at keeping the catch in balance with a stream's productivity, some to increase the sizes of fish. These include: catch-and-release, slot limits (commonly requiring the release of all fish between twelve and sixteen inches), use of barbless hooks and artificial lures (e.g., flies) only. Although most trout streams remain under general statewide regulations, be careful to acquaint yourself with this booklet and the streams that have special rules.

Another feature in the booklet of great interest to trout anglers, are the many streamside easements that have been negotiated with landowners, allowing angler entrance to fishing not previously available. While open to the public, these are nevertheless private lands; be sure to show respect if we want to keep them open.

Allowing more opportunity to enjoy your sport are many streams that permit winter fishing, usually January 1 through March 31, catch-and-release and artificials only. These are also located in the DNR booklet. Remember, in winter, good trout streams with groundwater sources are warmer than the air, and they flow freely. (This doesn't mean that the line guides on your fly rod won't freeze up!) Partake only if you have protected fingers. On the other hand, if you pick your day and its weather, there's nothing more bracing than being on the water on a crisp, sunny, midwinter day. Better yet, chances are you'll be all alone.

*   *   *

THE ROOT RIVER WATERSHED has been the subject of a new long-range hiking trail system. Starting near the town of Fountain, the Root River State Trail takes about six miles to drop down into the river valley and join up with the South Branch. An alternate beginning would be to start at the town of Preston where the Harmony/Preston Valley State Trail comes up from the south and runs for six miles along the river to join the Root River Trail at the same place. From there the Root River State Trail follows closely the rest of the South Branch and then the main stem of the river all the way to Houston, forty miles total. This would be the end of the trail, about twenty miles of river above the Mississippi. Of course, highway US 16 along the river is a bit of a bother, but woods and streams keep most of it separated by a reasonable distance.

A total distance of roughly forty miles along the spectacular Root with its cliffs and forested bluffs makes for a remarkable outdoor adventure. Many accesses and campgrounds are located along the way for stopovers or shorter hikes.

Trout Run Creek, tributary of the North Branch of the Root.
Highly productive of trout.

*   *   *

THE NAME, ROOT, FOR THIS REMARKABLE STREAM is not clear. There remain some families in the region with the name of Root, but there's no apparent connection. Most likely it comes from the Native Americans, the Dakota, whose name for the river, Hokah, was translated to Root. There is a Hokah Township in Houston County.

*   *   *

THERE REMAIN SOME PROBLEMS in the Driftless Area. Erosion and sedimentation are the main ones. The major source of such pollution is the many eroding streambanks, so common that they may seem part of the natural landscape. Some, of course, are due to natural processes, such as the erosive power of high water pounding away on the outside of normal meanders. But the reason why these common processes are so destructive is that natural protective vegetation and topography on surrounding land have been removed or greatly disturbed. Poor agricultural practice in the past and indiscriminate logging too close to the stream are the major factors. Others include disturbance by poor road placement, gravel mining, other development. Old flood-plains, laid down by floods in the long past, remain particularly susceptible to such erosion; modern management calls for no soil disruptive activity of any kind on floodplains.

However, good solutions are on the horizon. Trout Unlimited, the nation's major citizen organization of trout and salmon enthusiasts, has embarked on a major program of stream restoration in the Driftless Area. Well financed nationally, comprising thousands of members in hundreds of local chapters sensitive to the land's critical impact on stream and river quality, this organization now brings these nationwide forces with precise focus to the ambitious goal of improved coolwater streams in this resource so important in the upper Midwest.

But more than trout and smallmouth anglers can benefit, because a healthy watershed means not only higher water quality and better fishing, but also improved wildlife habitat, reduction of floods, more stable groundwater, and scenic beauty in the landscape—available to all of us who love and enjoy outdoor recreation in this very special region of North America.

You will find most of the Root River system in the CALE-DONIA PRIM map.

*   *   *

YOU WILL LOVE EXPLORING THE DRIFTLESS AREA. Especially take time to scout the remote valleys, with hiking, hunting, or hip boots, for there you will find solitude and beauty beyond your greatest imagination. Watch for the brilliance of a scarlet tanager; listen for the soft whisper of tiny springs; feel a summer breeze wafting down from overhead white pines. Bring only your tem-porary presence to the woods and wildlife habitats. Take away only your lovely photographs, maybe a brace of brook trout in your creel, or a ruffed grouse in your game pocket, and some wonderful memories.

Enjoy!

CONSERVATION NOTE
NUMBER 12

MEANDERS

EARLY SETTLERS CAME UP THE MISSISSIPPI and found the flat bottomland along rivers with its black, rich soil. Numerous smaller streams meandered toward the major river. With heavy rains, productive croplands became swamps, and crops were often destroyed. So, deep ditches were dug to line the fields, and meandering streams were straightened, to hurry more water downstream.

But something went wrong. The original streams had been clear and had held good fish populations, now lost. And a straightened stream tends to create meanders through excessive erosion of its banks, and so the straightened streams turned muddy.

Now, finally, land managers, fishery professionals, and even local citizens, have been putting the meanders back in place. It's not difficult, for many of the original banks are still visible.

Two projects in Minnesota come to mind. One was a lower reach of the Whitewater River, channelized into straight lines long ago. But now, winding across its floodplain it holds smallmouth bass, catfish, and probably a few large brown trout. Another one is Rice Creek in northern Ramsey County, straight as a string since the 1930s, now swinging lazily around bend after bend across a large wetland in the company of deer and ducks. Canoeing Rice Creek is getting more popular—right in our backyards.

Chapter 13

THE ST. CROIX—
WILD RIVER

The Rivers:
St. Croix, Sunrise

IT HAS BEEN SAID THAT THE REAL VALUE of wilderness lies in the comparison of its silence to the noise of civilization.

True too, of wild rivers—where the muted music of water currents replaces the raucous roars and rushes of busy streets and rumbles of engines—whether from semi's on the highway or recreational vehicles in the woods.

Legendary conservationist Aldo Leopold nearly a century ago railed against the "Great God Motor" as he saw the proliferation of roads—and therefore engines—in the wilderness forests of America. The late John Sawhill, longtime leader of The Nature Conservancy, reminded us that "...future generations will remember us not only for what we have created, but for what we refused to destroy."

Although appreciation of the beauty and silence of our nation's pristine rivers emerged long ago, the counsel of Leopold and Sawhill were largely ignored—and the natural character of many rivers indeed had been destroyed.

Then, only a few decades ago, the first steps of river advocacy were taken. The passage of the national Wild and Scenic Rivers Act in 1968 was a major milestone in the nation's treatment of its most valuable streams and rivers. The act divides these national treasures into three categories: *Wild, Scenic, and Recreational*, in decreasing character of wildness.

The St. Croix River, although not as remote and primitive as our western mountain streams, includes sections of *Scenic* and *Recreational*, adding an enormous element of river protection. Until recently, our special rivers were open to potential development and damming. Many had already disappeared beneath the waters of impoundments. The protection of the wild river system came just in time.

Soon after the national act was in place, a number of states developed their own systems of Wild and Scenic Rivers, and throughout the nation emerged hundreds of streams and rivers deserving of protection. Minnesota was one such state, with the enactment of its own Wild and Scenic River System in 1973. We'll take up details of Minnesota's selections as they pop up in this book, and for now consider the beautiful St. Croix. The Department of Natural Resource maps called Public Recreation Information Maps (or PRIM) include a wealth of opportunity for outdoor recreation, including rivers. See PRIM maps SANDSTONE, MORA, NORTH METRO, and SOUTH METRO.

*   *   *

THE DESIGNATION OF THE ST. CROIX in the national system was unusual in one important aspect: among eight initial rivers it was the only one close to a major metropolitan area, almost a suburb of Minnesota's Twin Cities. Consequently, recreational opportunities have been extremely popular for both day use and extended camping and canoeing. What this means is that special efforts have been, and will remain, necessary to maintain its scenic character. The National Park Service, as administrator, has steadfastly resisted plans for non-conforming development.

In the national wild river designation, the St. Croix River is divided into two major sections. The upper section, from its headwaters in Wisconsin, to Taylors Falls, Minnesota, and across the river, St. Croix Falls, Wisconsin, is about one hundred miles; the lower section, from Taylors Falls to the St. Croix's confluence with the Mississippi, an additional fifty miles. Most of the upper river is classified as *Scenic,* whereas the lower river, much of it in a lake environment, is mainly classified as *Recreational.* (See Chapter 9, Rivers in Your Backyard.*)*

*   *   *

THE ST. CROIX IS THE MOST POPULAR major river for recreation in the Midwest. Yet the great length available for river use means that on almost any day there is ample space for fishing or a pleasure float. Most of the upper river is restricted to non-motorized use, so canoeing is quiet.

All of Minnesota's St. Croix is a boundary, with Minnesota and Wisconsin sharing. The river runs along the eastern borders of Pine, Chisago, and Washington counties in Minnesota, and in the last of these it empties into the Mississippi at Point Douglas County Park.

An abundance of accesses and campgrounds dot the river throughout its length, especially in the upper river, on both sides. If you want to experience the entire Minnesota portion, start at the access and campground at the crossing of Wisconsin Highway 35 (a couple of miles above the states' border), for a complete trip of several days. From there downstream, the river flows through dense pine forest and, later, hardwood second growth.

The St. Croix River is nationally known for its smallmouth bass fishing. Of all freshwater game fish, the smallmouth is the most respected for its fighting ability, with repeated leaps into the air. The strength of this fish, especially on a fly line, is often difficult to believe, even for a relatively small fish. But the smallmouth is not alone, for walleyes and northern pike (also a leaper), are abundant in the river. The St. Croix is also one of the major locations for good populations of the lake sturgeon, a leftover from Jurassic times. There is some limited angling permitted for the lake sturgeon in these border waters; check your regulations.

*   *   *

THE ENTIRE ST. CROIX IS COVERED in a series of canoe route maps that include road accesses and both drive-in and canoe campsites, including five state parks, down to the Mississippi River, available from the Minnesota Department of Natural Resources (DNR). Other fine maps are available from the National Park Service, Breining's *Paddling Minnesota*, and Lynne and Robert Diebel's *Paddling Southern Minnesota*. The Diebels divide the main, upper St. Croix into six daily trips, each one described for a day's run with good put-in access and take-out with camping.

Also, see the DNR's website on the St. Croix River: www .dnr.state.mn.us/canoeing/stcroixriver.

The upper part of the river is classified in the scenic category, through St. Croix State Park, past the relatively new Wild River State Park, and to Interstate State Park (cooperative between Minnesota and Wisconsin). The river is quiet and pleasant floating. But at Interstate the river changes drastically.

First, a dam at St. Croix Falls must be circumnavigated. Immediately below the dam is the rapids at the upper end of the park, the only really rough whitewater on the river. Following is a stunning float through the Dalles of the St. Croix, a narrow, igneous-rock-bound run, downstream from which boat traffic increases greatly. The river from Interstate to William O'Brien State Park is larger, braided in part, containing many islands. Some of these permit camping. O'Brien may be the most popular state park on the river, the closest to the Twin Cities.

*   *   *

A SUPER ABUNDANCE OF TRAILS and campsites of many kinds in state parks line the river.

St. Croix State Park, as the largest in Minnesota, offers 130 miles of hiking trails, many along the 20-mile reach of the river within the park. In addition, other trails offer paved trails for bicyclists, trails for mountain bikes, and horseback riding. Winter trails are also available for skiing, as well as trails for snowmobiles that connect with other trails in Chengwatana and St. Croix state forests. Snowshoeing is allowed anywhere in the park.

Trails that follow along the river provide a wonderland of riverscapes. Over 200 campsites are available, most drive-in, plus backpack, walk-in, canoe and kayak sites, and a horse camp. A few cabins are also offered. For more information on St. Croix State Park, see: www.dnr.state.mn.us/state_parks/st_croix.

Wild River State Park is another large park, with more than 6,800 acres and eighteen miles of the St. Croix River. As the name suggests, this park features the wild river aspect of the St. Croix, with restoration of prairie and oak savanna, and many miles of river trails. A special trail guide lists details of over thirty miles of hiking and ski trails, and twenty miles more for horseback riding. Wild River's trail system is especially designed with a wonderful diversity in landscape and riverscape, including trails to remote campsites along the river.

Wild River State Park offers many modern features that provide privacy camping, like remote rustic campsites and a camper cabin, with emphasis on good stewardship. For more, see: www.dnr.state.mn.us/state_parks/wild_river.

Interstate, like the name suggests, is located on both sides of the river, Minnesota and Wisconsin. Administration of the two sides, however, is distinct. Admission allows entrance to both. Both are fascinating. We deal here, with the Minnesota side.

Although small among our state parks, at only 298 acres, it is in Minnesota's Interstate that you can experience one of the most fascinating geological elements of river formation. When the glaciers that once invaded Minnesota were melting back, the huge lake of meltwater, Glacial Lake Duluth overfilled the Superior Basin, and high volumes of water poured out through what is now the St. Croix Valley. Many glimpses of formations that were left as a result are visible from the river, such as the Dalles, where the river is narrowed between towering cliffs of lava rock. The abundance of "kettle holes," where swirling water with huge force and the help of rotating stones, like grindstones, carved out great round holes in the rock, now high and dry.

Boom site on the St. Croix River.

At a place on the St. Croix River where rocky streambanks narrow the flow, the hundreds of thousands of floating white pines were squeezed into a natural dam, causing them to slow their flow in the widened and quieter water, into many square miles of floating logs, often using sitka spruce from the states of Oregon and Washington.. The jammed logs were later surrounded by larger, tougher logs into "booms." This enabled owners to identify their own logs by their log marks. The "boom site" is today memorialized by a marker and rest stop along the highway.

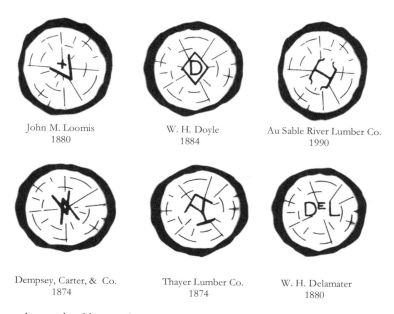

John M. Loomis 1880	W. H. Doyle 1884	Au Sable River Lumber Co. 1990
Dempsey, Carter, & Co. 1874	Thayer Lumber Co. 1874	W. H. Delamater 1880

A sample of log marks used by some logging and lumber companies.

Interstate does not have many hiking trails like other parks. The reason is the rugged landscapes created by the hard, igneous rock topography. Ten miles of trails are available, but they are mostly rugged and steep. Instead, emphasis is on the unique, rocky aspects of the river valley. Camping facilities are ample, however, with nearly forty drive-in sites and several group sites that accommodate larger numbers of persons.

Interstate is the first such park in the nation. Recognized for its rugged, scenic value, community leaders from both Wisconsin and Minnesota convinced their legislatures to cooperatively protect the area from mining and establish the park, Minnesota in 1895 and Wisconsin in 1900.

Interstate is a fascinating experience, helping us to understand the quality of Minnesota's natural heritage. For more information: www.dnr.state.mn.us/state_parks/interstate.

Although small as Minnesota parks go, William O'Brien State Park is close to the Twin Cities and immensely popular.

Annual visits number over a quarter million. So this is not your wilderness experience. Nevertheless, it is located in a lovely area, with magnificent riverscapes of the St. Croix. Many recreational amenities are available, but most of all are the views of the pristine river.

Several ponds and a small lake dot the park area. Fishing is good in both lake and the St. Croix, and canoe rentals and shuttle services are located on the river. A swimming beach is available on the lake. Many naturalist programs explain and demonstrate the ecology and geology of the diverse nature systems of the park region. A large island in the St. Croix River stands just off the park, accessible by canoe, for pleasant hikes, wildlife watching, and wildflower viewing.

O'Brien offers two large campgrounds, one on the river, plus two large, primitive group camps. Some winter camping available. One camper cabin is available, by reservation. A limited mileage of trails is available, but diverse in type—hiking, skiing, biking—ranging through a variety of natural features.

William O'Brien is unmatched as a recreational treasure so close to home. The park honors a lumber baron that owned large areas of land in the region, much of which was later donated by his family for a state park. See the DNR website: www.dnr.state.mn .us/state_parks/william_obrien.

The name of the St. Croix is uncertain. A prominent rock formation in the Interstate Park area, Wisconsin side, resembles a cross, but the more likely origin is from an early French fur trader.

$$* \qquad * \qquad *$$

THIS CHAPTER CONCLUDES WITH one more important stream, one with the lovely name of Sunrise River. Heading up in several tributaries in southwestern Chisago County, the Sunrise flows north to enter the Carlos Avery Wildlife Management Area (WMA) and traverses several large "pools," or impounded reservoirs, many marshes, and uncounted meanders, for about twenty-five miles.

*The Sunrise River, a gem of a small stream in a kayak, tributary to the
St. Croix. As the Sunrise drops down into the St. Croix valley at
increased speed, you may find some large boulders that give you trouble.
Its closeness to the Twin Cities attracts pressure from development,
so it needs special protection to preserve its natural values.*

Carlos Avery is a large wildlife area for public hunting, extremely popular for deer and small game almost next to the
metropolitan area of St. Paul. It is one of the largest wildlife areas
in the state, at 23,000 acres, or thirty-six square miles, the size of
an entire township. It comprises two separate units, the Carlos
Avery Unit (south) and the Sunrise River Unit (north); the Sunrise flows through the latter and continues north toward the St.
Croix River. Plenty of canoe landings are located within Carlos
Avery along the pools for access to hunting and bird watching.
Leaving the Sunrise Unit, the Sunrise then heads north and ends
at a landing on the St. Croix, in Wild River State Park.

Greg Breining, in his *Paddling Minnesota,* outlines a canoe
float on the Sunrise of about twelve miles to Wild River State
Park and take-out on the St. Croix a quarter mile upstream from

the Sunrise's mouth. He describes this section of the Sunrise as a small, intimate stream through shaded woodlands, with lively currents and easy rapids, although there are a couple of rough rapids when the river is higher than usual, especially as you approach its mouth.

The river's route runs through its namesake town of Sunrise (birthplace of motion picture star Richard Widmark), and continues to its junction with the St. Croix. While the junction with the larger river is in state park property, it is not near the central activities of the park, and the Sunrise is not actually a major feature. Fishing for smallmouth bass and northerns is reputed to be good in the last few miles of the Sunrise above the St. Croix.

The Carlos Avery WMA, so very near the Twin Cities metro area, is heavily used, not only by hunters but also by many other outdoors enthusiasts, such as hikers and birders and canoeists/kayakers on the stream.

Many species of wildlife inhabit Carlos Avery. The ubiquitous white-tailed deer is the major large game animal, but Carlos Avery is wild enough to hold a few black bears and coyotes, as well as the occasional gray wolf. Cottontail rabbits and fox squirrels are common, but little hunted. Waterfowl, ducks and geese, and pheasants are the principal game birds hunted, although ruffed grouse and woodcock can also be found along the river and wetland edges. Many other migrating birds stop over in season, and trapping regulations allow the take of several furbearers. Two refuge/sanctuary areas provide complete protection for wildlife in special locations.

While the nearness of Carlos Avery WMA to the cities means a short trip to favorite hunting grounds, this closeness also attracts development, threatening nearby wildlife habitat. In particular, the corridor of wild land from the north used by bears, wolves, and migratory birds such as waterfowl, jack snipe, and woodcock, may be irretrievable. A current proposal (2005) would allow a dense housing development too close to the wildlife area and so impact an especially important wetland that extends directly into the WMA. Environmentalists, developers, the DNR, and the city of Ham Lake currently try to work out an acceptable compromise. The choice, as usual, is between the integrity of our natural resources and the profits of development in the wrong places.

As is, Carlos Avery provides superb outdoor adventure of all kinds, close to home. It should be kept that way.

Two more major tributaries to the St. Croix, the Snake and Kettle, both with wonderful canoeing and fishing, enter the St. Croix in its upper reaches. We'll take them up in the next chapter.

CONSERVATION NOTE
NUMBER 13

HATCHERIES I

REMEMBER THE U.S. PRESIDENT who said, "so salmon are getting rare and endangered?" (P.S. The big cattle ranchers were complaining that they were not allowed to pasture their cows in the chinook salmon's spawning stream.) "I'll fix that!" the prez exclaimed. "We'll raise lots of salmon in our hatcheries, plant 'em out in all those rivers, and they won't be rare and endangered any more!"

Five salmon species occupy streams on the Pacific coast. Each species exhibits a different system of life cycle, thus keeping the five species separated through the years of evolution.

However, each of the five species includes a number of distinct genetic *stocks*, each stock spawning in its own natal stream where its parents spawned, often in the same gravel bed. Consequently, such a stock is treated just like a species in the "threatened and endangered" rules. Each stream associated with an independent stock must be carefully protected to preserve that particular stock.

If a stock is wiped out due to cattle trampling on its spawning gravels, that stock is gone forever. Extinct.

I think someone got to the president, as he later shut up about it.

Chapter 14

SNAKE and KETTLE RIVERS

THESE TWO TRIBUTARIES of the St. Croix River (on the Minnesota side) include some of the finest whitewater in our state: the Upper Falls and Lower Falls of the Snake, and Hell's Gate rapids on the Kettle. In low water they are just a bunch of dry rocks, albeit huge ones; in medium water levels these rapids are fun for the experienced paddler, especially with a kayak. But at highest water levels they go off the chart, life-threatening, but lovely.

Apart from these rapids and falls, the two rivers constitute some of the best canoeing in Minnesota; most river miles are easy but scenic. Waters in both rivers are unpolluted, good fishing, and with many sites for public access. Both are on the state's list of designated canoe routes, with maps available from the Department of Natural Resources (DNR) and in Greg Breining's excellent *Paddling Minnesota*. Lynne Smith Diebel's *Paddling Northern Minnesota* includes the Kettle, whereas the Snake is covered in Lynne and Robert Diebel's *Paddling Southern Minnesota*.

Although the Kettle has a state park on its banks, Banning, the Snake does not, but it deserves one. The Kettle River is one of Minnesota's Wild and Scenic Rivers, and the Snake desperately needs similar protection. Still, they make a wonderful pair.

Both streams have a history of severe harvest of timber, a devastation of land that was left with slash and stumps, and tragic fires. Scattered remnants of the great white pine forests can still be found here and there, probably the result of the loggers leaving a few that were small and young at the time. Now the combination of browsing white-tailed deer and white pine blister rust has effectively denied any chance of reforesting the white pine giants. Yet, time and new growth over several decades have brought a conifer-hardwood mixture that replaced the pine, to create a land rich in recreational opportunity—deer and small game hunting, stream fishing, canoeing, and new hiking trails.

This part of the St. Croix watershed gives us an unlimited source of outdoor enjoyment. It is essential that both rivers and their watersheds receive strong environmental protection.

*   *   *

THE SNAKE RIVER IS RENOWNED for its canoeing, one of Minnesota's most famous float streams. There's enough access, to be sure, although the upper sections are remote and wild for many miles, mostly through county lands and state forest.

The Snake begins a hundred-mile journey to the St. Croix River with slow beginnings in the swamps of Solana State Forest in Aitkin County, flowing south through Kanabec County, and finally sharply turning east through Pine County to its mouth in the St. Croix. (See PRIM maps AITKIN and MORA for the Snake River.)

In the uppermost headwaters, the stream is divided into East and West branches, both small, swampy streams. But near the town of McGrath a good access immediately offers the paddler steep gradients and swift currents. The river then contains many small rapids, rarely up to Class II, and life afloat seems to be a matter of dodging one boulder after another; of course a lot depends on river level. There's plenty of quiet water too, just don't go to sleep.

From McGrath downstream about six miles you can find the Aitkin County Campground, with good access. And farther down the Upper Falls of the Snake will greet the canoeist or kayaker, some of the most spectacular riverscapes in the state, Class V in high water. At one point, the river slams into a sheer granite wall. And only a few miles farther is the Lower Falls, similar to the Upper but different, even rougher in high water to Class VI in extreme levels. There's a long, well-used portage path, however, which is disdained by kayakers, who love to play among the cataracts. It too is lovely. Neither of these two rapids areas includes real waterfalls as such, but the whitewater is truly white. No drive-in access is available near either site. A primitive trail, on private land but kept open to the public, leads to the Lower Falls. Unfortunately, it has been badly damaged by ATV use.

Although a few road crossings mark passage downstream, the river remains wild for many miles, albeit including several canoe landings. In the Pine City area the Snake becomes more of a lake environment, backed up by a small dam. Here the river touches the south end of large Pokegama Lake, and then flows through Cross Lake, a long, wide quiet water with two extensions, north and south, to make the "cross." Both lakes are heavily used for boating and fishing.

Down from the Pine City area the river becomes almost a straight line, with frequent small rapids, down to its entry into the St. Croix. Good scenery is often absent in this section, with banks lined with cottages.

Canoeing on the Snake is usually best in spring with higher water levels, although good levels are sometimes up during the summer too, with sporadic rainfalls. The Snake is "flashy," meaning it comes up fast with heavy rain, and down again rapidly afterward. At lower levels in summer, passage can be difficult or impossible because of protruding large boulders.

Lynne Smith Diebel's *Paddling Southern Minnesota* gives us a richly detailed treatment of the Snake. Beginning at the Aitkin County Campground, she divides the river into six daily segments, ending at its mouth in the St. Croix.

The first of these includes the Upper and Lower falls, with good descriptions and warnings for this stretch of wild water. Further trips lead south with quiet pools, through the town of Mora, later Pine City. The stretch from Pine City to the St. Croix River she describes as a rocky maze, with many cabins and cottages but forested banks, and good smallmouth fishing. The Chengwatana State Forest Campground at the mouth offers rest after the river's run, as well as a put-in on the St. Croix.

Lower Falls of the Snake in high water condition becomes a roaring cauldron of whitewater. Man and dog enjoy the sight and sound.

Throughout the six separate daily trips, the Diebels give the paddler a rich assortment of river information, invaluable to the canoeist on rapids, islands, and pools, many accesses and camping facilities, detailed shuttle routes, stream gradient and locations of level gauges, and much more, including where to get a good burger in Mora.

Like many of our non-trout streams, fishing is often remarkably good in the Snake for warmwater species. Principal among these are smallmouth bass, northern pike, and walleyes.

Fishing pressure is light, which of course is favorable for those anglers willing to canoe or hike through wild countryside. Wading can be tough going because of the many shoals with slippery boulders. Nevertheless, fishing for smallmouth, pike, and walleyes is good. These three are predators—or piscivores, as the fisheries biologist would say—feeding on other, smaller fishes. Available as forage fish for the piscivores are many minnows and lots of small suckers.

In the lower reaches near Pine City, Cross Lake boasts good fishing for catfish and panfish such as bluegills, but little for walleyes; Pokegama Lake is known for good fishing for northern pike, walleyes, and crappies, but poor for other panfish.

The Snake is also home to a legendary monster, a living aquatic dinosaur—the lake sturgeon. (Don't be fooled by the name; this sturgeon is mostly a river fish.) You might catch one in the Snake (or Kettle), but it must be released. There is no open season for sturgeon in the Snake or Kettle; it is a long-lived, slow-growing fish, and it needs special protection. (See Chapter 13 on the St. Croix, where a limited angling season is open.) A canoe trip on the Snake River can be enhanced greatly with a spinning or fly rod!

Many tributaries empty into the Snake. Although these do not have good angling possibilities, they provide excellent access to northern pike in their springtime migration into the ponds and marshes required for spawning.

There's little in the way of camping facilities along the Snake. The Aitkin County Campground is located in the southern part of the county with good access to the river. (If you put in here, be aware of the Upper Falls a short way downstream.) At the mouth of the Snake in the St. Croix River is the Chengwatana State Forest campground; it's good for either a take-out from a trip on the Snake or a put-in for the St. Croix.

The name, Snake, derives from an unpleasant time in the history of Minnesota. Soon after the white Europeans began to settle the Minnesota region, the Ojibwe Indians provided with the white man's firearms, began a westward incursion into lands of the native Dakota. Pushing the Dakota upstream into the river's watershed, the Ojibwe applied their derisive name for kanabec—snake-in-the-grass—to the retreating Dakota. Kanabec eventually became the name of the county through which most of the Snake flows.

*   *   *

A MAJOR CHARACTER of the Kettle River lies in its great diversity, ranging widely from long reaches of quiet water to the violence of Hell's Gate Rapids in Banning State Park. Its wadeability for fishing also ranges widely, marked by gentle sandbars and slippery boulders the size of large cannonballs.

But the river presents some of the best scenery in Minnesota, with its mixture of hardwood and pine forests, lava and sandstone cliffs, and river-molded ledges. The Kettle is much more developed for recreational access than the Snake, with frequent canoe landings and campsites, including Banning State Park, one of Minnesota's most popular.

The Kettle begins in a maze of small tributaries in the northern part of its watershed, in Carlton County, sluggish and warm, mostly ditched. But these small waters soon merge into a single stream, initiating the main Kettle River. Ranging through Pine County, with its rapids and falls, the Kettle runs almost straight south into the St. Croix. (The Kettle is covered in PRIM maps SANDSTONE and MORA.)

In an upper stretch of about twenty miles, the Kettle receives the many small tributaries so that soon it is a moderate sized stream, appropriate for the wading angler, and full of smallmouth bass.

Then the Kettle receives its major tributary, the Moose River, almost the same size as the Kettle, so that its character changes abruptly into a remarkably more canoeable river.

The state-designated canoe route starts about midpoint in the upper section, and for about the next five miles it includes many small rapids, ideal for fishing, to the mouth of the Moose

River. From the Moose down to Banning State Park the Kettle is quiet water.

And then watch out!

Wolf Creek, a tributary of the Kettle, is hidden within its leafy cover, but you can find a trail. Banning State Park.

Without question, Banning's main attraction is the section of violent rapids, ranging up to Class IV. Kayakers love it, of course, but it is also the scene of tragic accidents. Some refer to the profusion of rapids together as Hell's Gate, although only the last of the series carries Hell's Gate as its formal name. The Kettle enjoys seventeen miles of hiking trail, some along the river offering dynamic views of the rapids. Camping includes drive-in sites, a backpack site, several canoe camps, and a camper cabin. Fishing is difficult in the rapids and not an attraction.

Hell's Gate rapids is spectacular in high water, and dangerous. Best in a kayak. Banning State Park.

Below the park the river quiets down again, but soon runs through the town of Sandstone's Robinson City Park. A mile farther is Big Spring Falls, Class IV, and shortly after that Sandstone Rapids, left when the Kettle River Dam (a former hydroelectric facility) was removed in 1995. For many miles the Kettle is again quiet water, but then in the lowermost stretch the Kettle runs through the Lower Kettle River Rapids to its mouth in the St. Croix.

More information on canoeing the Kettle can be found in Breining's *Paddling Minnesota*, in Diebel's exquisitely detailed *Paddling Northern Minnesota*, and in the DNR's canoe map and web site: www.dnr.state.mn.us/canoeing/kettleriver.

The Kettle was the first river to be designated in Minnesota's Wild and Scenic River system, established in 1975. Containing both Wild and Scenic designations, the Kettle aptly deserves this special protection against undesirable development.

Like "kettle holes" along many rivers, small pebbles that were whirled around by wandering river currents carved small holes in the Kettle's bedrock, enlarged by larger and larger stones through millennia to form ever larger holes. A profusion of such kettles along the stream's course led to the river's name.

Banning State Park carries the name of a former president of the St. Paul and Duluth Railroad, which served a sandstone quarry and the developing town of Banning. The town and quarry are long gone, but remnants of the old quarry's concrete walls still stand as a historic attraction of the park.

See more on this unusual state park: www.dnr.state.mn.us/state_parks/banning.

*   *   *

TOGETHER THE SNAKE AND KETTLE make up a pair of wonderful rivers for many types of recreation. They are similar physically and biologically, both contain excellent populations of smallmouth bass, and both have some violent, but beautiful whitewater.

CONSERVATION NOTE
NUMBER 14

HATCHERIES II

ONE OF THE WORST MISTAKES in the history of fisheries management was the introduction of exotic species into streams and rivers.

An outstanding example is the rainbow trout, introduced into small western streams where it hybridized with the native cutthroat. Soon the native cutthroats were gone from many streams.

The rainbow also destroyed many original brook trout populations in the Appalachians. Although hybridization between the 'bow and the brook did not occur, the rainbow, more aggressive in its feeding and growing faster and larger, simply crowded out the brook trout.

Today, rainbows are being removed from some streams, particularly in national parks such as Yellowstone and Great Smoky Mountains, kept as living museums of natural history.

There are other examples, like smallmouth bass stocked into Atlantic salmon rivers. The greatest error of all was the introduction of the Asian carp into North American waters where it has destroyed fish populations in innumerable lakes and rivers.

To the delight of trout anglers, however, the introduction of brown trout was highly "successful," although the native brook trout was pushed out in much of its natural range, to the dismay of some other folks.

Chapter 15

THE MINNESOTA — RIVER OF HISTORY

THE MINNESOTA RIVER and its broad valley will attract history buffs and reveal a major record of an important part of the state's past. Some of Minnesota's historical record is a story of the early settlers' independence and heroism. Other parts mark some of the valley's darker sides.

Yet, still others portray some of our worst environmental treatments of this once beautiful and bounteous part of Minnesota's soils and waters. Newspaper headlines yet proclaim: *Minnesota still a dirty river.* Modern efforts on the part of individuals and organizations, however, have emerged to make amends for the resource degradation and to make at least a start at environmental restoration, with some progress.

*   *   *

THE UNIQUE GEOLOGICAL HISTORY of the Minnesota Valley is intriguing and at first puzzling, especially as to what happened during a period spanning many centuries, about 10,000 to 8,000 years ago. The valley's floodplains, five miles in width, and the depth of the eroded valley of 250 feet suggest a past time of huge roaring torrents of swift and forceful water. But the relatively tiny stream today winding its way back and forth across the broad valley floor does not fit this picture—the river is just too small to have created the large valley. It remained a major geological paradox for many years.

The answer to this puzzle emerged after discovery of *glaciation,* an epoch of about two million years duration. During that time, most of the world's northern hemisphere was covered with huge lobes of ice up to two miles thick, slowly creeping southward from areas of snow and ice build-up in several far northern regions. Eventually, the climate warmed and glaciation ceased, about eighteen thousand years ago, and the glaciers began to melt back. The great meltdown and the icy waters that resulted were responsible for creating most of the earth's northern topography—including that of Minnesota and the strange nature of the Minnesota Valley.

During the melt, a freshwater lake of incredible size spread over much of northwestern Minnesota, North Dakota, and huge areas of Ontario, Manitoba, and Saskatchewan. Now this great lake of long ago is called Glacial Lake Agassiz, after a prominent geologist of the time, Louis Agassiz, the discoverer of glaciation. It was a water body so large that it would have dwarfed even Lake Superior, the largest expanse of fresh water on Earth today.

But Lake Agassiz had to have an outlet, somewhere. That turned out to be a spot near today's Browns Valley, Minnesota, where a great river was born. Cold water flowed south and eastward, later named the Glacial River Warren (after a United States Army engineer), carving the huge Minnesota Valley. Glacial River Warren flowed for about three thousand years, 12,000 to 9,000 years ago.

It was near the end of that period that prehistoric humans dispersed northward across the Minnesota landscape. Some lived along the shores of the lake, we know from skeletal remains uncovered from Lake Agassiz's dry bed, apparently the result of drowning. Many followed the melting ice, hunting the woolly mammoth.

Eventually, after Glacial Lake Agassiz found other, lower outlets leading to the Atlantic Ocean, this great body of melt-water drained away. The relatively tiny Minnesota River remained in the huge valley of River Warren. Geologists call it an "underfit river," the solution to the paradox.

River Warren's floodplains were colonized by early Native Americans, attracted by the lush growth of wild fruits and rich soils that could grow many types of cultivated foods. Invasion by white settlers followed later, as did also the agricultural community of today's Minnesota Valley.

*　　　　　*　　　　　*

PART LAKE, A FEW DAMS AND RESERVOIRS, and a winding course set deep in a five-mile wide valley, the Minnesota River gently meanders from high bluff to high bluff, in many places bordered by hardwood forest and productive farmland. From Browns Valley in Big Stone County, the Minnesota forms the borders of many counties. On its north side the river passes by Chippewa, Renville, Nicollet, Sibley, and Carver counties. On its south side, the river borders Lac qui Parle, Yellow Medicine, Redwood, Blue Earth, Le Sueur, and Scott, to its mouth in the Mississippi in Hennepin County and the Twin Cities, a total of 370 miles. It's the longest stretch of river entirely in Minnesota.

The source of the Minnesota River is Big Stone Lake, border between Minnesota and South Dakota for its first thirty miles, a long and narrow body of water. A few trickles start the river near Browns Valley. There are many boat accesses on the lake, reputed to be good fishing for walleyes. Near the lower end is Big Stone Lake State Park, also offering boat access, drive-in camping, and hiking trails along the lakeshore.

For more information on Big Stone Lake State Park, see: www.dnr.state.mn.us/state_parks/big_stone_lake.

Big Stone Lake was created long ago as sediment from tributary streams formed a natural dam on the primordial river, which backed up water to make a natural reservoir. Now a new structure at the town of Ortonville helps to control the lake's water level.

For canoeists, however, the paddling starts about five miles below the dam where the infant Minnesota begins as a meandering quiet river, and it then flows for more than another 300 miles to its confluence with the Mississippi.

The Minnesota River is the longest river in Minnesota with hardly a man-made dam. Its waters are flat but relatively swift.

Below this first access, however, several more large bodies of water are crossed by the river's currents. First is a large, lake-like marshy area in which is located the Big Stone National Wildlife Refuge, home to a great diversity of birds, mammals, and other wildlife. Established in 1975 after the United States Army Corps of Engineers (USACE) constructed a dam that enlarged the original wetlands area, now for a total of 11,500 acres or 18 square miles. The principal objective of the refuge is to conserve habitat for migratory, resident, and threatened wildlife species that use the wetlands and adjacent native prairie. No camping is allowed in national refuges, but the Big Stone Refuge offers hiking trails, wildlife viewing stations, an auto tour, some fishing in the Minnesota River (winding through the refuge for nearly twelve miles), and public hunting in designated areas for deer, waterfowl, and other small game.

See: www.fws.gov/midwest/minnesotavalley.

Downstream from the refuge lie two more large lakes heading the Minnesota River: Marsh and Lac qui Parle. Both were formed long ago by sediment deposited by tributary streams. Marsh Lake was thus dammed by sediment dropped from the Pomme de Terre River from the north, Lac qui Parle Lake by sediment of the Lac qui Parle River from the south. Lac qui Parle Lake is long and skinny, actually a wide part of the Minnesota River, about fifteen miles. Water levels in Marsh Lake are now regulated by a modern dam at the outlet; the Lac qui Parle exit was not further modified.

In the headwater wetlands of Marsh Lake starts the state's huge Lac qui Parle Wildlife Management Area, 27,000 acres, or 42 square miles, stretching downstream on both sides of both lakes. The two lakes are visited by hordes of Canada geese, around 150,000, in spring and fall on their annual migrations.

The wildlife area offers a great resource for public hunting and wildlife watching, mainly for the remarkable goose migration in autumn. There are also several boat accesses for fishing opportunities.

At the mouth of the Lac qui Parle River at the east end of the lake is Lac qui Parle State Park. Both the Minnesota and the Lac qui Parle rivers do much winding around inside the park, which includes drive-in campsites, walk-in sites, horse camps, and a large group camp. The campground is crowded in autumn during goose season. But also included are miles of hiking trail along the Lac qui Parle lakeshore and around a large oxbow backwater of the Lac qui Parle River. Wonderful birding opportunities here.

For more information on Lac qui Parle State Park: www.dnr .state.mn.us/state_parks/lac_qui_parle.

Early French explorers gave us "Lac qui Parle," their translation of the Dakota's "the lake that talks." Goose talk?

*   *   *

FOR THE MOST PART, paddling the Minnesota River is a sleepy, relaxed float. The degree of curling and winding on much of this journey is extreme.

Canoe routes through the entire river are described in Breining's *Paddling Minnesota* and the other excellent canoe maps from the Minnesota Department of Natural Resources (DNR). They cover the same portion of the river: starting near the lower end of Big Stone Lake and ending at the junction of the Minnesota and the Mississippi in St. Paul.

Both sets of maps are divided into four parts, although different in selections of starts and finishes. The DNR maps are more detailed with other information, such as river miles, county parks, nearby roads and highways, landings and campsites, etc.

Lynne and Robert Diebel, in their *Paddling Southern Minnesota*, have selected three shorter trips with much more detail in river character, accesses and camping, wildlife along the river, shuttle routes, gradient and water levels, and others. Each segment is a day's trip, with camping at each start and finish. These three sections of the Minnesota, they point out, lie in the Minnesota Wild and Scenic Rivers system, and rightly so.

The Diebels' first trip begins just south of Granite Falls and ends just short of the Upper Sioux Agency State Park at Skalbekken County Park, a quiet, lazy, remote section, nine miles. The second continues downriver about fourteen miles to a Renville county park, Vicksburg County Park. Also remote and quiet for the most, this trip ends with a long stretch of rough, boulder-filled water, Patterson's Rapids. The third trip runs from Renville Park to near Redwood Falls, thirteen miles. They describe this stretch of easy paddling with some whirlpools and eddies between bedrock outcrops that line the river. The Diebels' selections offer an excellent invitation to some of the Minnesota River's best.

*   *   *

AN UPPER STRETCH OF THE MINNESOTA, from Lac qui Parle to the town of Franklin, about ninety river miles, was incorporated into the Minnesota Wild, Scenic, and Recreational River System in 1977. It is divided into two segments classified as Scenic separated by one segment classified as Recreational. These are some of the more scenic areas of the river. Nothing much has been done in the way of management of the system since the time of its inclusion in the system, but it at least received the system's protective provisions. Further development of the system is promised, based on community-based plans. The Minnesota River deserves continued stewardship.

For more on the Minnesota's Wild and Scenic System, see: www.dnr.state.mn.us/waters/watermgmt_section/wild_scenic.

About fifty miles below the end of Lac qui Parle Lake, in the city of Granite Falls, canoeists will meet a small rapids and two dams that require portaging, the only obstacles on the river. Otherwise there is nothing much to obstruct either navigation or the view of forest surroundings. Much of the broad river flood-plain is in agricultural cultivation, but wooded banks are the norm, making the river environment pleasantly wild. (See the Diebels' three canoe trips above.) Landings and campsites are numerous, so that short trips as well as long can be arranged easily. Several state parks are located along the river's shore.

In its last thirty-five miles, the river flows through the Minnesota Valley National Wildlife Refuge, the Minnesota Valley State Recreation Area, and Fort Snelling State Park, large areas offering many kinds of outdoor activities.

Along the Minnesota's entire length, a river traveler is aware of the little stream in a big valley. So forget the geological history for the moment. Enjoy the pastoral scenery, modern history, and the huge recreation opportunities in the lower river.

*   *   *

A TRAGIC PERIOD in Minnesota's cultural history, and still troubling today, was the conflict between native people, the Dakota, or Sioux, and the white Europeans. In their westward push for colonization of the rich resources of the North American continent, white settlers and traders made inevitable contact between the two cultures, often violent.

In 1862, despite the national upheaval caused by the beginnings of the Civil War, unrest boiled over among the starving Dakota on Minnesota reservations. Enraged at the whites for their refusal to provide food and other provisions promised in recent treaties, the Dakota finally wreaked vengeance upon their supposed providers but who had become their tormentors.

Violence began at the Lower Sioux Agency, near present Redwood Falls, where the Indians had received humiliating insults. On the morning of August 18, 1862, the Indians attacked and left hundreds of agents, traders, and settlers dead. United States military battalions responded from the lower valley. The war swirled throughout the Minnesota Valley for over a month. Homesteads, agencies, and missions were attacked and destroyed, and murder was rampant. Throughout the upper Minnesota Valley, farmers and their families fled in panic toward the St. Paul and Minneapolis area for protection. Soldiers of the United States Army at Fort Ridgely, near New Ulm, under the command of Colonel Henry Sibley, finally brought an end to the Indians' march toward the cities. On September 23, the conflict was finished after a battle near Wood Lake, in Yellow Medicine County. Three days later, more than 200 white prisoners were taken under protection near Montevideo, soon termed Camp Release, and the last of the Indian warriors surrendered.

The final reckoning was up to 800 whites killed and an unknown number of Dakota. About 300 Indians were rounded up and sentenced to execution. Of these, however, all but thirty-eight were reprieved by President Lincoln; sentences were carried out for the thirty-eight by public hanging in Mankato, on December 26, 1862.

The Dakota Conflict of 1862 left lingering scars in the Minnesota Valley, now memorialized in many historic sites. State parks, monuments, and dedications of places where significant events took place, preserve the physical remains of war between the expanding white culture and the ages-old Native American populations, scattered throughout the valley.

*   *   *

BEGIN YOUR HISTORICAL JOURNEY at the old site of Traverse des Sioux if you will, near St. Peter, where on July 23, 1851, a treaty signed by Dakota leaders and the Americans, extracting millions of acres from the native peoples, promising in return sustaining provisions on their reservations. Later, when the promised food and other provisions were not forthcoming, it was at the Lower Sioux Agency, near Redwood Falls, where starving Indians made their unheeded pleas, and where war began. This historic Lower Agency site includes an excellent visitors center, which unfortunately is closed at this writing due to decreased support funds. But the site is still visible and accessible, and the story is told elsewhere.

At the site of the attack on the Upper Sioux (or Yellow Medicine) Agency, which had been quickly attacked, you can now find the Upper Sioux Agency State Park, on the Yellow Medicine River near Granite Falls. The park offers the usual facilities for camping, horse riding, and hiking, but also two tepees for a treat of something different for overnight lodging. An excellent interpretive center overlooks the broad Minnesota Valley.

For more information visit: www.dnr.state.mn.us/state_parks/upper_sioux_agency.

The battle at Fort Ridgely on August 20 brought a quick end to the Indians' advance toward the Twin Cities. Today's Fort Ridgely State Park, on a bluff top overlooking the Minnesota Valley, commemorates this military action. Remains of the old fort have been restored and preserved. The park includes hiking, horse trails, and campsites along Fort Ridgely Creek.

See: www.dnr.state.mn.us/state_parks/fort_ridgely.

Sites at Birch Coulee Battlefield, where an ambush and defeat of a party of federal soldiers took place on September 2, and Wood Lake, the location of the final battle on September 23, commemorate some of the most bitter fighting. That last day resulted in the capture of many Indian prisoners. All sites have monuments and markers.

These reminders are sobering. But all are relevant to the Minnesota Valley and to our state's past. If history is part of your interest in Minnesota, don't miss this important segment.

*   *   *

FISHING AND HUNTING OPPORTUNITIES abound in the Minnesota Valley.

For the hunter, the Canada goose is prime. The numbers of Canadas that annually drop in for resting and feeding to the upper lakes and river is truly impressive. Large areas are open to public hunting: in the upper sections of the river to some extent, but especially in the large Big Stone National Wildlife Refuge and the even larger Lac qui Parle Wildlife Management Area, more than twice as large. Hundreds of thousands of geese descend upon these areas in their autumn migrations to southern climes.

Although most not on the river, many state Wildlife Management Areas and federal Waterfowl Production Areas dot the landscape of the Minnesota River watershed, especially in western counties. In total, these smaller areas provide an immense public hunting resource for ducks, pheasants, gray partridge (formerly called Hungarian partridge), and cottontails.

Fishing in the Minnesota River can be mainly summarized in just one word: *catfish,* throughout the entire river. Actually, we refer to the channel cat here, although another species of catfish is also in the river, the flathead (or mud) catfish, much less common. Channel cats may be disdained by many folks, but their popularity is on the rise, for two simple reasons: they are easy to catch and they are good eating. The channel cat's unpopularity was due mainly to the fact that it's ugly looking—ugly, that is, until it's in the frying pan. They have to be skinned, best by nailing its head to a board, making a couple of skillful cuts, and using a pair of pliers.

A family relative of catfish is the bullhead (several species) in the Minnesota River. Bullheads are also easy to catch and tasty on the palate, but often small for the effort of skinning.

Fishing the headwater lakes is a different story, that is, more like lake fishing, which should not surprise us. Walleye, northern pike, bass, and panfish fishing is reported good, especially in Big Stone Lake.

The stretch of river from Lac qui Parle downstream to Granite Falls may be the best water for fish other than catfish. Mickey Johnson, in his *Flyfisher's Guide to Minnesota*, obviously favors this piece of the river. Smallmouth, walleye, and northern pike (the big three of warmwater) can be taken here, particularly below small rapids, at mouths of tributaries, and around and below the dams at Granite Falls.

Farther downstream on the river, particularly in the lower reach of river between Mankato and St. Paul, are walleyes, and a few largemouth and smallmouth bass.

But everywhere in the Minnesota River the catfish remains king.

*   *   *

SEVERAL MORE RECREATIONAL opportunities exist on this remarkable river.

From the town of Jordan downstream to the Twin Cities and the junction with the Mississippi, a river distance of thirty-four miles, lies one of the most unusual wildlife and natural areas in the nation: the Minnesota Valley National Wildlife Refuge. It is not a wildlife "refuge" in the strictest sense; its wider objectives include many other benefits to its users, the people of the Twin Cities, the state of Minnesota and, in the broader sense, all citizens. All national refuges throughout the country (543 of them!) provide outdoor recreation, most with special protection and habitat enhancement for some species. Minnesota Valley is focused on people, and their use and stewardship of a broader and unique area, with wildlife enjoyment as part of the whole. Great emphasis is placed on education and appreciation of our outdoor resource. The refuges have often been called "nature's classrooms."

The lower Minnesota Valley contains many so-called "floodplain lakes," bodies of water that are shallow, located close to the main river, and which receive floodwaters from the river periodically. Often they are created by the natural closure of oxbow lakes, and their fish fauna is a reflection of fishes in the Minnesota. Through this part of the river, three major recreation areas treat the users with almost unlimited opportunity of thousands of acres for outdoor activities: The Minnesota Valley National Wildlife Refuge, Minnesota Valley State Park, and Fort Snelling State Park.

See: www.dnr.state.mn.us/state_parks/minnesota_valley, and www.dnr.state.mn.us/state_parks/fort_snelling.

At 14,000 acres, the wildlife refuge is the largest of the three, including about twenty-five floodplain lakes, ponds, and marshes, laced with hiking trails, offering fishing, hunting, and birding. Fishing in the river is open under statewide regulations, and other fishing opportunities exist in special programs. Bird observation is probably the largest use of the refuge, a major stopover point for hundreds of migratory species. Organized into eight units, fishing and hunting are open in specified locations, as well as wildlife observation, varying among the eight units.

Canoeing and boating, as usual, is permitted on the Minnesota River but not on refuge property waters for protection of special wildlife habitats. As in all national refuges no camping is permitted but several campgrounds on state park area units are open nearby.

A modern, large visitor center is the gateway to the refuge. It provides information on all aspects of the area, many exhibits, a large auditorium, art gallery, bookshop, and classrooms for educational programs. A half-mile nature trail starts at the center and offers an excellent introduction to the refuge. Many trails are guided by naturalists in season. For further information, see: www.fws.gov/midwest/minnesotavalley.

*   *   *

THE EMPHASIS OF MINNESOTA VALLEY STATE PARK is much the same as the refuge: preservation of the natural values in the lower Minnesota Valley, including the forested bottomlands, floodplain lakes, wetlands, and bluff tops. It overlaps the refuge in many ways, with many connections, complementing each other. For example, camping is available in the state park but not in the refuge. Hunting is not permitted in state park lands but open in specified areas in the refuge.

The state park, or Minnesota State Recreation Area, runs roughly from Belle Plaine downstream to Shakopee; the Trail Center is located in Belle Plaine, campgrounds are near the old town of St. Lawrence, and the Park Center is in Jordan. Campgrounds offer many drive-in sites, several walk-in sites, and a horse camp with riding trails. Canoe campsites and fishing are available at several of the flood-plain lakes. Fifty miles of hiking trails make up an ample supply, scattered at all locations, plus paved and mountain bike trails. Cross-country skiing and snowmobile trails are abundant in winter. In addition, several canoe campsites and accesses are available along the state designated canoe route. The Diebels give excellent descriptions and directions for accessing these sites. Also see: www.dnr.state.mn.us/state_parks/ minnesota_valley.

*   *   *

THE MINNESOTA RIVER TERMINATES at its confluence with the Mississippi River. However, the character of the Mississippi below the junction, opposite to what you might think, is more like the Minnesota than the Mississippi above the confluence. This is because the Glacial River Warren, at the close of glaciation, did not terminate here but continued to flow downstream to create the character of the River Warren valley. That is, in a miles-wide valley hundreds of feet deep. Native Americans called the river, from Lake Itasca all the way to the Gulf of Mexico, the Mississippi, and we're stuck with it.

Fort Snelling State Park celebrates the land around this junction, incorporating extensive hiking, biking, and skiing trails. At nearly 2,000 acres, Fort Snelling offers many opportunities for wildland enjoyment, in river bottom forest, marshes, several lakes (including fishing and swimming), and of course along the two rivers—right in the middle of the metropolitan area. No camping in this park, but plenty of room, including developed picnic sites and rest areas.

Many species of wildlife, including an abundance of birds, small mammals, and white-tailed deer prosper in Fort Snelling State Park.

A short hike up to Historic Fort Snelling brings you to some of the most important history of Minnesota under the administration of the Minnesota Historical Society. One of the fort's major missions was to keep the peace among warring Dakota and Ojibwe tribes, upstream along both the Minnesota and Mississippi rivers. Original military buildings, many interpretive sources, and costumed soldiers and civilians that replay long ago ways of life and military routine, can be enjoyed almost any day.

See more of Fort Snelling State Park at: www.dnr.state.mn.us/state_parks/fort_snelling.

The abundance of state parks, the national wildlife refuge, fishing and hunting opportunities, river canoeing, historic sites, hiking and camping—all close to home along our heritage of majestic river and valley—offers us enormous recreational opportunity. Use it, take care of it, and enjoy.

*   *   *

STARTING AT THE SOURCE WATER of the Minnesota River, Big Stone Lake near Browns Valley, the Minnesota flows southeastward in the WHEATON PRIM map, and then through maps BIG STONE LAKE, WILMAR, MONTEVIDEO, GLENCOE, NEW ULM, FARIBAULT, and finally, the SOUTH

METRO map and the river's junction with the Mississippi, its total of 370 miles.

*   *   *

DESPITE THE LUXURIOUS QUALITY of the original valley, today's Minnesota River in certain ways comprises a cancer of poor water quality among the natural treasures of our state. Decades of uncontrolled, poor agricultural practice have resulted in a muddy river.

The valley of the Minnesota River was originally a land of fertility. Today, however, this once beautiful and bounteous river flows as the most sediment-polluted stream in Minnesota.

Loaded with soil from eroded cultivated row crops, drainage of the natural capacity of wetlands to soak up runoff, and the enormous tile systems in the profusion of farms, has left the Minnesota's waters despoiled and continuously turbid, loaded with agricultural fertilizers and pesticides that fill the river. The accumulated sediment and chemicals flow to the Mississippi and down to the Gulf of Mexico. There, excessive phosphorus and nitrogen compounds fertilize immense beds of algae, later to decompose and make large portions of the Gulf devoid of oxygen. Empty of fish, shrimp, clams, and other aquatic life, huge areas of the Gulf now have been degraded to a so-called *Dead Zone*. Even though far away, Minnesota contributes heavily to this scar upon the Earth's otherwise productive oceans.

More lately, many agencies, private organizations, conservation groups, and academic programs, having become alarmed, are currently seeking ways to resolve this problem. Federal programs result in setting aside thousands of acres to a return of natural vegetation instead of crops; new regulations now eliminate or reduce phosphorus (the worst contributor to the Dead Zone) in lawn fertilizers. Resource agencies help farm owners to restore natural wetlands that soak up the runoff of sediment and chemicals and urge crops alternative to corn and soybeans (the greatest contributors to soil erosion). Intensive research by state and federal agencies, the University of Minnesota, and private laboratories are striving for solutions. Environmental and conservation organizations continually urge our policy makers in congress and our own legislature for better regulations and assistance programs.

Above all, however, is the support by citizens, private stewards of our natural world who vote, join advocate groups, and pay taxes to support the improvement of our natural world, including the muddy Minnesota River.

"Minnesota," in the Native Americans' language, means "sky-blue waters," at least as we immigrants have translated it. But was it muddy even before European settlement? Some calculations suggest that it was, but not near as full of sediment and exotic chemicals as it is now. Since our blue skies are often masked by gray clouds, maybe the ancients saw the river waters as "cloudy."

Some things, like words and language, have a habit of changing through the centuries.

CONSERVATION NOTE
NUMBER 15

SPECIAL PLACES—U.S.

MINNESOTA IS LOADED WITH SPECIAL PLACES for public recreation, both state and federal, and many include streams and rivers.

Minnesota includes one national park, Voyageurs, along with two national monuments: Pipestone and Grand Portage. Voyageurs is almost entirely in lakes, memorializing the first explorers' track. Grand Portage also honors the early explorers and fur traders, heading up the Pigeon River toward the Northwest.

In a metropolitan segment of the Mississippi River the Mississippi National River and Recreation Area offers a wealth of parks, hiking trails, and boat and canoe landings.

Eight National Wildlife Refuges offer huge areas for hunting and wildlife observation: Agassiz, Big Stone, Crane Meadows, Minnesota Valley, Rice Lake, Sherburne, Tamarack, and part of the huge Upper Mississippi River National Wildlife and Fish Refuge. Most include some river sections, as well as small tributaries, especially on or along the big river.

The Minnesota Valley Refuge also includes many metropolitan sites on or along the river.

Chapter 16

TRIBUTARIES OF THE MINNESOTA

The Rivers:
Pomme de Terre, Chippewa, Lac qui Parle, Yellow Medicine, Redwood, Cottonwood, Blue Earth, and Watonwan

TWO LARGE EXTENSIONS OF THE MINNESOTA watershed provide much additional recreational opportunity. In a northern subwatershed, two tributaries flow south—the Pomme de Terre and the Chippewa, running somewhat parallel to each other.

South of the Minnesota and flowing north, five more rivers add their waters to the Minnesota—the Lac qui Parle, Yellow Medicine, Redwood, Cottonwood, Blue Earth and Watonwan.

In contrast to the pine and spruce forests of the north, most rivers draining into the Minnesota flow past hardwoods and across rolling plains, formerly covered by native prairie. Head-waters of tributaries on both sides of the Minnesota drain lakes and marshes, and consequently the upper sections are reasonably clear, but lower sections become more turbid.

Fish populations vary too. Several state parks and many county parks, particularly historic sites, are located on the main rivers, and accesses allow ample entry for canoeing.

*   *   *

IN THE NORTHERN SUBWATERSHED, the Pomme de Terre and Chippewa head up in lakes of Minnesota's central area of glacial moraines. The lakes are clear and offer typical warmwater fishing, good for largemouth bass, northern pike, and panfish. Some of the plunge pools below dams hold good numbers of fish but mainly small bullheads.

These two streams come tumbling down from lake to lake until large enough to canoe and fish. Most of the lakes have small outlet dams installed, primarily for maintaining stable lake levels and partly as barriers to the dispersal of unwanted fish species.

Many state Wildlife Management Areas (WMAs) and federal Waterfowl Production Areas (WPAs) have been established for public hunting in this region of Minnesota, and many of these are located along small tributaries of the two main rivers, connecting marshes, and some on the main streams as well.

*   *   *

THE POMME DE TERRE RIVER (from the French, "apple of the earth," or potato) is the western and smaller of the two. Heading up in Otter Tail County, the river follows through Grant, Stevens, and Swift counties to its mouth in Marsh Lake, an impoundment in the Minnesota River, for a total of a hundred miles.

*The Pomme des Terre (the potato) is native to North America
and prized highly by Native Americans.*

Several lakes in the headwaters offer good warmwater fishing
for bluegills, largemouth bass, yellow perch, and walleyes—best
in Ten Mile and Pomme de Terre lakes. Most fish species are natural to the lakes, although walleyes are routinely stocked by the
Department of Natural Resources (DNR). Pomme de Terre Lake
is large. Below the small headwater trickles and outlets of the
lakes, the Pomme de Terre becomes large enough for paddling.

The Pomme de Terre is included in Greg Breining's *Paddling
Minnesota,* in Lynne and Robert Diebel's *Paddling Southern
Minnesota*, and in the state DNR's designated canoe route map of
the Minnesota. (See PRIM map BIG STONE LAKE.)

Breining and the DNR map start the canoe route upstream
several miles from the town of Appleton. From there, the river
winds its way to its junction with the Minnesota River in Marsh
Lake—a total of about twenty-seven miles. In its lowest few miles
or so the Pomme de Terre flows through the Lac qui Parle
WMA, which surrounds Marsh Lake, open to public hunting.

Lynne and Robert Diebel describe a Pomme de Terre canoe route somewhat differently, in two segments of a day's trip each. They give more description of the surrounding countryside. They also warn of many obstacles, downed trees, snags, and even field wires strung across the stream. However, they also wax eloquent about the remote, wild few miles in the Lac qui Parle WMA, with its natural forest and abundant wildlife.

Numerous other WMAs and WPAs for public hunting are scattered nearby, including several along the river itself. (See PRIM maps WILMAR and BIG STONE LAKE for the Pomme de Terre River.)

The Pomme de Terre is the stream responsible for the old sediment deposits in the Minnesota River that dam up Marsh Lake.

*   *   *

THE CHIPPEWA RIVER, twice the flow of the Pomme de Terre, also heads up in lakes and ponds of Minnesota's central lake region, most in Douglas County. A major tributary is the East Branch, but the main stem (actually West Branch) is by far the largest and longest.

Several headwater lakes hold the usual warmwater fish fauna, especially Chippewa, Little Chippewa, and Devils lakes, deep and very clear. They hold good natural populations of bluegills, northern pike, largemouth bass, and yellow perch, and walleyes are routinely stocked.

The main stem of the Chippewa, like the Pomme de Terre, tumbles down from its beginning trickles, but farther downstream the river's currents level out considerably. Successively, through Douglas, Pope, Swift, and Chippewa counties, to its mouth, the Chippewa flows for a total of more than a hundred miles. However, the suggested canoe route is much shorter but still longer than for the Pomme de Terre. This route is described in Breining's *Paddling Minnesota,* in the state's designated canoe route of the Minnesota, and most of it in the Diebels' *Paddling Southern Minnesota.* Mainly it's a quiet, twisty run, with small

rapids, and with wooded streambanks and only interspersed agriculture making a scenic paddle.

*The Chippewa comes down from the north, parallel to the
Pomme des Terre, to empty into the Minnesota.*

Breining and the DNR start at the town of Benson and run
to a take-out up a couple miles from the town of Watson. From
Watson downstream to Montevideo, however, about ten miles,
many downed trees obstruct the river, and most canoeists avoid
this stretch by taking out at Watson.

The Diebels divide the Chippewa into two daily segments;
the second is the best, offering the most pleasurable river scenes
with forested streamside topography. As the river descends into
the Minnesota River Valley, riverside scenery improves with ever
higher bluffs welcoming paddlers, some over a hundred feet high.

A dam at Watson diverts floodwaters from the Chippewa
westward toward Lac qui Parle Lake, through an old glacial
channel. Modified by the Corps of Engineers, this channel is
known as the Watson Sag, and is normally dry except during high
water in the Chippewa. Not canoeable, of course.

Many state WMAs and federal WPAs are scattered in the Chippewa's watershed and along the river, open for public hunting for ducks, pheasants, and cottontails.

The name, Chippewa, is the former name of the river's namesake, the Ojibwe Indian tribe. (Note how close the two words actually sound.) (For the Chippewa River see PRIM map WILMAR.)

*   *   *

FROM THE SOUTHERN SUBWATERSHED of the Minnesota come five more tributaries with a wide variety of recreational opportunities: The Lac qui Parle, Yellow Medicine, Redwood, Cottonwood, and Blue Earth rivers. The first four head up on the southwestern Coteau des Prairie, a highland range of igneous Sioux Quartzite, extending northwest-to-southeast across much of South Dakota and the southwestern corner of Minnesota; the fifth, Blue Earth, is a gift *from* Iowa.

*   *   *

HERE WE DIGRESS BRIEFLY TO EXPLAIN the effect of the Coteau des Prairies on the streams that head up there. The Coteau des Prairies in Minnesota is a relatively small wedge of the Sioux quartzite, many millions of years old, and hard enough to resist erosion by the glaciers that scrubbed the rest of central North America only a couple of million years ago. Consequently, the Coteau looms above Minnesota's flat western plains by up to 800 feet, seeming much out of place. On top, the surface is rolling, and in contrast to most of the western plains, it contains an abundance of lakes, ponds, and marshes, holding fish, furbearers, and waterfowl. Because four rivers start here, they rush precipitously down the edge of the Coteau, creating rapids, waterfalls, and scenic, deep gorges. Many parks, picnic areas, and hiking trails are located along these river sections.

The Coteau des Prairies (French for "highland of the prairie") is a hidden, rich resource of recreation, waiting to be discovered.

Another major component of these streams is their fall into the Minnesota Valley, where scenic gorges with their rapids and waterfalls are repeated. We'll take up all of these for discussion, coming up.

*   *   *

THE LAC QUI PARLE RIVER is the smallest of the four, but its main attraction—its part in the Canada Goose migration—stands unique in Minnesota. Much has been written about this great avian resource earlier in this book, and elsewhere, so here we will concentrate on the river itself.

From its beginnings in small Lake Hendricks in Lincoln County (actually on the Minnesota/South Dakota border), the Lac qui Parle continues its flow northeastward through Yellow Medicine and Lac qui Parle counties to its mouth. After dropping about 250 feet off the Coteau, the river winds slowly across rolling plains, and drops another 200 feet into the Minnesota for a total of about sixty miles.

The final drop into the Minnesota Valley is over a river length of about twenty miles, so that its scenery is less striking than for the other three Coteau streams. Nevertheless, like most of the Coteau rivers, the Lac qui Parle presents some interesting effects of high gradient in both sections. In these sections, the river flows swiftly between heavily wooded banks. In this area Canby Creek and Ten Mile Creek are designated trout streams, stocked by the DNR. There are two county parks along the river, offering shady rest away from the summer heat of the western plains.

Neither the DNR maps nor Breining in his *Paddling Minnesota* include canoeing on the Lac qui Parle. It's small and often filled with obstacles in the form of debris dams and downed trees and branches. However, the Diebels in their *Paddling Southern Minnesota* do offer some canoeing. They emphasize lots of riffles and

Class I rapids, high bluffs along the stream, and abundant wild-life. From Lac qui Parle County Park to the Lac qui Parle State Park at the downstream end of Lac qui Parle Lake, it's about a thirteen-mile trip. They warn of wooded jams in the forested sections but praise the bird life in the marshy areas. If the river is very low the trip can be a long walk; in very high levels, she says, don't do it. Dangerous. But lovely. (See BIG STONE LAKE PRIM map for the Lac qui Parle.)

*　　　　*　　　　*

THE YELLOW MEDICINE is a much different stream. Heading in western Lincoln County in tiny Shaokatan Lake, it picks up two small tributaries, South Branch and North Branch, all of which drop off the Coteau and join to create the main stem in a north-western corner of Lyon County, then on through Yellow Med-icine County to the Minnesota River with a drop into the valley.

In the higher water of spring, these waters of the Yellow Medicine River turn to a froth, and canoeing becomes a sport of strength, knowledge, and quick reaction.

In the lower ten miles in its rush down to the Minnesota, the Yellow Medicine contains the main whitewater in the south-western plains. Especially in springtime, this stretch, favored by canoeists and kayakers for its challenging rapids and boulder-strewn cascades, seems surprising among the flat plains. See Breining's *Paddling Minnesota* and the Diebels' *Paddling Southern Minnesota* for further descriptions of this special recreational re-source. The Yellow Medicine is not covered by DNR designation or map. (See PRIM map MONTEVIDEO.)

The Upper Sioux Agency State Park memorializes the Dakota Conflict of 1862 (see Chapter 15). In addition to its historical significance, the park offers many recreational oppor-tunities. Unique among Minnesota's state park lodging facilities, two Dakota tepees are available for an unusual night's sleep. High points offer magnificent views of both the Yellow Medicine and Minnesota River valleys.

Yellow Medicine comes from the Indians' medical use of the yellow root of the moonseed plant, growing along river banks.

For more information on the state park, see: www.dnr.state .mn.us/state_parks/upper_sioux_agency.

*   *   *

THE REDWOOD RIVER is the largest and most scenic of the four streams draining off the Coteau des Prairies. From its highland source in Lyon County, the Redwood drops off the summit as a fast-flowing, bouldery stretch of river, much of it fed by cool springs. This river stays cooler longer than other streams of southern Minnesota. In high water the rapids are mindful of the rushing waters in northern parts. Located on this rapids reach is Camden State Park, an outgrowth of an area used in older times as public picnic grounds and community gatherings. The Redwood's valley here is wooded and cool. (See PRIM MAPS MONTEVIDEO and MARSHALL.)

Redwood River in Camden State Park.

Courtesy of University of Minnesota Press

This combination of characteristics results in stream conditions at least marginally suitable for trout, unusual but welcome in this predominantly prairie region. Although there is little or no reproduction, regular stocking is done by the DNR, and the occasional lunker brown trout is taken. A few remaining brown trout from earlier days of stocking now grace the walls of Camden State Park visitor center.

Downstream, the Redwood flows through Redwood County toward its mouth in the Minnesota. Where the Redwood drops down into the Minnesota Valley, the river presents some of the most scenic views among all of our southwestern rivers. The river literally leaps over hard rock ledges, cutting a deep gorge in some of the most ancient of rock formations. In this steep, wooded valley is Alexander Ramsey Park, the largest municipal park in the state. Originally established as a state park in 1911, it was later given to the city of Redwood Falls. A high dam upstream causes sediment in the muddy upper river to settle out, and consequently the water through the park is usually crystal clear.

Courtesy of University of Minnesota Press

Where the Redwood River drops down into the Minnesota Valley, erosion has created the highest cliffs in southern Minnesota.

In this steepest part of the river, rocky cliffs soar above the river, and nearby Ramsey Creek drops in a high, sheer falls to rival northern rivers, emptying into the Redwood. Campgrounds are plentiful and many trails wind through wooded settings, across bridges over the river, and up to scenic overlooks.

Canoeing seems to be unknown on the Redwood. Neither the state's DNR list includes it, nor does either Breining or the Diebels cover canoeing. Probably some adventurous soul in the future will give it a try and let us know how it goes. (See PRIM maps MONTEVIDEO and MARSHALL.)

The park and its cool river gorge make a large and very welcome oasis in this land of arid western plains.

The Redwood River is not a namesake of the giant sequoia of northern California. Rather, the name stems from the reddish bark of the red-osier dogwood bush growing along riverbanks, used by the Indians as "tobacco." (The fruits are favorite foods of ruffed grouse, so that thickets of red-osier dogwood also signal good places for old Spot or Tober to strike a point.)

*   *   *

THE COTTONWOOD RIVER is larger and longer, and with a different flow pattern than the other three Coteau streams. Heading in small Rock Lake in Lyon County, the Cottonwood winds around as a very small and often intermittent creek on top of the Coteau, then entering Redwood County it plunges down 200 feet through a deep, wooded course to the plains below. For about forty miles the Cottonwood flows slowly along the bottom edge of the Coteau, picking up small tributaries from the highland, and then it turns east across the plains in Brown County to the Minnesota River.

Along the Coteau a small stream, Plum Creek, enters the Cottonwood. This area is noted for scenes of Laura Ingalls Wilder's books, *A Little House on the Prairie* and others; memorial sites, a museum, and historical reconstructions abound here for those interested in this Minnesota literary history.

For another thirty to forty miles the Cottonwood winds and meanders toward the Minnesota River across a flat landscape surrounded by intensely cultivated fields; however, most of this section is pleasantly grown to wooded streambanks. Water flow is usually sufficient in this stretch, particularly the last twenty-five miles, for some pleasant canoeing. In his *Paddling Minnesota*, Greg Breining suggests a twenty-five-mile run to Flandrau State Park. The Diebels describe the Cottonwood in detail, noting some wild water in two daily segments, a total of twenty miles. (PRIM maps for the Cottonwood include MARSHALL and NEW ULM.)

In this lower reach, Flandrau State Park is a large, very popular park in a heavily wooded area on the north side of the river. Three campgrounds boast nearly a hundred sites, plus many miles of hiking trails that wind through the bottomland forest along the river. Surrounding bluffs provide views of both the Cottonwood and Minnesota valleys. A canoe landing is included.

The name of the river is taken from the many cottonwood trees along the river. Native Americans also had the name in their own language for the river.

For more on Flandrau State Park, see: www.dnr.state.mn.us/ state_parks/flandrau.

*   *   *

FARTHER DOWNSTREAM near the city of Mankato a lovely small stream, Minneopa Creek, empties into the Minnesota River. Here we can find Minneopa State Park, including two waterfalls, one of them a fall of about twenty feet. There are ample campsites, one camper cabin, and a very pleasant hiking trail that surrounds the falls area. One of Minnesota's earliest state parks, the name comes from the Dakota for "water falling twice." See more at: www.dnr.state.mn.us/state_parks/minneopa.

*   *   *

THE BLUE EARTH RIVER is one of few streams that originates outside our state and flows into Minnesota—although its waters ultimately flow back out as well. Except for the Blue Earth and a very few others, all of Minnesota streams and rivers that originate inside the state flow out. (Actually, when you come to think of it, all streams flow out. None really stay put in Minnesota.)

The Blue Earth, beginning in Iowa and then flowing north, is a fast run by canoe or kayak, with towering hills on all sides, only eight miles to the best take-out.

The Blue Earth flows about thirty-five miles in Minnesota. From the cornfield border with Iowa, the Blue Earth runs gently as a small creek northward through Faribault County, joining the Minnesota River in the city of Mankato. For about the first twenty-five miles, the Blue Earth runs through cultivated fields as a small stream, much ditched, to the Rapidan Dam, and then for its final miles it runs to its juncture with the Minnesota in Mankato, Blue Earth County. (See PRIM map NEW ULM.)

The Rapidan Dam is an old structure that no longer provides any practical benefit; the reservoir it impounds is filled with sediment and probably many other nasty substances that we had rather not talk about. For many years, much controversy about removing the Rapidan has swirled about; it remains useless, a problem that also threatens thousands of small dams across the nation–how to get rid of them. Like the others, the Rapidan Dam remains as a testament to past mistakes, to the failure of environmental principles not understood years ago.

Below the dam, however, the gorge of the Blue Earth stands as one of the most excellent of riverscapes and canoe experiences among those in southern Minnesota. The gorge is deep and the steep hillsides are densely wooded. Both Breining and the Diebels outline a canoe trip from below the Rapidan Dam to Mankato, about twelve miles. Put-in is available at the new Rapidan Dam Park below the dam (complete with a Dam Store offering food and such) and take-out in Sibley Municipal Park in Mankato. The state's Minnesota River canoe route also includes this section of the Blue Earth.

A canoe or kayak trip is rich with enough boulder dodging and Class I rapids to keep you awake and your paddle busy. The Diebels point out a take-out at about eight miles rather than continuing on through an uninteresting reach through Mankato's urban areas.

"Blue Earth" relates back to the early days of French exploration when some blue-tinted clay in the area was thought to be a compound of copper, with its imagined potential of untold riches. No such luck.

*   *   *

WEST OF THE BLUE EARTH, the Watonwan River arises in a number of small streams in Cottonwood County, flows eastward into Watonwan and Blue Earth Counties, and enters the Blue Earth River near the city of Mankato. Most of the Watonwan watershed has been turned into farmland by ditching and draining, relieved only by the occasional Wildlife Management Area. The region is fascinating with Indian legend.

It was along the Watonwan River that most of the Jesse James gang met their violent ends, following the gang's unsuccessful 1876 raid at the bank in the city of Northfield. A concrete and granite marker identifies the spot where a hail of deputies' bullets shredded not only the streambank vegetation, but the gang members as well, killing one and wounding the others. Jesse and his brother Frank escaped and fled to their home in Missouri.

Watonwan River in southern Minnesota.

In their excellent canoe guide, Lynne and Robert Diebel give detailed information on Watonwan canoeing in two daily segments. They describe at some length the last few miles as the Watonwan drops down into the steep Blue Earth valley, with many small rapids.

*   *   *

THE MINNESOTA RIVER and its tributaries make up a treasure chest of natural resources replete with recreational opportunities in all respects. Canoeing, hiking and camping, hunting and fishing, searching out the state's history.

For the most part, these resources are little used; you will find solitude if you want it. Natural landscapes and river scenes abound, where the only sounds are melodies of native birds, the gurgle of water currents, and the overhead breeze in the tops of bottomland forests.

Many state parks with their waters, woodlands, and riverside trails, a plethora of county and municipal parks (unnamed in this book), and a huge National Wildlife Refuge all invite your presence and pleasure. State and national park rangers are plentiful and anxious to help you find your way, along with maps of all kinds. Even if you don't camp out, there are fascinating old inns and B&B's to accommodate you near the rivers.

While summer crowds flock to northern lakes, resorts, and popular boating routes replete with roaring engines, isn't it time to explore the quiet riverine pleasures of southern Minnesota?

CONSERVATION NOTE
NUMBER 16

SPECIAL PLACES—MINNESOTA

MINNESOTA IS RICH with outdoor adventure, so we can only include a broad-sweep sample.

At the top of the list must be the state's 1,380 Wildlife Management Areas (WMAs), totaling more than a million acres. There's no camping permitted in WMAs, and no ATVs. All are open for hunting, hiking, and wildlife watching, a huge resource open to the public. WMAs are located in 86 of Minnesota's 87 counties.

Another large example is the Carlos Avery WMA (23,000 acres) almost at the edge of the Twin Cities now. There are several ponds through which the Sunrise River flows. But many WMAs are tiny, maybe a single marsh.

The Whitewater WMA (27,000 acres) in the southeast Driftless Area includes hunting, but also three branches of the Whitewater River that give us some of the best trout fishing in Minnesota.

Around 200 Scientific and Natural Areas (SNAs) preserve rare plant and animal habitat for scientific and educational purposes. On foot, of course.

Finally, some seventy-five state parks (many on rivers) offer a huge treasure of land and water for public use.

Chapter 17

RIVERS TO OUR NEIGHBORS

The Streams:
Des Moines, Upper Iowa, Cedar and Rock Rivers
Pipestone and Split Rock Creeks

Aᴸᴸ ʀɪᴠᴇʀꜱ ʜᴇᴀᴅɪɴɢ ᴜᴘ ɪɴ Mɪɴɴᴇꜱᴏᴛᴀ eventually flow out of the state to several of our neighboring states and provinces. Most exit Minnesota by way of the three major watersheds we have discussed already: Lake Superior and the Great Lakes, the Mississippi River, and the Hudson Bay drainage.

Some head up in Minnesota and leave, but not in our three major watersheds. Along our southern border some rivers run directly out of Minnesota and into Iowa (later to enter the Mississippi), and some leave Minnesota to South Dakota (later to enter the Missouri River). The huge Red River watershed drains north to Canada.

Southern Minnesota is becoming more popular for outdoor recreation. Additional recreational opportunities have increased greatly over the past few years with new parks, trails, and campgrounds being added. And there are still few crowds. You'll find good paddling, some excellent warmwater stream fishing, some fascinating history—and much of it along our streams and rivers.

Briefly, we will look at the Des Moines River, a bit of the Upper Iowa, headwaters of the Cedar, Pipestone Creek, Rock River, and Split Rock Creek.

Let's take a look.

*   *   *

THE DES MOINES RIVER is the largest, by far, of these southern Minnesota streams. Heading up in southern Murray County in Lake Shetek, high on the Coteau des Prairies (see Chapter 16) the Des Moines winds among many lakes and ponds characteristic of the Coteau. Farther south, the Des Moines flows down through Jackson County on its way to the Iowa border.

Shetek, at 3,500 acres, is the largest lake in southwestern Minnesota. Here is located Lake Shetek State Park, over a thousand acres, providing an oasis of water and woods in otherwise cultivated plains. An infant Des Moines River exits Lake Shetek at its southeast corner and flows southeastward. Then it's a hundred miles to the Iowa border. In our neighboring state, the Des Moines becomes Iowa's largest river, running across the entirety of the state to its confluence with the Mississippi. Relative to the Des Moines River as a whole, the Minnesota portion is part of the West Fork, but since it's the only part of the river in Minnesota, herein we'll just call it the Des Moines. (PRIM map FAIRMONT.)

About halfway down the Minnesota reach of the Des Moines, the river flows through a small portion of Talcot Lake, in the southwestern corner of Cottonwood County, the outlet of which is dammed up to maintain lake levels. The entire lake, plus a good deal of the river upstream from the lake northward, is the main feature of Talcot Lake Wildlife Management Area (WMA), one of Minnesota's most important wildlife areas, open to public hunting for ducks and geese, deer, pheasants, and cottontails, as well as wonderful birding.

The Des Moines is a designated canoe route in the Department of Natural Resources (DNR) list. Starting below the dam at the outlet of Talcot Lake, a canoe landing affords access to the river, the put-in for the state-designated route.

Breining, in his *Paddling Minnesota*, also starts this trip at Talcot Lake. Lynne and Robert Diebel's treatment of the Des Moines in their *Paddling Southern Minnesota* is much shorter, from the city of Windom to the city of Jackson, a distance of about twenty-five miles. They divide this reach of river into two segments, Windom to Kilen Woods State Park (about fifteen miles), and Kilen Woods to Jackson (about ten), for two daily trips. Above Windom, the river flows past flat farmland, and from Windom down the scenery improves remarkably, with high, wooded bluffs. The Des Moines flows largely through cultivated land, with little in the way of forest scenery. However, it is a quiet, pleasant float, almost always in complete solitude.

Below Windom, Kilen Woods State Park makes up the centerpiece of the Des Moines River route. The valley becomes deeper and narrow, entering a gorge with limestone bluffs 250 feet overhead. Small as Minnesota's state parks go, Kilen Woods nevertheless affords ample drive-in camping, along with several carry-in sites, good river access, and miles of hiking trails along the river gorge and through shady hardwood forest. This park is a true oasis in the spreading agricultural landscape of southern Minnesota.

Fishing in the Des Moines is for warmwater species, typical of the southern region—channel catfish, crappies, northern pike, perch, and bullheads—but mainly for channel cats.

The entire region is also rich with hunting opportunity. Talcot Lake WMA affords the largest area for waterfowl. In addition, the region is dotted with state WMAs and federal Waterfowl Production Areas (WPAs), particularly along the river in its upper reaches.

The name, Des Moines (the monks), comes by way of a very convoluted route from early French explorers who thought the Dakota's pronunciation of their word for the river sounded like "monks." The Indians actually named the stream after one of their villages in Iowa-land.

(See PRIM maps FAIRMONT and WORTHINGTON for the Des Moines.)

For more on Kilen Woods State Park, see: www.dnr.state.mn .us/state_parks/kilen_woods.

*   *   *

ALONG THE BORDER WITH IOWA, heading in Mower County for only a few miles, the Upper Iowa River enters Fillmore County and then into our neighbor.

At the border, the Upper Iowa follows a bizarre path. In Iowa, the stream seems to change its mind and loops back into Minnesota. Still not decided, it loops across the border four more times, back and forth, finally settling on Iowa as its chosen path. Flowing south into our neighboring state, the Upper Iowa River becomes one of the nation's most scenic rivers, meandering through clear pools below limestone bluffs up to 450 feet high.

Near the town of Le Roy, Lake Louise State Park offers a refuge among the sun-baked flatlands of the plains. The lake was formed by a dam built in the mid-1800s on the Upper Iowa to power a gristmill, grinding flour from the grains produced by early settlers. Later, the private land was donated to the village of Le Roy as a public recreation area, the oldest existing such gift of land for a Minnesota state park. The small lake, about twenty-five acres, offered swimming and beach picnics where no such amenities existed previously in the region.

The modern state park was established in 1962, enlarged now to over a thousand acres. It still offers respite from the surrounding plains with an ample campground. Twelve miles of hiking trails and ten miles of biking trails provide exploration around the stream and lake.

Lake Louise is shallow and partially filled with sediment from adjoining cropland and so is limited in its fishing opportunity. Crappies are common and, with some largemouth bass, provide most of the game fish, while the small but beautiful orangespotted sunfish adds a novelty to the angling.

The lake was named after a family member of the early property owners who originally donated land for public use.

The Upper Iowa offers some top-quality smallmouth fishing, one of Iowa's choice streams for this very popular sport fish. Even in the Minnesota loops the river offers Minnesotans some small-stream angling. And it is not likely you will find an idyllic day disturbed by competition.

Upper Iowa River. Mostly quiet water, but shady, and great for smallmouth action.

In all probability, "Iowa" is a translation of the Dakota name for the Iowa River, with the state, like Minnesota, later named after the area's major stream. The Indians had no concept of a "state." The *Upper* Iowa, being a northern tributary, naturally followed. (See PRIM map AUSTIN for the Upper Iowa.)

*   *   *

A MAJOR TRIBUTARY TO THE UPPER IOWA is the Cedar River. Although relatively short in Minnesota—forty miles—the Cedar joins other branches in Iowa to create one of their major rivers, flowing beneath huge cliffs of sandstone for some stunning scenery for canoeists, where it empties into the Upper Iowa. The Cedar begins in northern Mower County, collects many small branches, with the main stem flowing through the city of Austin, and continues southward to cross the border into Iowa near the town of Lyle. In the middle reaches of Minnesota, the Cedar runs across spreading plains, formerly covered by prairie grass where the buffalo roamed, but now mostly turned to agriculture. Catfish and smallmouth bass make up the main fisheries.

After passing through the city of Austin and its very pleasant city park, the Cedar River opens up to become big enough for a bit of canoeing and some smallmouth fishing.

*   *   *

IN THE FARTHEST SOUTHWESTERN CORNER of Minnesota, the Rock River heads in Pipestone County but flows south through Rock County, continues south into Iowa, and eventually into the watershed of the Missouri River.

The University of Minnesota's fish assessment in the Rock River shows species present in the Rock that are not found anywhere else in Minnesota. Of course, the Mississippi joins the Missouri at St. Louis, and it's a long way for fish to make the journey from St. Louis to Minnesota's Rock River, with its many obstacles. And apparently those Missouri River fish species now in the Rock just never made it all the way back.

The Rock River contains some fish species not found elsewhere in our state. That hill in the background is part of the Coteau des Prairies.

An unusual state park is located on the Rock River, Blue Mounds State Park. An outstanding feature of the park is a quartzite cliff on the Coteau des Prairies, a hundred feet above the river below. Prior to the white man's entry into Minnesota land, or so the stories go, the Dakota Indians used this cliff to drive bison to their death, a means of harvesting the animals for food and hide. In early spring, blooms of pasque flowers sprinkle the native prairie above the cliff and, later, the blossoming prickly pear cactus produces its showy yellow flowers. A herd of bison, remnants of the immense populations of the past, roams freely in the park.

Ample camping facilities include about seventy-five drive-in sites, several walk-in sites, and a group camp. Miles of hiking trails wind through restored native prairie and along the top and bottom of the cliff. The cliff, by the way, appeared bluish to western-bound immigrants, a landmark visible from long distances; they were the first to call it the *blue mound*.

Since the river originates on the Coteau des Prairies, the Dakota called it the River of the Rock, probably based on the high outcrop of the Coteau's Sioux Quartzite, the "Blue Mound." Explorer Joseph Nicollet is credited with the translation. (See PRIM map WORTHINGTON for the Rock River.)

For more, see: www.dnr.state.mn.us/state_parks/blue_mounds.

*   *   *

ALSO LOCATED IN SOUTHWESTERN MINNESOTA, the waters of little Pipestone Creek head up in Pipestone County and flow west across our border with South Dakota, and eventually into the Missouri River. The creek itself holds little note among the streams of Minnesota, but rather its inclusion in this book stems from its course through one of the most interesting geologically historic sites in Minnesota—Pipestone National Monument, a unit of the National Park Service.

The site is located on the Coteau, which covers the southwestern corner of Minnesota. *Pipestone* is the name given to a mineral layer of clay, hardened by the heat and pressure of geological forces, embedded as a vein in the quartzite of the Coteau. Visibly outcropping, pink or reddish in color, pipestone is also called *catlinite*, after artist George Catlin who, in the mid-1800s, produced a host of images of local Dakota Indians and of their ways.

Durable but easily carved, the mineral attracted Native Americans from across the continent. Their original carvings were of ceremonial pipes, smoked for sacred purposes such as burials, marriages, and intertribal agreements. Those were widely called "peace pipes," and so the material led to the name *pipestone*. Later, other shapes of carvings of such animals as bison and birds, and other objects important in their culture, were included in the Indians' use of pipestone. Today, only Native Americans may remove any of the pipestone.

Within the monument, a cliff of quartzite of about fifteen feet high overlooks the layer of pipestone deposit, and over this cliff Pipestone Creek drops to form small but beautiful Winnewissa Falls. Below the falls, the creek widens into small Lake Hiawatha, holding many aquatic animals including some small fishes, at least one of which is nationally listed as threatened. Down from the monument Pipestone Creek picks up North and South branches, and then continues on westward into South Dakota and the Missouri River watershed.

Pipestone National Monument commemorates this exceedingly important part of Native American history, particularly since it was truly of national significance, with trade and peaceful intercourse among many tribes. Visitors can walk a self-guided trail to view the pipestone quarries and Pipestone Creek, observe local Dakota at work in their carving, and enjoy the excellent visitor center, full of ancient pipes of many kinds and other historic artifacts. Modern carvings of pipes and other subjects are available for purchase in the center.

The name of the stream, of course, originates from the local mineral. (Pipestone Creek can be found on the WORTHINGTON and MARSHALL PRIM maps.)

For more on the national monument, see: www.cr.nps.gov/nr/travel/pipestone/pnm.htm.

*   *   *

A SMALL STREAM, ALSO FLOWING into South Dakota from Minnesota's Pipestone County, along with some special recreational attributes is Split Rock Creek (not to be confused with Split Rock River on the North Shore). The little creek flows across rolling plains of former sweeping prairie.

The main focus of its watershed lies in Split Rock Creek State Park, open year-round. A large dam built in 1938 by a federal program in the Great Depression era backed up a reservoir of eighty acres to provide much needed water-based recreation, such as swimming, boating, and fishing.

Today the park on Split Rock Lake includes thirty-five modern campsites, mostly drive-ins, some walk-in sites for privacy, and a group camp. Since the original prairie grew no trees, some were planted years ago and now provide pleasant shade to the picnic and camping areas, especially welcome in the heat of a western Minnesota summer.

Walleyes, stocked regularly by the DNR, attract most anglers, but good populations of crappies and bluegills produce the major catch. Present in lower numbers are northern pike, largemouth bass, and yellow perch. A species rare in Minnesota waters is the orangespotted sunfish, present only in small sizes and scarce, but beautiful to behold.

Hiking trails follow parts of the stream and around Split Rock Lake. Visitors can view the sweeping expanse of former prairie from a small hillside still holding native soil and plants. Autumn is a special time to visit Split Rock, when the prairie flowers bloom their brightest.

The creek has in the long past eroded some small, narrow gorges in the Sioux Quartzite bedrock near the village of Jasper, accounting for the village name. Mined outcrops of the reddish/pink quartzite in the area have provided a beautiful building stone.

(See the WORTHINGTON PRIM map for this fascinating little stream and park.)

*   *   *

So OFTEN WITH CULTIVATED FIELDS stretching to the horizon, as well as with its lack of crystal lakes and pine-scented forests, we tend to pass by the land and its flowing waters in our state's far corner.

We must not forget that it's also a land that holds many treasures of its own. Here are placid streams and rivers that hold their own beauty, much of our remaining native prairie, a profusion of wildflowers not found elsewhere, rare migrating birds, and a land so greatly important in Minnesota's early history.

The land invites us.

CONSERVATION NOTE
NUMBER 17

STREAM MONITORING

IT SEEMS THE COUNTRY'S ALIVE with little kids and teenagers, even grownups, out splashing around in creeks and rivers. Wide-eyed, they examine the undersides of stones they have plucked from the bottom of a stream's riffle or from a collection of detritus in long-handled nets.

Here they find tiny snails and clams, immature mayflies and caddisflies, and shrimp-like crustaceans anglers call scuds. They learn that these bugs are the food for fish. They peer through long tubes to check for sediment. They write down data in their notebooks, just like a real scientist.

Oftentimes in their nets they find small fish they never saw before—with strange names like muddlers, darters, and shiners. Some sparkle like silver, and some are colored like a rainbow.

For many of the students, the experience will be the first time they learn of new kinds of life in the outdoors they never before imagined—an opening glimpse into the natural world that will bring desire to know more.

Most importantly, this hands-on outdoor experience may inspire appreciation of a larger world, leading to careers as science teacher or environmental lawyer. Maybe a politician sensitive to Earth's resources.

Part Three

THE
HUDSON BAY

Where Rivers Run North

THE RIVERS
OF MINNESOTA

Recreation · Conservation

INTRODUCTION TO PART THREE
THE HUDSON BAY

THE WATERSHED OF THE HUDSON bay drainage in Minnesota, with rivers running north, occupies a huge area nearly matching that of the Mississippi: the entire border country in the north, almost all of western Minnesota, and the entire northwestern part of the state. That the streams run north, to the upper border of the map, may seem strange to some of us. But it's true enough.

The Hudson Bay basin in Minnesota falls easily into two parts. Both are offsprings of the glaciers that covered this land from about two million years ago to their ending only ten thousand years ago.

First, marking our western border with North Dakota, the Red River flows through a great flat area that we in Minnesota call the Red River Valley—so, the common joke is it's so flat that anyone wanting to play a game of billiards doesn't even need a pool table.

Of course, there are local exceptions. But if you stand almost anywhere in this area and squint your eyes a bit, the horizon seems as flat as, well, a pool table. And the reason is that the Red River Valley unlike the deep valleys of the Rockies or even the Mississippi was formed as the dried up bottom of the largest freshwater lake ever to have existed on Earth. Today the ancient lake is known as Glacial Lake Agassiz, named after Louis Agassiz, geologist credited with the discovery of glaciation.

The northern flow is into Canada, where the old western song *Red River Valley* with its haunting melody, had its birthplace. Here the Red flows into large Lake Winnipeg (a remnant of Lake Agassiz), the outlet of which initiates the Winnipeg River; this stream, also flowing north, changes into the Nelson River, whose flow ultimately enters the salt water of Hudson Bay, part of the Atlantic Ocean.

Although the "valley" may seem flat and uninteresting, many local sites, little publicized, include some choice recreational opportunities: canoeing on the Otter Tail, Red Lake River, and the Red itself, offering hundreds of miles to paddle. A number of rivers and streams, heading up in the lake country of central Minnesota, flow westward toward the Red, some with wooded valleys and rushing rapids.

Fluctuating water levels of the old glacial lake formed high beaches during long periods of thousands of years, backing up huge marshes rich with waterfowl and shorebirds. Although many of these marshes have been drained for agriculture, some remain. Streams flowing through the beach ridges cut their own valleys, where now woodlands prosper, and where state parks have been developed to provide respite from the open plains in their oases of shade and flowing water.

Fishing in the Red River includes primarily catfish, some huge. You might also catch a rare species of our evolutionary past, the lake sturgeon. There's a large, new state park on the Red that grew out of the flood-ravaged remains of the worst flood disaster ever. Add two more state parks and a host of county and municipal parks, located on the swift, forest-lined tributaries flowing through the ancient beaches. Later, we'll take these up in detail.

*   *   *

THE HUDSON BAY WATERSHED, totally different from the Red River Valley, makes up our northern border with Canada. Comprising a vast mixed-conifer forest, a thousand lakes rich in some of our favorite sport fishes, and a few of the most beautiful canoeing streams in Minnesota—destination of hundreds of thousands of visitors from Minnesota and around the country. Here we call it the *Rainy River Country*, for the Rainy is the stream that drains it, but most of it is known nation-wide as the Boundary Waters Canoe Area Wilderness (BWCAW) and, across the border in Canada, the Quetico Wilderness Park.

Much of this wild country lies north of the Lake Superior watershed, incorporated into the Superior National Forest and many smaller Minnesota state forests. Voyageurs National Park, in addition to the BWCAW, defines this vast area of deep, cool, pristine waters.

The abundant lakes in the Rainy River country trend northeast to southwest, scoured by glaciers that ground and scraped out lake basins as the ice slowly crept southwestward across the Precambrian Shield of ancient lava from their source in Labrador on the North Atlantic.

We may call it the Rainy River watershed, but not because a single stream flows from its source to its mouth. Rather, the basin begins where the Pigeon River also begins, in the spreading forest of eastern North America. The Pigeon flows south and east to Lake Superior, whereas the Rainy's headwaters flow west toward giant Lake of the Woods, which is part Canada, and onto the Hudson Bay.

Granted that the recreational resources of this area are mainly in lakes, river-based recreation is endless. We'll take up details in separate chapters.

The cultural histories of these two strikingly different regions are also greatly different. Escaping from despotic landowners in Britain, uprooted Scots and Irish immigrated to North America via Hudson Bay, then south to the fertile plains of the upper Red River. On another route, French and English explorers and fur traders arrived in North America via the St. Lawrence River and the Great Lakes. They ventured west through the lakes in their quests, first for the (nonexistent) passage to India and the Orient, and second to exploit the vast interior of the Northwest for beaver, preferred for the fur hats of Europe. Many residents of these two regions still reflect their different ancestral sources.

Waters of the two river basins, from the Red River plains to the Rainy's conifer forests, eventually meet and mix. We'll finish up how the Rainy's water joins the Red's and continues on to Hudson Bay, ever northward.

Chapter 18

RED RIVER VALLEY

The Rivers:
Red, Bois de Sioux, Otter Tail, Buffalo, Middle, Roseau

I T MAY SEEM STRANGE TO BELIEVE that one of our major rivers actually *flows north*. After all, most streams and rivers all over the country join the Mississippi and *flow south*. When we plan a trip to our lake cabin, we call it *up north,* and all our maps run *down* from the north to the southern bottom of the page. They behave themselves. The errant flow of the Red, northward, seems unnatural, as if we think the Army Corps of Engineers ought to do something about it.

Of course, we feel we must distinguish it from the Red River in the South, Texas and Oklahoma, so we call ours *the Red River of the North.*

*   *   *

IF YOU VISIT THE RED, just to see it, you might be turned off by its looks—muddy, slow, winding around interminably.

But looks can be deceiving. So much has been improved, so much has been discovered, so much done in conserving and preserving its natural values. The great flood of 1993 taught us many lessons. Not all of which have survived, but many have been acted upon with vigor, and the result has given us more access for recreation to the river and its floodplains. The potential for flood damage has been reduced, and access, parks, campgrounds, trails, canoeing opportunities, and other green spaces have replaced the flood damage potential. Of course, we're not finished. The added floods of 1997 and 2009 have proved that.

The Red River of the North. As the border between Minnesota and the North Dakota, fishing regulations may differ.

The Red is a border river between Minnesota and North Dakota for its entire length in the United States. Along this western margin of Minnesota, the river passes from its beginning in Traverse County north into Wilkin County, where the Otter Tail River joins the Red. Continuing north, the river runs past Clay,

Norman, Polk, Marshall, and Kittson counties, and thus into Canada.

Across the river, the changes on our neighbor's side have resulted in similar beneficial results to their recreation access and quality. So we must keep in mind that what we do on the Minnesota's side may also affect the North Dakota side, and vice versa.

*   *   *

BEFORE WE GET INTO THE PARKS, fishing, and canoeing on the Red River, it is necessary to briefly review its fascinating geologic history, so significant to the modern river and its opportunities for outdoor recreation, on both sides.

The series of long-ago events that created the river and its valley is directly linked to the melting of glaciers, ten thousand years ago. The melting was the result of a warming climate and the end of glaciation after the two-million-years-long Pleistocene Epoch. The melting itself took many thousands of years, and the immense body of meltwater that resulted changed the topography in a huge area of North America.

Melting began in the Minnesota/North Dakota region about eighteen thousand years ago. North of today's town of Browns Valley, meltwater began to accumulate into a large lake. Modern geologists call it Glacial Lake Agassiz after geologist Louis Agassiz who is credited with the discovery of glaciation. From a tiny pond at Browns Valley, it grew to become the largest body of fresh water ever to have existed (as far as we know).

With a warming climate, the edge of melting ice slowly moved northward, and Glacial Lake Agassiz increased in response. To the east, lower outlets that might have carried meltwater to the Atlantic Ocean were blocked, still covered by ice. So, with continued melting, the impounded waters continued to rise, simply because accumulated meltwater had no place to go. The lake grew to cover up to some 200,000 square miles, much larger than today's combined Great Lakes. With variations in size and shape, the lake existed for about eight thousand years.

Eventually, however, ice melted to expose the eastern outlets such as the Great Lakes and the St. Lawrence River. Water poured through to the Atlantic Ocean, and Glacial Lake Agassiz ceased to exist. Some of the largest lakes in North America have been left as today's remnants of Glacial Lake Agassiz.

The entirety of the glacial lake did not exist all at one time. Nor did decreasing water levels fall at a consistent rate. Rather, it was in fits and starts as one after another a new outlet to the Atlantic Ocean was uncovered. At various times, stable levels remained for hundreds or thousands of years, and sand and gravel accumulated as dunes at lake edges due to wind and wave action. So when lake levels dropped further, these beaches, or strandlines, remained up to twenty-five feet above the rest of the flat plains, still with us today.

The most prominent strandlines in Minnesota are the Herman and Campbell beaches. Herman Beach, the earliest and farthest east, and at the highest lake level, marks the most eastward edge of Glacial Lake Agassiz. It runs as a ridge near its namesake town of Herman at its southern end, then northward through Grant, Otter Tail, Clay, Norman, and Polk counties, where it swings eastward to surround the Upper and Lower Red lakes. Campbell Beach, the latest and farther west, at a lower lake level, begins near its namesake town of Campbell at its southern end, and then courses through Wilkin, Clay, and Norman counties, to near Roseau at its northern end. Incidentally, both lakes are remnants of Glacial Lake Agassiz.

These two beaches give us some of the most notable locations for stream and river recreation, particularly on the tributary streams that have carved valleys of their own as they rushed through the higher ridges of the beaches.

At these highest lake levels, water emitted at the location of Browns Valley rushed across southeastern Minnesota-land, carving Glacial River Warren, the precursor of the Minnesota River. (See Chapter 15 on the Minnesota.)

But later, when glaciation of central North America and Glacial Lake Agassiz was in decline, more and more dry land became exposed near the southern edges, as well as across the continent.

It was in these times that prehistoric humans invaded the newly exposed landscape, hunting the mastodon, woolly mammoth, and other large mammals, following the edge of the melting ice.

*　　　*　　　*

TODAY, THE NORTHWARD FLOW of the Red River produces some dire results. After a cold winter that leaves the river frozen, in the spring it's the southern headwaters that thaw first, sending meltwaters rushing downstream, northward, where the river is still frozen. The existing ice stops the flow, and major floods result.

Don't forget, while we're paddling the river and think we might be going in the wrong direction, floating downstream toward the top of the map. Remember? We call it the Red River of the North.

*　　　*　　　*

AS WITH OTHER RIVERS, we're going to start at the beginning of the Red River and work our way downstream—that is, to the north.

The north-flowing waters of the Red River begin near the town of Browns Valley, Minnesota, close to the North Dakota border. These waters start out as the long, narrow Lake Traverse, not as the Red River. Lake Traverse reaches northward for about twenty miles, where it meets an Army Corps dam, stabilizing the lake's surface level. Water exiting from the dam forms Mud Lake, which, in turn, runs north for about three or four more miles, meeting yet another Corps dam. But the exit from this dam forms a river, albeit slow and shallow, the Bois des Sioux (woodlands of the Sioux). The Bois des Sioux flows north for twenty-some more miles where, at the city of Breckenridge, it is joined by the much larger and more river-like Otter Tail River.

North of the Red Lake River junction the Red River winds and twists its way north to leave the United States and enter Canada after its long journey of 400 miles.

          *   *   *

THE RED RIVER MUST BE THE WORLD'S most tortuous river. Winding back and forth it seems you are traveling in circles, and in fact that is almost true. The bends, meanders, and oxbows are endless. If you travel by car on US Highway 75 from Breckenridge to Georgetown, pretty much paralleling the river on the way, you would put on about sixty highway miles. From the canoe put-in at Breckenridge, however, the Red flows to Georgetown for a hundred and thirty river miles. Characteristic of its entire length, the river flows about twice as far as the crow would fly. Early DNR's canoe maps described only the route between Breckenridge and Georgetown, but recent additions continue description of the longer route up to the North Dakota city of Pembina and a couple more miles to the International Border. The entire state-designated canoe route now comprises three separate guide maps, free for the asking from the Minnesota Department of Natural Resources. Nearly four hundred miles.

In his *Paddling Minnesota*, Greg Breining describes the Red as incredibly flat and wormlike, with no rapids, but several man-made dams to contend with. (Some of these dams have now been removed or modified to allow free passage.) Breining covers the whole of the river, from Breckenridge to Canada, but without much detail. The entire route, should you opt for it, would probably take about three weeks.

The route includes many landings for access to the river; some are boat ramps. Rest areas and campgrounds are ample too. Of course, similar facilities are located on the North Dakota side. Some dams still obstruct the river that must be portaged or otherwise avoided.

One adventurous river-lover made the entire trip from Breckenridge, Minnesota, to Selkirk north of Winnipeg, Manitoba, 550 miles, by canoe. The Red River Valley was the home ground of the paddler, and he felt the challenge to emphasize the environmental and recreational value of his beloved stream. (See Jim Dale Huot-Vickery, *A Sense of Place: Going with the Flow, Minnesota Conservation Volunteer*, March-April, 2001.)

Although the Red River is placid with no natural rapids, we have created a few. Dams at East Grand Forks (on the Red) and Crookston (on the Red Lake River) have recently been removed or modified, replaced with bouldery rapids, opening up the river to give fish and kayakers free passage. The new rapids are beautiful sights to see, after so much flat water. More to come.

Here on the spreading plains of the West, once with its vast herds of bison and waving prairie grasses (now mostly sugar beets and soybeans), you can still find respite down this quiet stream lined with woodlands of silver maple, box elder, and cottonwoods.

You'll find some fascinating historic sites along the river, for it is here that the Hudson's Bay Company early on established fur trading stations, outposts of the company's far-flung enterprise in the great Northwest.

And it was here, too, that immigrants and traders from northern settlements labored across the prairie with their squealing, wooden-wheeled Red River oxcarts, sometimes following the old beach ridges, to found and colonize the city of St. Paul. To visit these icons of North American history by canoe or boat is a rare treat.

* * *

MUCH ATTENTION HAS BEEN GIVEN recently to the recreational potential of the Red River. Parks and special environmental sites, boat and canoe accesses, and fisheries management have all increased significantly.

The new Red River State Park is an outstanding example. Located at and near East Grand Forks and Grand Forks, North Dakota, this park is a direct outgrowth of the devastating flood of 1997 that hit both sides of the river with great damage. For example, almost all homes in East Grand Forks, Minnesota, were inundated. Hundreds of houses subject to future flood damage were bought and removed from the floodplain. The result is a "Greenway," over 1,200 acres, now empty of buildings. The park now provides campgrounds, fishing sites, boat and canoe accesses, and other facilities, that we can now enjoy, along the river. The Greenway, of course, is located on both sides of the river.

We were a long time recognizing that *floodplains* are not called that for nothing, and that floods are a natural result of topography and climate that we cannot change. Instead of dams and levees, parks make much better use of lands subject to inundation. When the flood retreats, parkland remains intact. And we have increased river recreation opportunity to boot.

In the Red River Greenway, instead of flood-prone buildings we now have campgrounds, two golf courses, many playgrounds and shelters, canoe and boat landings, over a dozen trailheads and accesses with picnic grounds, and a beautiful river rapids where once stood a useless dam.

It was a tough lesson to be learned, the hard way, but now we can be thankful that we did learn it, at last.

County and municipal parks are also scattered along the river. About fifteen parks, plus other accesses, golf courses, camp and picnic grounds, hiking trails, and historic sites are located in the Breckenridge to Georgetown reach alone, on the North Dakota side as well as Minnesota. And there's more to come.

*   *   *

FISHING ON THE RED IS DIFFERENT than on our thousands of lakes and miles of other rivers. The water is much warmer and muddier than our trout and smallmouth streams.

Catfish are supreme, the major sport fish, and there's lots of them. Catfish can prosper in muddy water because of their barbels (whiskers) that have an olfactory sensing function, enabling them to detect their food in the dark.

There are two species: the channel catfish and the flathead (also called mudcat). The flathead grows larger than the channel cat, but both grow larger than catfish in other waters. You can tell the difference between the two species by the fact that the flathead has, well, a flatter head; more distinctive, however, is that the channel cat has a sharply forked tail, and the flathead's tail is almost square.

Channel cats, with their sensitive barbels, locate their food by its *smell*, often at the river bottom where muddy water is the thickest. The Red River provides this habitat aplenty. So bait it is, on the bottom. Some of the smelliest, specially prepared baits are often the most effective. (But better hold your nose.)

The flathead catfish feeds much differently, mainly on live, small fish, and avoids dead bait. We call it a piscivore, feeding on other fish. Here you can drag out your walleye lures again.

Most fish-eating anglers prefer the channel cat, in the one-to-two pound size. Maximum is around thirty-pounds; flatheads are caught up to much larger sizes, with angler-caught specimens up to seventy pounds, commercial catches over one hundred pounds.

If you're after trophy catfish (up to thirty pounds), fish the lower river stretches, that is, nearer Canada. You will catch smaller catfish (like good eating size) in the upper or southern, reaches.

The Red River is the best producer of catfish in the state, although the channel cat is also very popular in the Minnesota River and the muddier sections of the Mississippi and St. Croix.

Many other fish species prosper in the Red River. Northern pike, that ubiquitous denizen of practically all waters everywhere, is common in the Red. Walleyes provide good fishing if you are experienced in knowing where and when. Because they will not spawn and reproduce in the Red's waters, walleyes are heavily stocked by the DNR.

Other warmwater fishes are present too—sunfish, crappies, bullheads—but not seriously sought after.

Another Red River fish, not commonly seen these days, is the lake sturgeon. Despite its name, it's really more of a river species, requiring rocky riffles for spawning. Commonly called a "heritage" fish, it is a primitive leftover from the dinosaur days, millions of years ago.

Once they were so common that local folks would net them in the rapids during spawning in quantities enough to fill the bed of a farm truck. But today there are almost none to be found.

A "fingerling" lake sturgeon. For many fish species,
this size is attained after the first year of growth.
(Photo courtesy of Minnesota Department of Natural Resources.)

The culprit was the profusion of dams that prevented fish movement. Each spring, mature sturgeon must ascend upstream reaches to gravel riffles in smaller streams for spawning, and when dams filled the Red and tributaries, sturgeon reproduction ceased.

Now, much fish management effort by the Department of Natural Resources (DNR) is directed toward restoring the lake sturgeon. Most of the dams in the Red River have been removed or retrofitted to allow fish to move up to their old spawning sites.

Restoration has also been carried out in tributary streams, such as the Otter Tail, Wild Rice, Buffalo, and Red Lake rivers. In their efforts to restore this rare species, the DNR stocks hundreds of thousands of young sturgeon each year. But they are long-lived, taking twenty years to reach maturity, so to assess success will take time. Restoration projects are also under way in other streams of Minnesota, once holding native-bred sturgeon like the St. Croix, Snake, and Kettle.

Who knows, Minnesotans may be lucky enough to land at least a small sturgeon in a Red River watershed stream in the near future—a sample of our heritage from long ago. If you do, it must go back.

Keep in mind that the Red River is the border between two states and regulations may differ from inland waters. Such interstate regulations are often more liberal.

Although the Red River is naturally muddy or turbid, its water quality is good otherwise. The river is not as badly polluted as it may look. Good eating is the result.

Tip: Check out *Fishing on the Red River of the North,* a valuable booklet available from the DNR's Information Center, 651-296-6157.

*   *   *

A MAJOR TRIBUTARY OF THE RED RIVER is the Otter Tail River, entering at Breckenridge and considered by some as the real headwater of the Red River. It's true that only below the junction of the Otter Tail and the Bois de Sioux is the main stem called the Red, and it's the water of the Otter Tail that makes up the greatest volume of the Red River downstream. Early Indians had named the stream we now call the Red River as the Otter Tail all the way up. Geologically however, the headwaters lay directly south where the Red's waters initiate at Browns Valley. In any case, we are going to discuss the Otter Tail from the perspective of its importance as a recreational river—which is great indeed.

The Otter Tail is a river of lakes. This doesn't mean that you'll be on flat water all the time, for a canoe ride can be broken up into short reaches offering trips of great variety.

The Otter Tail heads up in the lake country of central Minnesota, in small trickles in the southwestern corner of Clearwater County, flows southwestward, and then swings west to join the Bois de Sioux and gives birth to the Red. In its long course, the river flows through a host of lakes, some big (like Otter Tail Lake, at over twenty-one square miles), many smaller. Initiating the main river, the Otter Tail exits long-stretching, north–to–south Elbow Lake, at the northern border of Becker County, to begin its journey to the Red. Shortly below Elbow Lake the river flows through Round Lake near the Otter Tail's entrance into Tamarac National Wildlife Refuge.

The Otter Tail River is mostly a series of lakes, so upper reaches are always clear.

At 43,000 acres, or 67 square miles, Tamarac National Wildlife Refuge is one of the largest in Minnesota. Whereas the Otter Tail does flow through the refuge, it runs mostly through the refuge's wildlife sanctuary, where public activities, including canoeing and fishing are prohibited. An exception is that fishing from the banks near county road crossings is permitted, and your canoe may be launched in Bluebird Lake, near the southern border of the refuge, for further paddling down the Otter Tail. All national refuges have similar sanctuaries where all animals and their habitats, particularly waterfowl and their breeding areas, can live and reproduce undisturbed.

Fishing opportunities, however, are abundant in several of the refuge lakes for which there are about fifteen boat and canoe landings. Wauboose, Lost, and North Tamarac lakes are a few; species include the usual list of warmwater lake fishes, such as bluegills, largemouth bass, northern pike, and walleye. Height of Land and Many Point lakes, large and better known, abut the refuge and are open for public fishing.

While you're there, other recreational and educational opportunities abound. The mission of Tamarac, like other national refuges, is primarily for restoration and management of wildlife populations and their habitat. Sustaining a healthy diversity in habitat is essential to both productivity and variety of wildlife species.

Tamarac provides a wondrous opportunity to observe a large natural area for understanding many wildlife species and their place in diverse natural environments. Tamarac includes over twenty lakes, some closed to provide undisturbed habitats for waterfowl in their breeding season. There are miles of hiking trails—some along the Otter Tail—wildlife observation posts, a self-guiding auto wildlife drive, and a large visitor center where many of the refuge objectives and activities are explained and demonstrated.

Like many other National Wildlife Refuges, Tamarac offers a treasure chest of birding opportunity. Because of the several lakes on the refuge, many species of waterfowl and shore birds nest or migrate through the refuge's marshes, ponds, and wetlands; included are Canada geese, pelicans, swans, loons, twenty-species of shorebirds, fifteen birds of prey, such as the bald eagle, osprey, and owls, ten hawks and falcons, and more than twenty species of ducks. Over a hundred small songbirds populate the forest and wetlands. In total, about 275 bird species are seen on the refuge. Of course, many are rare or just casually seen, but over a hundred nest and breed on Tamarac.

Small game, deer, and waterfowl hunting is allowed in specially designated areas and, for the most part, under regular statewide regulations, demonstrates the place of regulated hunting in the normal ecology of many of our native wildlife species. Areas open for hunting are plentiful, in most of the refuge, primarily for white-tailed deer, waterfowl of several species, ruffed grouse and woodcock, and small game such as squirrels and rabbits. Part of Tamarac includes some of the White Earth Tribal Reservation, wherein special tribal regulations apply. Otherwise, statewide regulations apply, although non-toxic shot only may be used for all species in the refuge.

Much of the refuge is forested with deciduous woods, and the autumn colors are spectacular. Visit in the fall when the bird migrations are in full swing and the maples are blazing with red and orange.

*   *   *

BELOW THE REFUGE, many miles of the Otter Tail River await you. You can start a canoe trip with a refuge landing on Bluebird Lake, near the southern border of the refuge. There are many more lakes through which the river flows, including Height of Land, Pine, and Otter Tail, all large. A few more miles of placid water and the river enters Fergus Falls, and it is here that Breining begins his suggested trip of thirteen miles through what is the most interesting section of the Otter Tail River.

At Fergus Falls a diversion dam directs the Otter Tail's water through a shortcut that avoids a big bend of thirteen miles. However, plenty enough water remains around this tortuous, winding path for a good day's canoeing. The river is placid for most of the trip, but the lower third contains enough rapids to satisfy most of us, up to Class II. Breining also describes some hazards in this lower third. Here the Broken Down Dam rapids (Class II) marks the location of a large dam built in 1908, collapsing a year later and causing a devastating flood in Fergus Falls. Several additional canoe landings may be accessed in this run, and take-out is back on the river's original channel.

In her *Paddling Northern Minnesota*, Lynne Smith Diebel describes more of the Otter Tail, adding twenty miles of river, in two sections for two daily trips for good canoeing. She describes this section as having strikingly clear water (usual below a dam) and excellent smallmouth bass fishing.

Downstream the river swings west and runs into Orwell Reservoir, backed up by an Army Corps flood-control dam. From this dam the Otter Tail continues west to flow over the flat bed of Glacial Lake Agassiz, through the town of Breckenridge, and then north as the Red River of the North.

＊   ＊   ＊

OTHER TRIBUTARIES HEAD UP IN THE LAKES of higher country outside the flat glacial lake bed, flow westward, and empty into the Red River to swell its flow northward toward Hudson Bay.

Notable among these tributaries is the Buffalo River. It heads in Tamarac Lake in the Tamarac refuge. Where the Buffalo falls through the Campbell Beach, near the town of Glyndon, Buffalo River State Park was established in 1937, primarily to preserve some of the tallgrass prairie that grew so high and so lush on the surrounding flat plains. On the Campbell Beach, the river's waters fall through the ravine carved into the beach, providing recreational opportunities along the wooded riverbank, rare on the otherwise flat plains. The park is also noted for native prairie, some of the largest and best bluestem prairie in the state, laced by miles of hiking trail. Furthermore, at nearly 1,300 acres, the nearby Bluestem Prairie Scientific and Natural Area is one of the largest remaining native prairies in the nation, protected by The Nature Conservancy. Hiking trails wind through the spreading native prairie inside the park and along the tumbling waters of the Buffalo, shaded by river-bottom woodlands of ash and cottonwood trees.

Onion Creek, A small tributary of the Otter Tail winds around in some greening, springtime woods, brightening up the dullness of surrounding dry plains and fallow fields.

Next downstream (up the map) the Red Lake River comes in to join the Red River. This stream is the largest and longest of the Red River Valley rivers, and its origin is much different. Rather than heading in upland lakes or trickles out on the plains, the Red Lake River begins as a full-blown river emitting from huge Lower Red Lake, far to the east, a leftover from Glacial Lake Agassiz. We'll take up this stream in Chapter 19 coming up next, but in the meantime we'll continue downstream on the Red.

*   *   *

THE MIDDLE RIVER, A LITTLE STREAM that actually starts on the old lakebed itself and, flowing across extremely flat land with almost no gradient, follows through a maze of tortuous bends and meanders. Flowing west over the lakebed, the Middle River ultimately empties into the Snake River very near the Red.

The only break in its leisurely flow, like other streams on the flat lakebed, is where it tumbles through an eroded valley in the Campbell Beach ridge. Here you will find a most welcome stop-over, Old Mill State Park, a delightful reminder of pioneer days on the prairie.

In the late 1800s settlers found the site to be suitable for a dam and a water-powered grist mill (grinding wheat to flour). After several changes in the mill's power source, Old Mill State Park was established in 1958. Today the mill is operated with an old steam engine as the power source, fired up once a year to demonstrate an older way of making flour, so important to early settlers; visitors may purchase samples. A restored old cabin reminds us of an earlier day.

An extensive system of hiking trails of about eight miles winds along the river as well as out on the plains. Of special interest is a self-guided trail of over a mile in length that winds through native tallgrass prairie that once covered such vast areas of the Red River Valley. You will also walk through some examples of aspen parkland, oak savanna, the Campbell Beach ridge with remains of the old oxcart trail, and the forest-lined banks of the Middle River. This trail may very well offer the park visitor the best example of western native Minnesota landscape in the state, illustrating the reason for the park's original location, the water power of the Middle River.

You can't help but get the feeling of what the surrounding plains looked like, and felt like, when the first mill operated on the river's water power.

*   *   *

IN THE FAR NORTHWEST CORNER OF MINNESOTA, the Roseau River arises on the old glacial lakebed. Small trickles head in Beltrami and Lake of the Woods counties, and the mainstem Roseau runs northwestward across the entire width of Roseau County and through a tiny corner of Kittson County for a total of about 150 miles in Minnesota. The Roseau then flows north into the Canadian province of Manitoba, eventually emptying its waters downstream on the Red River.

In the eastern part of Roseau County, on a far upstream reach known as the North Fork of the Roseau, Hayes Lake State Park provides welcome recreation in a region without other such opportunities. A dam on the river years ago created Hayes Lake (after an early settler) to provide more water-based recreation, and the state park was established in 1967. Swimming and fishing are available in the lake. Many miles of trails line the lake and river, providing some excellent scenic views of lake and stream. Obviously the main recreational focus of the park is on the lake, but on streamside hiking trails you can enjoy the riverine landscape as well.

At about two-thirds of the river distance downstream, the Roseau River flows through the town of Roseau. A dam here backs up an impoundment, but a public access below the dam allows the best canoe travel from this point on down to near the Canadian border, a distance of about fifty miles. Several canoe and boat accesses are available through this stretch for shorter trips.

The Roseau is generally shallow with moderate turbidity and a sand bottom. Much of this reach has been channelized and straightened by the Army Corps of Engineers for flood control. Many natural oxbows on the river were cut off and banks lined with dredge spoil, all of which helps to rush floodwaters away downstream (into Canada, of course). However, snowmelt and heavy precipitation can still cause rapid flooding with muddy water. On the other hand, midsummer water levels may be too low for watercraft travel. Late spring is best, or after some fall rains.

Most of the river between Roseau and the border is through the Roseau Wildlife Management Areas (WMAs). There are two: the first (farthest upstream) is the Roseau Lake WMA of 6,000 acres (nine square miles). The lake has been largely drained and exists now as wetland. The second, farther downstream, is the much larger Roseau River WMA at 74,000 acres (115 square miles), through which the river flows for fifteen miles. It's one of the largest WMAs in Minnesota. (Only the expansive Red Lake WMA is larger, at 400,000 acres.)

Both areas include extensive wetlands, remnants of Glacial Lake Agassiz, and a large area once known as the Big Swamp. At one time these wetlands were widely ditched and drained for agriculture, but now they are incorporated into wildlife habitat that remains in wetland. Four large "pools" are maintained by detention structures to create open, shallow water. Surrounding areas of brush land, grass, and open land, and conifer and deciduous forest, are managed for a diversity of wildlife habitat, a major objective of the area.

Canoeing the Roseau River may not be attractive to the canoeing community, and neither Breining in his *Paddling Minnesota* nor Diebel in her *Paddling Northern Minnesota* include the Roseau as a suggested canoe opportunity.

Fishing for northern pike remains famous. The reason is the vast area of pike spawning habitat so plentiful in the marshes and pools in the two WMAs. Anglers congregate in droves in the early season, fishing from the banks of the river and by watercraft in the open pools, both for northerns and walleyes.

In spring, northern pike ascend small streams or rivulets of running water to marshes and ponds where they broadcast fertilized eggs among aquatic vegetation. They then return to their larger waters. Small hatchlings remain, however, to feed and grow on the rich plankton of shallow pond water and reach fingerling size by fall. Fingerlings move out of the shallow marshes into the river or deeper water for they cannot survive the low oxygen levels of winter under the ice.

Many accesses to the river and pools are located in the Roseau River WMA, including a number of campsites, both on the river and on wetlands located away from the stream.

Although the northern pike is the major sport fish here, anglers enjoy good walleye fishing too, especially in downstream reaches closer to the Canadian border where walleyes predominate.

A major lake sturgeon restoration is under way with the stocking of hundreds of thousands of sturgeon fry in the Roseau. It is part of the sturgeon recovery project in the Red River system to recreate a self-sustaining population throughout the system, such as that before dams in the Red River and tributaries prevented mature fish from reaching their spawning areas. Lake sturgeon require about twenty-six years to reach maturity, so the project is long-term. There's no open season on lake sturgeon in the Red River system now, but hopes are high for the future.

The main emphasis of the management area is on wildlife and public access for sport hunting. The big draw for hunters is the many species of waterfowl that stop over on their annual migrations, including Canada geese and many species of ducks, woodcock and snipe, and several shorebirds. Many of these breed within the WMA itself. Some mammals are also common, white-tailed deer, black bear, and moose; one of the most dense populations of moose in Minnesota exists in the Big Swamp. Both ruffed grouse and sharp-tailed grouse are abundant in the aspen and willow edges and islands in the wetlands, and in brush and grasslands that surround the pools and wetlands. Many miles of hunting trails wind among the great diversity of habitat.

For birders, the Roseau River WMA is a paradise with over two hundred species that either reside year-round or pass through in spring and fall, including sixteen species of ducks, and a wealth of other water birds such as herons, cranes, swans, sandpipers, and other shorebirds.

An excellent way to observe wildlife in the area is by canoe, whereby the silent approach least disturbs animals in both water and bank cover. The many cutoff oxbows on the river contain much more emergent vegetation than the river, where still water allows a quiet approach to ducks and, particularly, moose.

The Roseau River and its associated wetlands provide a wealth of outdoor recreation in an area so large that you will have no trouble finding your own quiet recreation.

The origin of the Red River name seems to be the stuff of legend. The Ojibwe term for it suggests its reflection of a summer sunset, and so the French called it Riviere Rouge. The search for such a sunset and reflection would surely be a pleasant quest.

The Red River Valley in its entirety can be viewed in PRIM maps WHEATON, CROOKSTON, FERGUS FALLS, MOOR-HEAD, ADA, CROOKSTON, FOSSTON, THIEF RIVER FALLS, and HALLOCK.

*   *   *

Red River at Grand Forks, North Dakota, and East Grand Forks, Minnesota after partial dam removal to allow fish passage.
(Photo courtesy of Minnesota Department of Natural Resources.)

THE RED RIVER VALLEY SPANS such a large area of Minnesota that it is difficult to characterize it in a single chapter, or even including the Red Lake River in another chapter. And even with an emphasis on streams and rivers, huge opportunities exist in other areas of the natural environment. Upland hunting, wildlife observation, and birding in grassland, lakes, and marshes offers an immense scope of outdoor adventure. A profusion of public lands and waters in Wildlife Management Areas, national refuges, and state forests, provide for public uses of great variety no matter where one's particular interest lies.

Sometimes the huge areas involved lead us to feel that no problem of resource degradation can possibly occur. That is furthest from the truth. Serious problems do exist, such as too much tampering with our rivers with dams, ditches, and levees.

We now know that these physical modifications, once well meaning, can be devastating to the viability of water quality and the lives of aquatic life we love. It is gratifying to know that more knowledgeable management of rivers are now restoring many streams and rivers, particularly in the Red River Valley by removal and modification of dams.

Full removal of a dam on the Red River at Fargo now allows fish passage upstream and canoeing through the small rapids downstream.
(Photo courtesy of Minnesota Department of Natural Resources.)

We have a long way to go. Hundreds of unnecessary dams still obstruct our streams, and obsolete agricultural practice still needs upgrading to preserve viable stream life and the quality of our outdoor recreation.

We've made a good start in the Red River and its tributaries. The more we enjoy the wonderful outdoor opportunities here, and understand the dependence of the viability of these resources upon our own actions, the greater will be the forces for continued and increased river stewardship.

CONSERVATION NOTE
NUMBER 18

TAKE A KID FISHING

SOME YEARS AGO, AN OLD SAW in the fishing business was "Take a kid fishing." Good advice, but why? Beyond just having a good time out fishing, it was never explained. Of course, it was aimed at kids without a father or uncle to take them.

I was lucky. My dad was passionate about fishing, and he towed me along to instill in me a passion just as strong. Those early images remain: the clear water, some bugs under a stone in a riffle, and the view from a high bank of an unsullied valley stretching far away into a misty distance. But mostly, there was that silver flash as a hooked rainbow trout leaped high into the air. I'll never forget it.

I'll admit it: those early experiences were responsible for my choice of career.

There must be scores of kids living near any experienced angler, who are not so lucky. Sure, maybe they will grow up to be doctors and lawyers, but we'll need more conservationists, too.

So take a kid fishing. Standing in a rushing riffle, mention the need for that clear water. Turn over a stone or two to discover some mayfly nymphs. Think of him or her not just as a kid going fishing, but also as a future scientist, or a senator, or maybe even a judge hearing a water pollution lawsuit.

Today, there must be new meaning to that old saw: "Take a future conservationist out fishing."

Chapter 19

RED LAKE and CLEARWATER RIVERS

EMITTING FROM HUGE LOWER RED LAKE, the Red Lake River winds its often-tortuous path of two hundred miles across Clearwater, Pennington, Red Lake, and Polk counties to empty into the Red River at East Grand Forks. Its entire course is located on the flat bed of ancient Glacial Lake Agassiz.

With its origin in Lower Red Lake, the Red Lake River flows for many of its first miles in the Red Lake Indian Reservation (non-Indian fishing not allowed). About midway, at Crookston, an old dam has been modified to allow fish passage, leaving some rapids, rare on these flat plains. Paddlers can shoot the rapids to diversify their trip, which has been pretty quiet water. Beyond Crookston, the river winds and turns unceasingly westward toward the Red River of the North.

On its way, the river first flows through part of the reservation, extensive northern bog country, some excellent walleye fishing, one lovely rapids-strewn canoe or kayak section, and a meandering passage across the old lakebed to the Red River. It's the longest and largest tributary in the Red River Valley.

At the outlet of Lower Red Lake, an Army Corps dam maintains the lake's stable level; here's where the Red Lake River begins its two-hundred-mile journey. But the first twenty miles lie in the Indian reservation and is open for public fishing only with a tribal permit. Walleyes are the main target, but many sheepshead (freshwater drum) are caught, too. However, this first twenty-mile section of the river has been heavily channelized as it flows slowly through spreading marsh, and may offer little interest to canoeists. (See PRIM map FOSSTON.)

In the remaining 180 miles, over a dozen canoe and boat landings offer ample opportunity for short or long trips along the rest of the river's course.

Upon leaving the confines of the Indian reservation, the Red Lake River cuts across the southwest corner of the GRYGLA PRIM map and heads northwest into the THIEF RIVER FALLS PRIM map, towards the town of Thief River Falls. Here it picks up the Thief River, running down from the north out of the Agassiz National Wildlife Refuge. Greatly meandering, the Thief flows southward to Red Lake Falls in the CROOKSTON PRIM map, through a rapids stretch at Huot, and the city of Crookston. From Crookston northwest, a long, twisting final stretch of forty-five miles, the Red Lake River makes its entry into the Red River of the North.

*   *   *

A HOST OF CANOEING INFORMATION is available for the Red Lake River, which is a state-designated canoe stream. An excellent guide map for the entire river can be obtained from the DNR Information Center, by phone at 651-296-6157, or email request at info@dnr.state.mn.us. Or look up the map on the web at www.dnr.state.mn.us/canoeing/redlakeriver.

Two other excellent river guides, in greater detail, are: *Red Lake River Canoe & Small Boat Brochure*, in seven parts, from Red Lake River Corridor. See: www.redlakerivercorridor.org. And also check out *Discover Northwest Minnesota on the Red Lake River by*

Canoe or Kayak, also in seven parts, from the University of Minnesota, Crookston.

While most of the Red Lake River is quiet and placid, an exception is the boulderly reach between the towns of St. Hilaire and Huot. Here the river drops down through the old Campbell Beach on an ancient shore of Glacial Lake Agassiz. Paddlers will enjoy this thirty-six mile run, the section recommended by both Breining and Diebel. Forested, with high banks, faster water, and boulders to dodge make it an enjoyable paddle. (See PRIM map CROOKSTON.)

Both Greg Breining's *Paddling Minnesota* and Lynne Smith Diebel's *Paddling Northern Minnesota* include this section. Diebel breaks it up into two daily runs, stopping for the night at a campground in Sportsman's Park in Red Lake Falls, about midway.

After running the rapids reach, visit the Old Crossing Treaty State Historical Park at Huot, site of the 1863 Indian treaty where a vast western prairie of millions of acres were ceded to the white man's thirst for land. The site also includes remains of the old ox-cart crossing of the river.

With the exception of the rapids, paddling through most of the river is quiet, with placid water, greatly meandering. Some reaches are shielded by riverbank forest, but most of the Red Lake River is surrounded by cultivated farmland, with scattered rural residences. It passes through a number of small towns, at most of which you can find camping facilities, good accesses (including boat ramps in the lower reaches), and opportunities for replenishing supplies.

*   *   *

UPSTREAM FROM THE ST. HILAIRE-TO-HUOT section, the Thief River joins the Red Lake River at the town of Thief River Falls. The Thief comes down from the north, through western Marshall County, having emitted from Thief Lake, the centerpiece of huge Thief Lake Wildlife Management Area, one of the state's largest. Thief Lake, a huge marsh, is habitat for many waterfowl species.

Farther downstream, the Thief enters a small part of the Agassiz National Wildlife Refuge, located in a transition zone of coniferous forest, tallgrass prairie, and prairie potholes. Although the river reach is very short, and is closed to fishing and canoeing, the refuge otherwise is a treasure of ecological interest.

At over 61,000 acres, the Agassiz refuge covers a large area of the lakebed of Glacial Lake Agassiz, containing an amazing diversity of wildlife habitat—lakes, marshes, wetlands, grassland, shrubland, forest, and black spruce-tamarack bog. A significant portion is designated as wilderness under the *National Wilderness Preservation System*. Still, many opportunities exist for public access to wildlife observation, such as hiking trails, a driving trail of several miles, observation platforms, and a visitors center. Deer hunting is permitted and plans for expansion of hunting opportunities are under way. Bird life is terrific, both in abundance and with around 280 species. The refuge is surrounded by state Wildlife Management Areas where additional hunting is available, plus hiking and camping.

Clearwater River, a tributary of Red Lake River.

In Red Lake Falls, the Clearwater River, the Red Lake River's largest tributary, comes in at Sportsman's Park to join the Red Lake River. Running up from the south, the Clearwater tumbles down from Minnesota's central lake country and creates a stretch that is good trout water, a designated trout stream. It is stocked regularly with brown trout and rainbows, for there is almost no natural reproduction. But it's a pleasant, easily waded, pretty little stream offering good fly fishing in its succession of riffles and pools.

Clearwater River. Probably the minimum for a canoe stream, but a good way to case out some good pools for trout fishing later.

At Crookston, an old dam on the Red Lake River had created an obstacle to upstream movements of fish and a safety hazard to canoeists. Recently the dam was removed and the river converted back to rocky rapids, open to fish, safer for canoeists, and a lovely sight to see.

Such dam removals, and their conversion to riffles and rapids, have been completed at several river locations in the Red River Valley, benefiting river recreationists, and spawning fish migrations, most particularly for lake sturgeon. This technique, making good use of obsolete, often abandoned dams, is the brainchild of Dr. Luther Aadland, a DNR fisheries scientist, whose foresight is responsible for this remarkable sample of progress in Minnesota's management of our natural resources.

From Crookston to the town of Fisher and the next takeout, twenty-five miles without access, the river becomes even more winding. Meanders seem to go around in circles, and nearly do. From Fisher to East Grand Forks, another thirty miles with no access, is similar.

To paddle these last two segments may be more work than pleasure. It's quiet and easy going, although the days get long, and might be better traveled in a small motorboat or canoe with electric motor. But the fishing's good, excellent for catfish, interrupted by the occasional walleye or northern pike.

By canoe or motorboat, the trip is worthwhile just to experience this western prairie stream winding through a vast, spreading part of Minnesota's landscape—where nobody else goes. (See PRIM maps FOSSTON, GRYGLA, THIEF RIVER FALLS, and CROOKSTON for The Red Lake River.)

Origin of the Red Lake River's name derives from Red Lake, the name of which in turn lay in the reddish color of a sunset reflection viewed when the lake's waters were still and quiet, at least so the legend tells us.

CONSERVATION NOTE
NUMBER 19

WILD AND SCENIC RIVERS—US

ON OCTOBER 2, 1968, THE U.S. CONGRESS passed the *National Wild and Scenic Rivers Act*, setting up the *National Wild and Scenic Rivers System*. Eight "instant wild rivers" were included, among them the St. Croix, border between Minnesota and Wisconsin.

Congress declared that certain rivers possessing outstanding "remarkable scenic, recreational, geologic, fish and wildlife, historic or other similar values, shall be preserved in free-flowing condition, and that they and their immediate environments shall be protected for the benefit and enjoyment of present and future generations."

The act was widely hailed as a major step in natural resources conservation nationwide.

Soon many Americans created *American Rivers*, a strong and effective citizen group that grew to thousands. *American Rivers* lobbied hard in congress to add more rivers. At this writing (2009) there are more than 200, but over 300 counting tributaries.

With the national system in place, many states followed with their own system, including Minnesota. Although some used different names, all state systems had as their purpose the protection of the natural character of their special streams and rivers.

Chapter 20

RAINY RIVER and THE BWCAW

ALTHOUGH THE RAINY RIVER'S WATERSHED shares the Hudson Bay drainage with the Red River of the North, the watersheds of the Red and Rainy are vastly different. The Red River's watershed, as we have discussed in the last two chapters, comprises an immense, spreading region of flat plains and prairie where catfish reign supreme in the Red River's waters.

The Rainy's basin is much different. It can be divided in turn into two regions, upper and lower. Although the lower is similar to the Red River in that the Rainy runs flat and slow across the glacial lakebed, it differs in its northwoods flavor in its densely forested setting and sport fisheries of walleyes and northern pike.

Like the Red River watershed whose waters are shared with neighbor North Dakota, the Rainy's is shared with its neighbor Canada. In Minnesota, the Rainy's drainage basin begins in the far eastern corner of Cook County near the North Shore of Lake Superior where it continues into Canada. The river then runs west through Lake, St Louis, and Koochiching counties, and ends in huge Lake of the Woods, in Lake of the Woods County, all the way bordering Canada on the north.

The upper region is vastly different from the lower. Here, the Rainy's headwaters flow through a dense conifer-hardwood forest, in topography that is rough and rugged. Like the river's water, we'll start with this upper region, and work our way down-stream.

Among a thousand lakes varying from little ponds to huge water bodies that you cannot see across, all connected with a lacery of short streams and rivers, the upper Rainy's watershed is Minnesota's wilderness playground, a recreational treasure un-matched in the nation. This wild lake region provides canoeing, camping, and fishing opportunities in wealthy abundance, and it collects several tributaries with some of the most beautiful river-scapes you will ever see.

Almost all the upper Rainy's watershed lies within the Superior National Forest and several state forests north of Lake Superior. Broad at the western end north of Duluth and tapering to a point at the eastern end where Lake Superior meets the Canadian border, this region is roughly in the shape of a huge triangle, known affectionately as the "Arrowhead." The Arrowhead includes a few scattered towns, but mostly it's dense forest and shining water.

(A large, detailed map of the national forest can be obtained at modest cost from the forestry headquarters in Duluth, in person or by mail: Superior National Forest, 8901 Grand Avenue Place, Duluth MN 55808.)

*   *   *

THE RAINY RIVER'S FIRST tiny flow begins as the outlet of North Lake, a small body of water on the Canadian border near the wooded tip of the Arrowhead. Over Height of Land portage east-ward lies South Lake, a headwater of the Pigeon River, Lake Superior, and the Great Lakes.

From North Lake, these infant waters flow through a maze of forest-lined lakes and unnamed streams for 210 miles, mostly in the national forest. Included are the myriad lakes of the Boundary Waters Canoe Area Wilderness (BWCAW), a large component of the National Wilderness Preservation System. The BWCAW encompasses 1.6 million acres (2,500 square miles). (See PRIM maps ELY and CRANE LAKE.)

Beyond the BWCAW, Voyageurs National Park holds much larger lakes, Minnesota's only national park. Voyageurs is mainly a "water park" and can be fully enjoyed only with a watercraft, motorboat or canoe. (See PRIM maps CRANE LAKE and INTERNATIONAL FALLS.)

Finally, water in all of these lake outlets join in huge Rainy Lake, at the outlet of which the accumulated waters dropped over old Koochiching Falls. Years ago the power of the falls was harnessed with a dam to provide power to run paper mills, using the product of logging the spreading forests upstream, and the city of International Falls developed as a consequence.

The real Rainy River begins below the dam, forming the large stream still bordering Minnesota with Canada. Here we enter the lower Rainy, running across the flat glacial lakebed, still forested. The river waters continue westward for some eighty miles, leading to huge Lake of the Woods, also shared with Canada. (See PRIM map INTERNATIONAL FALLS.)

*　　　　*　　　　*

LET'S KEEP IN MIND why we are using the terms "Boundary Waters" and "Voyageurs."

Beginning in the mid-1600s, European explorers and fur-traders found their way through this lake-studded region to reach the great Northwest, rich with beaver, and so it was hoped, they'd find a passage to the Orient. The route left Lake Superior at the mouth of the Pigeon River. Roughly parallel to the river, a nine-mile portage avoided an impassable twenty miles of waterfalls and rapids, located with the help of the local Ojibwe Indians. Beyond, the voyageurs passed northwestward into the wilderness of northwestern North America, winding from lake to lake with many portages.

Traders left Montreal in Quebec with their trade goods, such as kettles, blankets, knives and axes, muskets and lead balls, and trinkets. They found their way through rushing rivers to Lake Huron and then Lake Superior. The trip across the big lake to the mouth of the Pigeon River was fraught with the dangers of Lake

Superior and its violent storms, but at the mouth of the Pigeon the voyageurs entered a large, quiet bay with bright colors flashing and loud, happy singing.

This was the annual mid-summer rendezvous near the river's mouth that meant weeks of celebration. Here the traders exchanged goods for beaver pelts, brought down from the northern wilderness after a winter of trapping and trading with the Indians by voyageurs called Northmen. Their destination was Grand Portage, first a fort of the English North West Company, later John Jacob Astor's American Fur Company, where north met east.

On the voyages from Montreal to the Pigeon River, and from Grand Portage to the northern wilderness, voyageurs paddled the canoes and carried the goods on portages. They were small but tough French-Canadians, and they carried normal packs of 180 pounds, sometimes more. (Hernia was a common problem among the voyageurs.)

On the route from Montreal and on the Great Lakes, canoes were large, for carrying heavy loads and withstanding the storms of Lake Superior. But from the north, over the many lakes, small streams, and rough portages, the Northmen used a smaller craft. The canoes on the two segments, although differing in size, were manufactured in the woods, from the tough, white, readily available bark of the paper birch tree. Canoes were not carried across the long portage that connected the north woods with Lake Superior as were their backpacked loads.

From all accounts, the rendezvous at Grand Portage was a pretty wild affair.

*   *   *

GRAND PORTAGE NATIONAL MONUMENT was named after the nine-mile-long path that avoided the lower stretch of the Pigeon, including the restored Great Hall. The twenty miles of river is as wild and beautiful today as it was then. And so is the rugged portage. For more on the national monument, see: www.nps.gov/grpo.

Minnesota recently established Grand Portage State Park that now allows us to view the 120-foot Big Falls on the Pigeon, the highest on the American North Shore (of course shared with Canada). The view is spectacular. (Kakabeka Falls, on the Kaministiquia River, Ontario, is the highest on the North Shore including Canada.)

For more on the state park, see: www.dnr.state.mn.us/state _parks/grand_portage.

Visitors can also hike the nine-mile portage, or at least part of it. Try tramping in the footsteps of the moccasins of voyageurs, those which for two centuries packed down the same soil now beneath your feet. Through your very own shoes, you will feel history come alive.

*   *   *

ALTHOUGH THIS BOOK IS ABOUT RIVERS, we'll also try to do some justice to the Boundary Waters Canoe Area Wilderness in its most treasured paddling, camping, and fishing opportunities—and solitude—in the most beautiful area of forest and lakes in the nation.

The lakes offer unparalleled angling for walleyes, northern pike, and lake trout. Small tributary streams can harbor some of those beautiful, brightly colored brook trout that prosper in cooler waters. See especially Mike Furtman's book, *A Boundary Waters Fishing Guide*, (Birch Portage Press, Duluth) for excellent information that will increase your creel and the pleasures of filling it.

With the exception of some important tributaries, the streams in the BWCAW and Voyageurs that connect the many lakes do not offer extensive river trips. But we will consider here some major tributaries, specifically the Vermilion and Kawishiwi rivers and, emptying into the river downstream from the lake region, the Big Fork and Little Fork rivers. The Vermilion holds some of the wildest water in Minnesota, a real gem; we'll include a separate chapter for it. The Kawishiwi, a river of lakes, includes one of the strangest features in river geology, and we'll take a look at that, too. The waters of both the Vermilion and Kawishiwi end up in the boundary waters. The last two streams, the Big Fork and the Little Fork, emptying into the Rainy down from the BWCAW, and being so special, also warrant a separate chapter.

Lynne Smith Diebel, in her *Paddling Northern Minnesota*, includes an excellent description of the BWCAW's main route, with all its detail of lake and stream, portages, scenic sights, and campsites. From Bearskin Lake to Moose Lake, she divides the entire route into two major regions, East and West, plus a day's "loop." Then, each region is divided into several day trips. Total: 17 days, 180 miles. Diebel also includes a short section on Voyageurs National Park. Additionally, she includes canoe routes on the Vermilion, Big Fork, and Little Fork. "Grab your paddle," she says, "and discover..."

Know too that there is a host of lakes in the BWCAW other than those on the voyageurs' route. These are most often accessible with a portage, offering paddling, camping, and fishing aplenty. Many detailed guide books and maps, available in any large bookstore, will lead you to these additions to your northwoods adventures. These may emphasize canoeing routes for sure, but also camping methods and fishing information. There are no modern, developed campgrounds in the BWCAW; after all, this is a natural wilderness, and it's managed to keep it that way. Permits must be obtained from Superior National Forest stations for all entries into the boundary waters.

*   *   *

MANY RECREATIONAL OPPORTUNITIES are available outside the BWCAW in large areas of the Superior National Forest and several Minnesota state forests. These include sites with varying degrees of camping facilities. Most are located on lakes, as might be expected, but there are a few on streams and rivers as well. Camping facilities range from fully developed campgrounds with all amenities, fee charged, to rustic campgrounds with some facilities, no fee charged, to backcountry sites where you're on your own. Take good care of them. If they are clean when you get there, it's because someone else cleaned them up before you arrived.

Developed campgrounds number over twenty, on lakes and rivers, providing a wide range of recreation, camping from RVs to pup tents, hiking trails, and canoe and boat accesses. Fees charged. River sites include those on the Temperance, Little Isabella, and Kawishiwi rivers.

Seventeen rustic campgrounds in the national forest provide the minimum of fire rings and tables, and although RVs are OK at a few but not all, all sites will accommodate tents that will fit. No fees. These include sites on the Cascade and Poplar rivers.

Backcountry camping may be preferred by many folks wanting solitude and wilderness. This is much like BWCAW camping, except these are single sites, no fees, permits, or reservations, and no crowds. Sites have a fire grate and a somewhat level space for a tent, but that's all. Again, most of these are on lakes, but some routes include stream sites on Island, Dead, Hunting Shack, Vermilion, and St. Louis rivers. However, in wild areas without designation, off the beaten trail, primitive camping with tent is allowed (called "dispersed camping").

A wealth of information is available from the US Forest Service for the asking. Contact headquarters at Superior National Forest, 8901 Grand Avenue Place, Duluth MN 55808, or phone 218-626-4300.

For more descriptions of back country routes and maps, contact specific Ranger Districts: Gunflint Ranger District, 2020 West Hwy 61, PO Box 790, Grand Marais MN 55604, or phone 218-387-1750; Kawishiwi Ranger District, 118 South 4th Avenue East, Ely MN 55731, or phone 218-365-7600; LaCroix Ranger District, 320 North Hwy 53, Cook MN 55723, or phone 218-666-0020; Laurentian Ranger District, 318 Forestry Road, Aurora MN 55705, or phone 218-229-8800; Tofte Ranger District, 7355 West Hwy 61, PO Box 2159, Tofte MN 55615, or phone 218-663-7280.

Take care to be good stewards and follow the forest principle of LNT (Leave no Trace).

*   *   *

FISHING IN THE BOUNDARY WATERS LAKES is renowned for its walleye and northern pike found in all lakes. In addition, smallmouth bass are fairly common. In the eastern part of the BWCAW, North Lake and Saganaga, for example, lake trout are the prized catch. Farther west, more fishes in warmer lakes— sunfish such as crappies, bluegills, rock bass—are common in such lakes as Lac la Croix, Namakan, and Rainy. Many lakes in addition hold good populations of yellow perch, lake whitefish, and tullibee (or cisco).

Northerns get big in the boundary lakes, pushing up to twenty pounds. For scrappy fighting, however, none can beat the smallmouth bass. But for eating, especially for shore lunch, it's the walleye. Here and there some brightly colored brook trout can be found in small tributary creeks.

While you're enjoying the paddle on your way to the next campsite, or after supper on a rocky point, get your line wet.

*   *   *

AT THE WESTERN EXTREMITY OF RAINY LAKE, the river used to plunge over the great Koochiching Falls, a drop of thirty feet. It was an important obstacle to the historic fur trade and required a tough portage in both directions. Now these falls have been modified and industrialized with a large hydropower dam, providing electricity to the city of International Falls and, across the river, the Canadian city of Fort Francis. The great falls marks the location where the upper Rainy's waters drop down from the rocky Canadian Shield of the boundary waters to the plains of Glacial Lake Agassiz's lakebed, a profound change in the character of the Rainy's watershed.

Lower region of the Rainy River.

The genesis of the Rainy's name, like so many of Minnesota's names, came from the Indian's lexicon, *Koochiching*, as referring to the constant spray of mist from the falls.

After draining the vast area of all the lakes and streams of the upper watershed, it might be expected that the Rainy will be a large river. It is. And after its passage through the hydropower dam in International Falls, the Rainy runs another eighty miles to its mouth in Lake of the Woods. Accesses, canoe and boat landings, and campsites abound. Franz Jevne State Park, with camping, access, and some hiking trails by the stream, is located about midway along the river.

The Rainy's waters become lost in the huge body of Lake of the Woods—most of which belongs to Canada. But they continue on out through the lake's northern outlet as part of the Winnipeg River. Farther on, the Winnipeg joins the waters of the Red River of the North in Lake Winnipeg, and from there they flow down Canada's Nelson River to the salt water of Hudson Bay.

*   *   *

THE WHOLE REGION OF THE BOUNDARY WATERS, Koochiching Falls, the Rainy and its eighty miles of big river, and huge Lake of the Woods, is rich in history. Thousands of voyageurs traversed the river, starting at the mouth of the Pigeon and the Grand Portage, winding their way through the maze of the boundary lakes to the Rainy, while millions of beaver pelts were carried out.

For thirty years in the late 1800s, steamboats plied the Rainy's placid waters, carrying supplies to settlers and lumber camps, and logs from the surrounding pinewoods to their destinations at the paper mills of International Falls.

In the northwestern corner of Lake of the Woods, the Rainy's waters must wind around a small peninsula, a bit of Minnesota now isolated by water from the rest of the country. Called the Northwest Angle, it sticks up on the map of North America as the northernmost part of the conterminous United States.

The reason for its existence is one of the strangest stories in the geographical history of North America. In 1783, soon after American independence, the international boundary was being planned by treaty between the new United States and Canada in this region of the upper lakes and Lake of the Woods. An international commission decided to follow the voyageurs' "water route." This track continued to Lake of the Woods and to the lake outlet at the northwest corner, following the voyageurs' route. Then the commission drew an imaginary line westward and declared it to continue to the Mississippi River. A problem, as we shall see, was that the commissioners didn't know where the Mississippi really was. The location of the border farther west across the continent was deferred to later determinations. After the War of 1812 this remainder of the border between the United States and Canada was decided along the line of latitude 49 degrees.

Then, explorer Henry Rowe Schoolcraft "discovered" the Mississippi's origin in 1832, well south of latitude 49 and the line exiting Lake of the Woods. Of course the two lines of latitude did not match, with a difference of about twenty-eight miles. The solution was to drop a line straight south from the big lake's corner to meet latitude 49 degrees. This left that little peninsula of United States territory sticking out into the lake, isolated from the rest of the country, today's Northwest Angle. You can get to it all right, but you either have to go by water or drive through part of Canada.

They don't seem to mind.

*   *   *

HEAVILY POLLUTED IN THE PAST from the paper mills in International Falls, the Rainy has been greatly cleaned up and now yields one of the largest catch of walleyes in the state. Many anglers crowd its shores in mid-May to participate in an annual celebration of opening day, but the greatest walleye fishing of all is in a special season just after the ice goes out in March and April.

While some ice may still remain on the lower Rainy's surface, Minnesota anglers by the hundreds crowd the shore landings and open water with their boats and motors to participate in this earliest of open-water walleye fishing. At this time of year, mature walleyes migrate into the river from Lake of the Woods, and the rush is on. The unique special season is for only a couple of weeks, while other regulations dictate only two keepers per day and none over 29.5 inches. But no matter, the catching is incredible with anglers happily busy with catch and release. It's an annual Minnesota spring tradition. Once badly polluted, the Rainy's new fishery is an outstanding example of progress in river care.

Keep in mind we share the Rainy River and Lake of the Woods with Canada. As such, these border waters have other special regulations, mostly applying to walleyes, but to other species as well. Be sure to familiarize yourself with these rules, different from inland waters, as detailed in your Minnesota fishing regulations booklet.

In addition to walleyes, northern pike probably constitute the next most important fishery in the Rainy. Pike are common throughout the river, although not abundant.

The fish species attracting the most passionate anglers, however, is the lake sturgeon. Tight restrictions allow you can keep one fish per season but only in a specified size range.

Four happy anglers with a day's catch of sturgeon on the Rainy River.
(Photo courtesy of Minnesota Department of Natural Resources.)

Sturgeon are abundant in many streams and rivers in Minnesota, especially in large warmwater rivers. So common that harvesting them a hundred years ago was only a matter of using seines or traps of some kind and taking them by the truck load. However, the sturgeon is very long lived, and specimens many years old are the norm. So when large mature fish were taken, reproductive potential was seriously reduced. Sturgeon also have strict requirements for spawning habitat—rocky riffles, most often in tributaries of large rivers. When dams were built by the hundreds in Minnesota, for water supply, flood control, and electric power, spawning areas were cut off. Sturgeon populations dropped precipitously. Now the Department of Natural Resources (DNR) is actively working to restore this magnificent fish in several major rivers of the state; stocking of large numbers of young fish and removal of dams have been the major methods of bringing back the sturgeon.

Fortunately, the Rainy is the one river in which the sturgeon still prospers naturally, as it does in Lake of the Woods, mainly because mature fish have access to the main river and its tributaries for spawning. Some real monsters have been caught.

A recent Rainy River catch in 2005 was probably a record breaker: seventy-one inches long and weighing well over a hundred pounds. We say, *probably*, because all sturgeon of this size must be immediately released. It was measured, but the weight had to be estimated from length and girth, and official recording was not possible.

Landing something that size sounds like hard work, doesn't it?

*   *   *

THE KAWISHIWI RIVER BEGINS in Kawishiwi Lake, in northeastern Lake County. The lake is accessible by a forest service road and there's a developed access and a national forest campground. It's a popular entry point to the BWCAW. You could canoe the Kawishiwi for about sixty miles, within the BWCAW, to near Winton, for the next landing, but this route is almost entirely through a succession of small lakes. Which wouldn't be all that bad, with "dispersed camping" along the way.

Meanwhile, at Kawishiwi Lake, try the fishing. It's a relatively shallow lake but abundant with walleyes, northern pike, and yellow perch.

The course of the rest of the Kawishiwi is also mainly through lakes. Very little actual river exists. About ten miles before reaching the town of Winton, the river splits into an unusual diversion called the South Kawishiwi. Here it angles southwestward for about twenty miles and then back north about fifteen more. Passing through large White Iron Lake, and then to Farm Lake, the South Kawishiwi rejoins the main stem. The Kawishiwi River, now complete, continues through Garden Lake, then Fall Lake (where there's a national forest campground), and then north into the BWCAW, a major entry point into the boundary waters. A bit farther north, the Kawishiwi empties into Basswood Lake on the border.

For the Ojibwe, Kawishiwi meant a river with many beaver. It must have attracted many fur trappers.

(See PRIM maps BAUDETTE, ELY, CRANE LAKE, GRAND MARAIS, and INTERNATON FALLS for the entire Rainy system.)

For something different in "river" canoeing, take a week and consider the South Kawishiwi. In a true wilderness setting, with tall pine and spruce forest near on both shores, a few camps on the way (and no crowds), superb fishing, and a favorite companion, it could turn out to be one of your most memorable canoe adventures in the north country.

**CONSERVATION NOTE
NUMBER 20**

**WILD AND SCENIC RIVERS
MINNESOTA I**

WHEN IN 1973 I HEARD THAT THE MINNESOTA legislature had passed a state Wild and Scenic Rivers Act, I was overjoyed.

Immediately, a dozen rivers came to mind. I joined a Sierra Club "task force" headed by Ford Robbins, an environmental attorney, to study, visit, and recommend special Minnesota rivers. In 1976, the Kettle River was the first to be established in the new Minnesota Wild and Scenic Rivers System.

Five more rivers were soon added: Cannon, Rum, North Fork of the Crow, and parts of the larger Mississippi and Minnesota rivers. I felt the Minnesota program was the greatest advance in natural resources that had ever occurred.

More rivers were on the agenda. The task force began studying the Cloquet with a canoeing expedition, and the Snake was going to be next.

But controversy and hostility broke out. At a public meeting on adding the Cloquet River, in the town of Cloquet, several tires were slashed on Department vehicles.

Further development of the Minnesota Wild and Scenic System came to a screeching halt.

For thirty years, not a single river was added. Even the position of a system director remains empty.

What went wrong?

Chapter 21

VERMILION RIVER

FOR NORTHWOODS PADDLING and spectacular river scenes, nothing can beat the Vermilion River in huge Kabetogama State Forest. The Vermilion personifies the wildness of the north woods, holding its recreational potential in remote river beauty. Flowing from its huge lake source, its water clarity and stability of flow are assured. There's plenty of quiet water, too, surrounded by wilderness pine and spruce forest (with lots of places to take out ahead of the rapids).

Readily accessible between its many canoe landings and parking spots, the crystal waters and dark conifer forests will bring you peace and quietude, river bend after bend. Yet the splendor of its thundering cascades and waterfalls (viewed safely from a hiking trail) will hold you in thrall.

The Vermilion's primordial flows begin quietly in central St. Louis County as little Sand River, which empties into Lake Vermilion. The lake is extraordinarily complex, replete with uncounted bays and points, with the Vermilion River running out of it and then north through St. Louis County for about forty miles to Crane Lake and the border.

In its rough-and-tumble reaches, the Vermilion River produces some of the most beautiful and spectacular rapids, cascades, and waterfalls that you will find anywhere. Canoeing for much of it is for the *expert only* (up to Class VI, which is suicidal). Huge rock outcrops along the river are common.

Although canoeing is the main draw, hiking on foot along the rapids and falls offers breath-taking scenes of the rapids and falls and magnificent overviews.

The river can be divided into three parts. First, an upper quiet stretch of about six miles that can give you a pleasant, forest-lined lake-like paddle, known as the Chain of Lakes. However, before this, there are some wild rapids just out of Lake Vermilion, and more of the same at the lower end of the Chain.

If you want to avoid this upper reach of quiet water and the two rapids altogether, a landing below them will get you started on the main river, the second major sector. For the next twenty miles it's river all the way. There are a few small rapids, of course, but nothing wild. It's a full day's paddle, or better take some time off and enjoy a rest, fishing, or a little hike, and a good night's sleep beneath the stars. There are a half-dozen designated stops, with canoe landings, also useful for shorter trips. Check out Lynne Smith Diebel's *Paddling Northern Minnesota* for her suggested daily trips.

The third section includes some more quiet water, lake-like but still scenic, about five or six miles. But the quiet water ends with High Falls rapids, Class VI. (Don't even think about it.) Below High Falls, the last four miles make up a section that is the most awe-inspiring piece of river in Minnesota, again up to Class VI. You can drive to near The Chasm by way of a forest road, then walk a short distance through some woods and get great views from an observation deck, where the white, roaring water is right below your feet. (Don't fall in.) You could also get to the lower end for a hike by putting in on Crane Lake, near the river mouth, and then paddle or motor up to the base of The Chasm. It's dazzling.

The Vermilion River, rushing northward toward the Hudson Bay,
thunders through The Chasm of the Vermilion and on to Crane Lake ,
entry to the Boundary Waters Canoe Area Wilderness.

Overall, the Vermilion offers plenty of diversity. In addition
to the rapids, you can enjoy the quiet stretches too, through remote areas, as you drift easily through the wilderness of the state
forest. Hiking opportunities are everywhere. Throughout, there
are plenty of campgrounds and remote sites where you can pitch
a small tent.

There's also plenty of canoeing information. Breining, in
Paddling Minnesota, divides the river into six sectors, separating
whitewater and quiet water. Diebel, in *Paddling Northern Minnesota*,
divides it into three. Each offers a single day's trip. Both guides
give much welcome detail, stressing the need for frequent portaging. The Vermilion is also a state-designated canoe river, with
the usual handy folding map of the entire river, also with many
details. You might get wet, but you won't get lost.

In the minds of a host of Minnesotans, the Vermilion River
with its wildness, its hiking and canoeing opportunities, and its
roaring rapids and falls, is a prime jewel of river recreation.

*   *   *

FISHING IN THE VERMILION is minimal. Northern pike, walleyes, some smallmouth bass, and yellow perch are the main species, and most abundant in the lake-like areas, the Chain of Lakes, and the wide waters upstream from High Falls. The wild rapids areas are difficult or impossible to fish.

Below the Vermilion Dam would be tough for angling, but in the Chain of Lakes you will find northern pike (some large), walleyes, smallmouth bass, lots of yellow perch and rock bass, and several other panfish. If you're fishing with bait on the bottom, there are plenty of suckers and redhorse. There are no catfish or carp.

Generally, the main river probably will not yield a lot to the angler. Some of the swifter water and below small rapids and riffles may provide some smallmouth and rock bass.

But as long as you are in the area, and if you are in for northern pike and walleyes, you might give Lake Vermilion a try. In the Vermilion, the exploration for fish can be as much fun as catching them. It's a marvelously diverse lake, with a huge concentration of bays, points, narrows, and islands, possibly the most complex lake in Minnesota.

At this writing, it looks like Lake Vermilion is going to be the newest addition to Minnesota's state parks. Maybe the river, its wild waterfalls, and the final chasm will be included. We should hope so.

The PRIM maps VERMILION LAKE and CRANE LAKE cover both the lake and river.

The origin of the river's name is not specific and seems lost in its ancient use. It appears that the Ojibwe's term for Lake Vermilion and the river is simply the same as for Red Lake, from the reddish reflection of sunset.

CONSERVATION NOTE
NUMBER 21

WILD AND SCENIC RIVERS
MINNESOTA II

I WAS GREATLY DISAPPOINTED. Here we had a program that could save and protect our choicest rivers in Minnesota under a state law, and yet everybody seemed against it.

After I had had a guest column published in the *Minnesota Star and Tribune*, praising the legislation that created the new wild and scenic system, an attorney specializing in land law had a contradictory letter in a following issue, complaining about my use of the word "unique" in my column. Actually, I had not used "unique" at all! It seemed to me that the attorney's statement was a simple and deliberate untruth. (Possibly a mistake reflecting his great passion against the program. Possibly.)

Most other states have set up protected river systems, using various titles. Michigan uses *Natural Rivers Program*; Wisconsin, *Wild Rivers System*; Iowa, *Protected Water Areas* (all rivers). And many others.

In a 2004 plan prepared by the DNR's Division of Waters, the section on the Mississippi that is in the current Minnesota Wild and Scenic River System is replaced by terms such as Rivertown and Rivertown Extension, which would functionally remove the Mississippi from the wild and scenic system altogether—and leave it open to more development.

Chapter 22

BIG FORK and LITTLE FORK

R EMOTE AND WILD—AND BEAUTIFUL—the Big Fork and Little Fork rivers are the jewels of the Northwoods.

Heading up in north-central Minnesota's lake and hill
country and flowing north, they drop down through a profusion
of rapids and pools to the forested plains of the old lakebed of
Glacial Lake Agassiz. There they wind their way through quiet
meanders between stream banks lined with pine, spruce, and
white birch, to the Rainy River.

In downstream reaches, the watersheds are heavily covered
by spreading bog. In drainage emanating from acid soils comes
the brown stain of the waters of the Big Fork and Little Fork,
common in many northern streams. Neither river is polluted,
although their waters are sometimes made turbid by runoff from
eroding streambanks.

The Big Fork and Little Fork are renowned for their scenery
and the quality of the canoeing. A major waterfall on the Little
Fork and two large falls on the Big Fork, unrunnable for most
paddlers, as well as a profusion of canoeable rapids, provide some
of the finest riverscapes in Minnesota. River levels are suitable for
paddling most of the year, but high water might be encountered

in spring and fall. Many campsites and accesses are available on both rivers.

Both Breining and Diebel include the two rivers in their respective canoe guidebooks, with some differences. Both include details of rapids, landings, and campgrounds, but Diebel includes more in the way of additional river information. Both rivers are included in the state's list of designated canoe streams, and excellent maps are available from the Department of Natural Resources (DNR) Information Center, phone 651-296-6157, or visit: www.dnr.state.mn.us/canoeing/bigforkriver.

*   *   *

THE BIG FORK RIVER, westernmost of the two, begins with water flows from a myriad of lakes in northern Itasca County, although its main flow is from Dora Lake, a shallow water body surrounded by marsh and famous for its wild rice. Continuing north through Koochiching County, the Big Fork arrives at the Rainy River after a total of 165 miles. Fifteen canoe landings and fifteen campsites are open for public use along the river.

A Chippewa National Forest landing at Dora Lake provides initial access. For several miles downstream, paddling is mainly through wild rice beds, but in ten miles the first campground, Harrison Landing, is perfect for ending a short, first day's trip.

For about the next fifty miles the river courses through several small rapids, past campsites and landings, including the town of Bigfork. Then we find one of the two major waterfalls on the Big Fork, a spectacular scene of whitewater, Little American Falls. The river shoots over a six-foot drop through a ten-foot-wide channel between massive rock, rated Class IV-V. The brief portage around the Little American affords you the chance to view the beauty of the scene. Rest a while. Mom and Dad and a junior or two can camp overnight—and sleep to the magical sound of the rush of river.

Little American Falls of the Big Fork River.

After another fifty miles northward, the river meets up with Big Falls, thundering over four separate drops for a total pitch of forty feet in only a quarter mile, rated Class IV. The portage around it may seem long at a half-mile, but camping is easy at a city park in the town of Big Falls for a rest. The river here is another beauty. At least, enjoy the roaring whitewater on the hike.

Big Falls marks the end of the upper rapids sector. The flat land of the old glacial lakebed lies ahead, and only one small rapids marks this passage through the last fifty miles. So it's mostly quiet water, but still forested and wild. Fewer landings and camps are available. The longest stretch without landings or campsites of twenty-five miles lies near the end of the Big Fork route. Quiet water, but it's heavily wooded and beautiful in its way, with plenty of solitude for the weary spirit.

In his *Paddling Minnesota,* Greg Breining covers the entire Big Fork River in three sectors, from Dora Lake down to its mouth in the Rainy. In *Paddling Northern Minnesota,* Lynne Smith Diebel is more selective. Avoiding the marshes of Dora Lake, she starts the Big Fork route a few miles down, at Harrison's Landing. After seven separately described trips, she stops her treatment at Big Falls, below which the river is less interesting in its monotonous flow across the bed of Glacial Lake Agassiz. She likes her rivers to be *real river*.

A fortunate circumstance surrounds the Big Fork. The Big Fork River Association of river stewards have joined many skills and different objectives to enable good management of the river. Included in their mission is a comprehensive plan for land use and development standards, water quality objectives, and preservation of wetlands and historic sites.

*   *   *

THE LITTLE FORK RIVER is similar to its twin in some respects, but in others significantly different. The two are roughly parallel, of similar length, of similar origins and topography and, despite their names, are of similar size and flow.

The Little Fork begins in marshlands in western St. Louis County, runs northeasterly for about forty miles to Koochiching County, and finally north another hundred miles to the Rainy River, for a 140-mile total.

The Little Fork is beautiful in its distinctive character. More rapids, wilder country, longer distances between landings, more do-it-yourself camping. If you select the Little Fork, expect some wild rapids, more portages—and more solitude. For many paddlers, a greater sense of wilderness and the beauty of forest and rushing river give a greater connection to the past, to our own place within our natural world.

Heading in marshland, the Little Fork begins as a specific entity at the town of Cook, soon joined by Rice River, where the Little Fork enlarges significantly. In fact, the beginning of river travel can start more conveniently at a landing a few miles up the Rice River. This beginning will avoid a six-mile stretch below Cook, in which the river flows under five bridges (hardly wilderness).

From the junction of these two streams, the Little Fork runs through a lot of wild river—many rapids Class I and II—to its major waterfall, Hannine Falls, up to Class VI, a sloping, very rough pitch of fifteen feet, for all practical purposes unrunnable. Canoeists may end a day's paddle above the falls at the Ax-Handle Hound Campsite at a county road bridge just upstream. Walk down for a spectacular view. Or, to continue on the river, try a put-in just below Hannine Falls by way of a county road coming down to the river from the north (no crossing).

Hannine Falls on the Little Fork River.

Downstream there's a lovely one- or two-day stretch attracting many paddlers. More rapids, Class I and II, follow quickly and dot the river for about twenty miles—crossed by several county roads—to Samuelson Park and camping.

Many paddlers consider the next stretch, from Samuelson's to the Dentaybow landing, the best part of the Little Fork. It offers a momentous canoe trip through the major wilderness section of the Little Fork, nearly fifty miles without a road or bridge. Primitive camping will be required and the fishing is great. Just before Dentaybow is Deadman's Rapids, Class II, that marks the approximate point where the Little Fork drops down onto the flat lands of the old glacial lakebed. So from here on it's almost all quiet water, much meandering, and slumping, slippery clay banks, for most of the way to the town of Little Fork, and twenty more meandering miles to the Little Fork River's mouth in the Rainy. (Unfortunately, these eroding banks are responsible for causing muddy water. They're fixable with modern techniques, but expensive.)

Breining and Diebel both give excellent descriptions of the rapids-filled stretch from Cook to Hannine Falls (unrunnable) and on down to Samuelson Park. Diebel describes a rocky portage around the falls, but many of the other rapids have no portage around. Diebel ends her treatment at Samuelson Park, but Breining and the DNR's designated route continues through the fifty-mile wilderness stretch, and then down to the Little Fork's mouth as well. This last part of the river, with its slow, meandering course across the glacial lakebed, may not attract many paddlers.

Call the DNR Information Center for their canoe map of the Little Fork, 651-296-6157, or visit: www.dnr.state.mn.us/canoeing/littleforkriver.

∗   ∗   ∗

ALTHOUGH MOST VISITORS to the Big Fork and Little Fork rivers are there for the paddling, some of the best fishing in northern Minnesota is to be had in these two streams.

The rivers are similar in their fish populations and angling possibilities. Preeminent are walleyes, northern pike, smallmouth bass and, more rarely, muskellunge, in both streams. Lucky anglers might hook on to a giant lake sturgeon, a whale of a fish that, if landed, must go back.

The Big Fork is noted especially for its consistent catch of walleyes, throughout the entire river. Spawning habitat is good in all reaches. In contrast to many other northern streams, however, northern pike are not abundant. Preferred pike spawning habitat, marshes and ponds, is nearly absent in the Big Fork. Some are big, though. Muskellunge, though rare, attract passionate muskie anglers, searching out these monsters of the deep pools; each is a trophy. Smallmouth bass, interestingly, used to occur only below the Big Falls, which of course is a barrier to fish movement; apparently, this species never made it upstream past the falls during early distribution of the species. Smallmouth may have been transferred by now, however. Where present, this aerial acrobat provides some the Big Fork's most spectacular fishing.

Yellow perch are present in abundance, some ranging up to ten or twelve inches, but their main value is in the principal diet of walleyes, one of the major reasons for the walleye's success here.

Similar to the fish fauna in almost all warmwater streams is the abundance of several members of the sucker family, comprising maybe three-fourths, or more, of the fish biomass. They run big, like walleyes, so if you fish with live bait you'll surely catch your fill of suckers. They're not bad eating, especially in early spring. But learn how to remove those annoying forked bones, just like you also do for northern pike.

The Little Fork's angling opportunities compare similarly to that in the Big Fork, with a few minor differences. The walleye, again, is the main sport fish, especially in the downstream sectors below the Indian reservation, where spawning habitat is best for walleyes. Sauger, a smaller relative of the walleye, appears a little more commonly in the Little Fork than in its brother. Northern pike are present throughout the entire stream, and although angling may be best in the upper parts of the river, like the Big Fork northern pike are not abundant. Smallmouth anglers will be pleased to know that this hard-fighting bass is in good numbers throughout the course of the Little Fork. In a rapids area, or anywhere there are stones and boulders, is often the best.

*   *   *

THE BIG FORK SOMEHOW GETS ITS NAME from an Indian term for Bow String, with the Bowstring River a major tributary in the Big Fork's headwaters. The Little Fork is really not smaller in its discharge or length, but must have appeared that way to the Native Americans.

(You can find the Little Fork River on PRIM maps VERMILION, BIG FORK, and INTERNATIONAL FALLS, while the Big Fork River is on the BIG FORK and INTERNATIONAL FALLS maps.)

Big or Little, these two streams offer some of the best river recreation in Minnesota. Sure, they are a long way from the Twin Cities, but that very circumstance is partly responsible for their unique quality, with canoeing for all levels, solitude and good fishing, and a plentitude of wilderness adventure. Great places for families to get away just by themselves for a while.

These river resources will continue to offer their quality to us, so long as we maintain our custody of them with strong stewardship. We can be thankful that the Big Fork enjoys the care of citizens in the Big Fork River Association; but the Little Fork is critically in need of similar protection, like inclusion in the Minnesota Wild and Scenic Rivers System, or something like it.

CONSERVATION NOTE
NUMBER 22

WILD AND SCENIC RIVERS
MINNESOTA III

THE MINNESOTA WILD AND SCENIC RIVER system was created by the experts. Left out were the citizens who felt the experts' regulations violated their private property rights.

Antagonism by the people spread to the Department of Natural Resources itself, and much of our protected river system soon lay flat.

Can we restart with some other system? A different name?

Start with a grassroots initiative—instead of with the experts? By a few citizens who are passionate about their rivers and who can spread that passion among their neighbors?

We can get help from *American Rivers* and *River Network*, national organizations that assist other river groups. We can copy models, like the Big Fork River Association. It must be a citizen-led effort, leading to strong state laws the citizenry helped to develop, and from which they themselves find benefit.

The late John Sawhill, who led The Nature Conservancy for many years, warned us: ". . . our society will be defined not only by what we create, but by what we refuse to destroy."

The time has come to nurture—and refuse to destroy—those streams and rivers that we love so much, and which so profoundly enrich our lives.

THROUGH AN OPEN WINDOW —
FINAL PERCEPTIONS

SOMETIMES, WE WHO LOVE THE OUTDOORS stop at the edge of a favorite river and rest on a convenient sitting log. Or we might pause to shuck our pack for a moment after a climb up a rocky trail to view a distant, green valley. Or just sit quietly on a sandy beach while small waves of crystal water lap on our toes.

The feeling must come, then, to wonder what the future holds for these precious moments outdoors.

Will the waters always be crystal clear? The valley always green? Try as we might to view the future, as through some kind of open window, it might be difficult to see what we can do to preserve our outdoor treasures.

We might be able to overcome that difficulty by, say, looking backward.

* * *

AS LITTLE AS FIFTY YEARS AGO, environmental conditions in Minnesota were not good, or across the country for that matter. The West had still not recovered from the dust bowl days, and farmers still plowed in the fall, so winter's winds raged upon fallow fields and blew their productive soils away, to produce dust storms as far east. High dams on major rivers were still being built, cutting off spawning migrations of fish and destroying thousands of miles of beautiful river beneath stagnant reservoirs.

Without contour plowing and grassed waterways, sediment drained unheeded from agricultural fields; the absence of fences or riparian buffers on pastured floodplains allowed massive erosion and sedimentation in hundreds of rivers in the agricultural Midwest.

America's most important river, the Mississippi, was putrid with sewage and other wastes, emanating from Minnesota's Twin Cities. Fish smelled foul and were inedible. DDT was still being spread over the land to control mosquitoes and gypsy moth larvae, without regard for its effect on fish and wildlife—or humans—and numerous species of our most valued birds were brought to the brink of extinction.

In the years following the Second World War, many of the nation's rivers were still being used for disposal of raw sewage. Wastes from the industrial cities of Toledo and Detroit seriously polluted Lake Erie, which was then considered biologically dead. Throughout the United States, the nation's wetlands, so important in maintaining good quality groundwater and preventing floods, were being destroyed at an alarming rate, at thousands of acres per day.

In 1969, the Cuyahoga River in Cleveland, Ohio, caught fire—from floating industrial petroleum effluent.

Isn't there any good news?

Yes. There is.

*   *   *

WHAT SEEMS SO LONG AGO NOW, Theodore Roosevelt, United States President in the early 1900s initiated the country's national parks, our system of national forests, and the huge national wildlife refuges. By the late 1960s more seeds of stewardship were sown, and a few more voices had been raised in defiance of environmental destruction.

Early in the 1920s, Ernest Oberholtzer, pioneer advocate for the preservation of the northern Minnesota wilderness, had begun a struggle for the protection of the Quetico-Superior region, an effort that lasted for the rest of his life—and resulted in today's Boundary Waters Canoe Area Wilderness.

In the 1940s, Aldo Leopold was raging against the destruction of our wild lands, rivers, and forests. Leopold was unheeded then, but today he is revered as a conservation legend of gigantic proportions.

Closer to home, Richard J. Dorer, Supervisor of the Bureau of Game in the Minnesota Department of Conservation campaigned after the Second World War for restoration of the river valleys of southeast Minnesota, devastated by earlier erosion and sedimentation. His efforts were instrumental in establishing our beloved Whitewater Wildlife Management Area and today's Richard J. Dorer Memorial Hardwood State Forest in southeastern Minnesota, which now protects hundreds of miles of fine trout and smallmouth streams.

By the late 1960s, the rapid dwindling of our outdoor resources had become more apparent. Previous technological advances, made of necessity during the war, had given America the confidence to believe we could apply science to anything, including going to the moon.

We conquered long-standing diseases; we created chemical fertilizers that increased agricultural production. New automobiles gave us the mobility and speed to whisk around the country in our daily business and pleasures. Jet airplanes whisked us even faster, not only from coast to coast but around the world, in just a few hours. The neighborhood grocery store gave way to the supermarket. New poisons killed off annoying insects. Every conceivable electrical gadget that the engineers could imagine became readily available to us all, including television, air conditioning, garbage disposals in our very own kitchens, and electric clothes washers and dishwashers. Detergents replaced Ivory soap in household chores, hugely increasing the ease and efficiency of dish washing and laundry. Nuclear plants were replacing coal, with unbelievably cheap power, seemingly inexhaustible. Electrical gadgets from power toothbrushes, to garage door openers, to wireless telephones, became not just entertainers and labor savers but necessities in our homes. Plastic, lighter and more durable, replaced wood and metal.

Life was good, wasn't it? We called ourselves the "affluent society."

But we forgot something.

All the modern gadgets, chemicals, and materials that made life easier, faster, and more fun produced *wastes*. Wastes of many kinds, which at first were only annoying, we easily "discarded."

There was a price to pay. Fast cars and airplanes depleted our fuel supplies and polluted the air we breathed. The poisons that killed annoying insects and made our food supplies abundant and cheap also poisoned our water, our birds and fish—and our children. Energy supplies to feed our cars, planes, and electrical gadgets dwindled, and we have to burn more and more coal in more and more power plants, emitting more pollution into our oxygen-threatened air.

These emissions now threaten us with the greatest environmental specter imaginable: a change in planet Earth's climate, along with its associated disasters of more violent storms, droughts, floods, and fire.

Supreme Court justice William O. Douglas, the most active environmentalist in the history of our nation's high court, termed our modern civilization the "effluent society." But we ignored his warnings. Gone from us now, Douglas's words will remain prophetic.

There were a few others. But, by and large, these efforts by early environmentalists (before the term was invented) were ignored by congress, state legislatures, and the general public.

But it was also in the 1960s that major national efforts to conserve and preserve the values of our natural resources arose. In 1964 the National Wilderness Preservation Act was passed by Congress, and in 1968 the National Wild and Scenic Rivers System was created. Wisconsin Senator Gaylord Nelson founded

Earth Day on April 22, 1970—a concept that swept the nation with its message of stewardship.

Earth Day ushered in a remarkable decade. As if a precursor for good things to come, and in rapid succession, the Clean Water Act in 1972 and the Clean Air Act in 1973 were enacted by Congress. Three dozen states quickly followed the National Wild and Scenic River System with protection systems of their own, including Minnesota.

We've become aware that such protective systems are not only in geo-political areas like counties and states, but effective systems must be without such borders, and essential in *watersheds* that cross states and counties. Now five major regional initiatives are currently going forward in the United States: one for eastern brook trout, one for southeastern aquatic resources, another for native trout in the West, one in Alaska for salmon and migratory/inland trout. Heavily involving Minnesota, the fifth region is the Midwest Driftless Area Restoration Effort, spearheaded by Trout Unlimited. The Driftless Area (named because the latest ice-age glaciers did not cover it and thus left no glacial drift) is a huge area, 24,000 square miles (over 15 million acres). It includes a large portion of southwestern Wisconsin, some bits of Illinois and Iowa, and all of the southeastern trout and smallmouth bass streams in Minnesota. Each of these five initiatives proceeds by involving many people, organizations, and agencies in a partnership mode.

The State of Minnesota is wonderfully blessed with its natural resources. So much so, it seems, that we often fail to realize their fragility, and we become apathetic.

We may be awe-struck while walking beneath the towering native white pines that still grace some of our state parks, but it would be easy to decide that clearcutting the forest would create jobs. We may glory in the pristine waters of our (more than) ten thousand lakes, but find it necessary to fertilize lakeside lawns until those same waters become murky-green with algae.

First among all the many threats to our rivers are erosion and stream sedimentation, the most important river pollution in the United States. Agriculture, with its cultivated crops, has long led the list of polluters, plowing too close to streams and in riparian areas. And row-crop cultivation (the most sensitive to surface erosion) increases with corn for ethanol. Livestock grazing and drainage of wetlands still contribute to the sediment problem. We see some improvement, but not enough. Many techniques have been devised to improve farming procedures, but implementation of these techniques is still widely ignored. New laws are aimed to protect wetlands and river shorelands, but enforcement is poor and variances commonly permit more and more residential development and shopping malls with their asphalt roofs and concrete parking lots that prevent infiltration into the ground but rather, whisks them off to sewers and our rivers.

Continuing development of our state's Wild and Scenic Rivers system, so important in the protection of our special rivers, remains stalled in the Minnesota Department of Natural Resources. Since the initial inclusion of several rivers (in 1973), no additions to the system have been made for these past more than thirty years, while some of our most beloved rivers cry out for this protection. Also troubling is that effective enforcement of regulations in rivers already in the wild-and-scenic system is largely lacking.

We are faced with new threats. Among the most destructive are the animal wastes from concentrated foodlots, numbering in the thousands now throughout Minnesota; the problem is not just the concept of the foodlot, but also the lack of adequate protection from manures reaching nearby streams.

Sediment, the most important stream and river pollutant in the nation, both in quantity and in its economic losses, continues to pour uncontrolled into our rivers from eroding streambanks, while highly developed techniques for prevention have been worked out but go unused. Name almost any river, and keep your eyes open, and you will find eroding streambanks.

Motorized recreational vehicles, ATVs and souped up four wheel drive trucks, increase by the thousands each year, with the potential of ripping up our state forests. Such mistreatment of our state forests continues. It's not just the vehicles that cause the problem, but reckless, uncontrolled use by riders insensitive to natural values. These lands are admired by many other outdoor enthusiasts, far more numerous, in the quiet sports of hiking, camping, hunting, and others, who may then be prevented from using these same woodland resources. Fortunately, the Minnesota Department of Natural Resources has embarked upon strong resource management programs, not only to provide riding trails designated specifically for motorized use, but also stronger enforcement to stay on those trails. Most important, however, is locating the designated trails away from our rivers and streams and other environmentally sensitive areas like wetlands and wildlife habitat. These current efforts hold much promise for better control over motorized recreation.

More general is the increase in commercial development that results in paved streets, rooftops, parking lots, and concrete driveways, preventing the infiltration of precipitation into the groundwater. Profit-hungry proponents of such development every day seek variances from environmental rules, intruding into river corridors and riparian zones, so important in the protection of our streams and rivers. Our beloved Boundary Waters Canoe Area Wilderness, may someday be threatened by current searches for gold proceeds, because other factors in the soils and bedrock of this area include some of the most important characteristics that promise gold.

Money talks, and often wins over natural resources.

Again, although we have invented techniques and management styles to prevent or reduce such environmental losses, we fail to implement them sufficiently.

*   *   *

WE MAY STILL THRILL TO OUR WILD RIVERS, their clear waters, exciting rapids, leaping trout, spectacular waterfalls, and still waters that shelter us with the quietude of spirit and bring us peace. In the cool of early morning, changing light on the river's currents brings an anticipation of adventure to the coming day;

and there's a pleasant mystery in the shadows that descend upon the river with the fall of twilight at the close of day.

Utopia? Perhaps.

A goal? Definitely.

Attainable? Possible, but who will do it?

Better than peering through an open window, perhaps, is to try to look through a mirror and, like Alice, wonder what's on the other side. The image in the mirror, of course, will tell us who must do it.

There are many ways. Join a river conservation organization; there are thousands throughout the nation, a hundred or so in Minnesota. Create one.

See that your kids are exposed to the wonder of our natural world. Take them out camping, fishing and hunting, hiking and paddling, and point out the beauty and fascination of their outdoor scenes and the need for stewardship. There are stream monitoring programs by the score that will give them the opportunity to experience first-hand the importance of the plants, insects, and fish in our streams. If your school does not have such a program, see the school's biology teacher and ask for one. Remember that our youngsters are the teachers, scientists, politicians, and environmental lawyers in our nation's future.

Our clear waters and green valleys will continue to provide us inspiration and adventure, so long as we also exercise stewardship for our lakes, wetlands, forests, and rivers. They are treasures beyond measure.

OTHER RIVERS

IN ADDITION TO THE RIVERS IN THIS BOOK, there are scores more in Minnesota that deserve your attention. How many? Probably uncountable. Anyway, you'd never run out.

Many offer wonderful canoeing and kayaking. Many are quiet for beginners or family, some provide thrills with a few rapids, and there are even a few for the whitewater experts who enjoy risking their lives.

Here are a few more streams (not in this book) but covered by Greg Breining in his *Paddling Minnesota:*

Boy River, Cass County (also in Diebel's *Paddling Northern Minnesota*)
Le Sueur River, Blue Earth County (also in the Diebel's *Paddling Southern Minnesota*)
Midway River, Carlton County
Rice River, St Louis County (also in Diebel)
Sand Creek, Scott County
Sturgeon River, St Louis County (also in Diebel)
Tamarack River, Pine County
Turtle River, Beltrami County (also in Diebel)

*   *   *

TO THOSE, ADD MORE RIVERS IN THE CANOEING GUIDEBOOKS by Lynne Smith Diebel (*Paddling Northern Minnesota*) and its companion book, (*Paddling Southern Minnesota*) with her paddling photographer husband, Robert. These guides are all mentioned frequently in the book you have in your hands. They're in the form of day-trips, giving you specific information you'll need for a single day's paddle (or several days), including access and take-out locations, campsites, hazards, skill required, outfitters, shuttle directions, excellent photographs, the time for each day's travel, and more. If you canoe or kayak, these single day-trip guidebooks are indispensable.

Here are the rivers described by the Diebels but not covered in this book or those covered by Breining:

Big Cobb River, Blue Earth County
Hawk Creek, Renville County
Long Prairie River, Todd County
Maple River, Blue Earth County
Pike River, St Louis County
Prairie River, Itasca County
Shell River, Hubbard and Wadena counties

*   *   *

MOST RIVERS OFFER SOME FISHING, not only for trout and smallmouth bass, but also for northern pike, sturgeon, walleyes, catfish, rock bass, yellow perch, and more. Plus there's a growing cadre of anglers pursuing carp and other unpopular fish, and with flies no less. With some tiny rods and lines, some folks have actually taken up flyfishing for chubs and shiners, as both rise readily to flies.

There are lots of little streams that are super for fishing while wading, although too small for paddling. Mickey O. Johnson, in his *Flyfisher's Guide to Minnesota*, suggests many more streams on which to try out your tackle and skills.

*   *   *

TRY EVE & GARY WALLINGA'S *Waterfalls of Minnesota's North Shore: A Guide for Sightseers, Hikers & Romantics*. They list more than 130 waterfalls on rivers of Minnesota's North Shore.

Explore the City of Duluth's city creeks, there's a bunch, and the city has been working hard to protect and enhance them. They're lovely: Amity Creek, Chester Creek, Lester River, Miller Creek and Tischer Creek.

There's a rapidly increasing number of small parks on our rivers, especially by new county park agencies. And the number of trail miles along rivers is also on the increase. Many state and national trails wind along rivers.

You can also find even more rivers, not included in this book, in my *The Streams and Rivers of Minnesota*. About 350 listed in the Stream Index. And, of course, check out the streams that *are* included in this book—about 150.

*   *   *

RECREATION ACTIVITIES AVAILABLE go way beyond just canoeing, fishing, hiking, and camping. There's photography, drawing and painting, writing poetry and songs, and—well, you can use your imagination.

Make a hobby out of collecting—what?—aquatic insects from the bottoms of streams, or small, lovely fishes like darters, sculpins, and minnows, and small sunfishes that anglers never see; some are truly beautiful for your aquarium, aquatic plants (some, seen only with a magnifier or microscope, have lovely, tiny flowers). There's a myriad of tiny animals, crustaceans, that live on the bottoms of streams and rivers, fascinating in their size, life history, and beauty, which become visible under a magnifier—we call them *meiofauna* (my-oh-fawna, little animals), very important as food for insects and newly-hatched fish that may be only a half-inch long. Try for some photos of birds that relate to rivers, like kingfishers, herons, water ouzels, and sand pipers.

Or, just a lazy day hanging out beside a lovely river, or a tiny brook, all alone or with someone special (with a bottle of wine and loaf of bread?), can be great for the soul.

*   *   *

NEED MAPS? Try these:

Canoe and boating guides for thirty rivers designated by the Minnesota Department of Natural Resources (DNR) include excellent maps of whole rivers, with lots of other stuff included. They're free. And in color. Phone: 651-296-6157, or 1-888-646-6367. Email: info@dnr.state.mn.us

The DNR also publishes Public Recreation Information Maps (PRIM), which include rivers, lakes, Wildlife Management Areas (WMA), Scientific and Natural Areas (SNA), state and national forests, state parks, and much more. Fifty maps cover the state. Available from Minnesota's Book Store, for a modest price, 651-297-3000, also at the DNR gift shop, 500 Lafayette Road, St Paul MN 55155. PRIM maps are cited throughout this book for all major rivers.

Brochures for all 75 state parks contain maps of campgrounds, trails, lakes, and rivers. Ask from the DNR Information Center, 651-296-6157, or see descriptions of all state parks at: www.dnr.state.mn.us/state_parks.

The Wallingas' book on North Shore waterfalls includes excellent trail maps for hiking up to hidden falls (and some not so hidden).

The Superior Hiking Trail Association has some super maps of the trail along the North Shore, with many streams and rivers to cross that run to Lake Superior. Join up: 218-834-2700.

Don't forget about Minnesota county highway maps. Everything you always wanted to know about how to get around in rural Minnesota. Good for rivers and a lot more. There are 127 sheets that cover all 85 counties (large counties have several sheets). Call the Minnesota Department of Transportation at 651-366-3017 for ordering information.

*   *   *

INTO TROUT FISHING? See three guidebooks that include trout streams of the Driftless Area (and elsewhere), with maps, by John Van Vliet, Ross A. Mueller, and Jim Humphrey/Bill Shogren. Also, you can find trout streams in Minnesota under the individual trout names in the General Index in this book. Plus a few smallie streams under the entry "smallmouth bass" in the General Index.

Good luck!

ACKNOWLEDGMENTS

MINNESOTA IS A LARGE STATE, blessed with an abundance of wonderful natural resources. Minnesotans enjoy a richness of outdoor recreation that is immeasurable to any accurate degree.

With thousands of lakes and millions of acres of public forest, Minnesota offers enormous opportunity for recreation in our natural resources. Add 70,000 miles or so of streams and rivers (that's three times around planet Earth, folks), and we have a huge wealth of river-based recreation.

Consequently, any author who undertakes a statewide writing project about just part of those natural resources must be presumptuous indeed. And so it was with me in preparing this book on rivers. I admit it.

It was necessary for me to depend heavily upon the Minnesota Department of Natural Resources, similarly huge, with many of its widespread staff across the state. Without that line of communication, this volume could not possibly have had the coverage and detail that it did. With the advent of the Internet, only a few years ago, access to almost unlimited information about our natural resources within the Department became readily available. But even so, just the Department's wealth of data was not enough, not enough without the personal assistance of scores of its staff who literally jumped to help.

It would be impossible for me to list them all, but here's a small sample.

Jack Wingate, supervisor of fisheries research, was always available at the touch of a telephone, to tell me where to proceed and who to contact for what I needed. Mark Ebbers, supervisor of trout and salmon management, and Steve Persons, Area Fisheries Supervisor, Grand Marais, provided a wealth of survey and management reports on the North Shore streams. To my many phone calls, Vicky Schiller responded by mailing copies of old reports that sometimes filled a good-sized box. (The Department's website is enormous, and though replete with survey data on lakes, reports and surveys on rivers are not.) I telephoned repeatedly to someone on the other end to ask for names, addresses, and phone numbers of field staff.

I included critical information on many state parks, a major source of outdoor recreation. (Did you know that most state parks are on rivers?) I am indebted to the many managers and assistants who provided me with that information; they always responded enthusiastically to my phone calls and letters.

Special thanks are due to the managers and biologists at several national wildlife refuges for their essential assistance, whose duties extend far beyond concern for river recreation. These large areas provide public access to the spreading wildlife habitats within the refuges, including access for hunting, birding, and wildlife observation. Through educational programs on the great diversity of wildlife habitats found in large areas, they emphasize the needs of the hundreds of animal and plant species for which the refuges provide homes. For those refuges included in this book, which cover at least some streams and rivers, assistance was received from Becky Carlson, Agassiz National Wildlife Refuge; Jeanne Holler, Sherburne National Wildlife Refuge; and Barbara Boyle, Tamarac National Wildlife Refuge.

I am especially grateful for a number of new friends who gave a day's time (or more) to provide some of my most memorable field experiences—canoeing some of Minnesota's streams and rivers. These include Dawn Doering, founder of Friends of the Sunrise River, with whom I paddled several times on the Sunrise and the Snake; Julie Westerlund, from the Minnehaha Creek Watershed District who, with her husband Andy in his kayak, canoed with me on Minnehaha Creek, to learn more about this most noted metropolitan stream; Kriste Ericsson, Friends of the Rum River, and Mark Riverblood, devoted river advocate, made possible or canoed with me on several excursions on the Rum River. I was assisted by Daniel Huff, Friends of the Mississippi River, for valuable information about canoeing and fishing in the Rice Creek Chain of Lakes, in the Anoka County park of that name. And, with leadership of Dawn Dubats, Rice Creek Watershed District, I joined a group of supporters on a canoe trip for a short but fascinating time on a restored section of the previously channelized stream. To top off my field experiences for this book, a summer day's paddling the clear waters of the Crow Wing River with my daughter Elizabeth was an unmatched delight.

Elizabeth spent many hours and days meticulously editing images and text, changing sentences that didn't make sense, and here and there choosing a better word. She carefully followed the Chicago Manual of Style from the placement of a lowly comma to replacement of a whole paragraph. She also obtained ISBN, other numbers, and cataloging details from the Copyright Office and Library of Congress with skill and speed. All of which resulted in a better book. Thanks, Liz.

In the more than thirty years I spent at the University of Minnesota, I gained as much from my students as they from me, probably more. Certainly the days and nights we spent together in the field, in hip boots or canoe, or around a campfire at night, contributed mightily to my perceptions of life on this planet and my relationship to it—whether discussing ecological principles or trout streams and favorite flies. They are too numerous to list here, but if they read this book they will recognize themselves, and a Minnesota river or two.

And finally, once again, I am grateful for the loving memories of the thousands of days spent together with my late wife, Carol, in our grand outdoors, so many of which were enjoyed on or near the rivers of Minnesota.

BIBLIOGRAPHY

Books and other publications referenced in this book

Arthur, Anne. 1998. *Minnesota's state parks: How to get there, what to do, where to do it.* Adventure Publications, Inc., Cambridge.

Breining, Greg. 1999. *Paddling Minnesota..* Falcon Publishing, Helena, Montana.

Breining, Greg. 2000. *Wild shore: Exploring lake Superior by kayak.* University of Minnesota Press, Minneapolis.

Buchanan, James W. 1980. *The Minnesota walk book.* NodinPress, Cambridge.

Diebel, Lynne Smith. 2005. *Paddling Northern Minnesota: 86 great trips by canoe and kayak.* Trails Books, Black Earth, Wisconsin.

Diebel, Lynne and Robert. 2007. *Paddling Southern Minnesota: 85 great trips by canoe and kayak.* Trails Books, Madison, Wisconsin.

Engrav, Timothy J. 2005. *County parks of Minnesota: 300 parks you can visit featuring 25 favorites.* Trails Books, Black Earth, Wisconsin.

Henderson, Carrol L.. 1997. *Traveler's Guide to Wildlife in Minnesota.* Minnesota's Bookstore, St. Paul.

Holling, Holling Clancy. 1951. *Minn of the Mississippi.* Houghton Mifflin Company, Boston.

Holschlag, Tim. 1990. *Stream smallmouth fishing: A comprehensive guide.* Stackpole Books, Harrisburg, Pennsylvania.

Holschlag, Tim. 2005. *Smallmouth fly fishing: The best techniques, flies, and destinations.* Smallmouth Angler Press, Minneapolis.

Humphrey, Jim, and Bill Shogren. 2001. *Trout streams of Wisconsin and Minnesota: A fly-angler's guide to more than 150 rivers and streams. 2nd edition.* Backcountry Guides, Woodstock, Vermont.

Huot-Vickery, Jim Dale. 2001. *A sense of place: going with the flow.* Minnesota Conservation Volunteer, March-April.

Johnson, Mickey O. 2005. *Flyfisher's guide to Minnesota.* Wilderness Adventures Press, Belgrade, Montana.

Linsenman, Bob. 2005. *Best streams for Great Lakes steelhead: A complete guide to the fish, the tactics, and the places to catch them.* The Countryman Press, Woodstock, Vermont.

MacGregor, Molly. 1995. *Mississippi headwaters guide book. A guide book to the natural, cultural, scenic, scientific and recreational values of the Mississippi River's first 400 miles.* Mississippi Headwaters Board, Walker, Minnesota.

Morton, Ron, and Judy Gibbs. 2006. *A Walking guide to the Superior Hiking Trail: natural history, scenery and other trail features.* Rockflower Press, Knife River, Minnesota.

Morton, Ron, and Steve Morse. 2007. *Gooseberry Falls to Grand Portage: A walking guide to the hiking trails in Minnesota's North Shore state parks.* Rockflower Press, Knife River, Minnesota.

Perich, Shawn. 1994. *Fishing Lake Superior: A complete guide to stream, shoreline, and open-water angling.* University of Minnesota Press, Minneapolis.

Perich, Shawn. 1995. *Fly-fishing the north country.* Pfeifer-Hamilton Publishers, Duluth, Minnesota.

Pukite, John. 1998. *Hiking Minnesota.* Morris Book Publishing, Kearney, Nebraska.

Red Lake River Corridor. Undated. *Red Lake River canoe and small boat brochure.* [Brochure].

Superior Hiking Trail Association. 2004. *Guide to the Superior hiking trail: Linking people with nature by footpath along Lake Superior's North Shore. 4th edition.* Ridgeline Press, Two Harbors, Minnesota.

Tester, John R. 1995. *Minnesota's natural heritage: An ecological perspective.* University of Minnesota Press, Minneapolis.

University of Minnesota, Crookston. Undated. *Discover Northwest Minnesota on the Red Lake River by canoe or kayak.* [Report].

Wallinga, Eve and Gary. 2006. *Waterfalls of Minnesota's North Shore: A guide for sightseers, hikers, & romantics.* North Shore Press, Hovland.

Waters, Thomas F. 1977. *The streams and rivers of Minnesota.* University of Minnesota Press, Minneapolis.

Watson, Tom. 2005. *The best in tent camping—Minnesota: A guide for car campers who hate RVs, concrete slabs, and loud portable stereos.* Menasha Ridge Press, Birmingham, Alabama.

Watson, Tom. 2007. *60 Hikes within 60 miles: Minneapolis and St. Paul, including hikes in and around the Twin Cities. 2nd edition.* Menasha Ridge Press, Birmingham, Alabama.

FOR FURTHER READING

Additional publications that may be of interest

Allan, J. David. 1995. *Stream ecology: Structure and function of running waters*. Chapman & Hall, New York.

Anfinson, John O. 2003. *The river we have wrought: A history of the upper Mississippi*. University of Minnesota Press, Minneapolis.

Boling, David M. 1994. *How to save a river: A handbook for citizen action*. Island Press, Washington, D.C.

Burke, William J. 2000. *The upper Mississippi valley: How the landscape shaped our heritage*. Mississippi Valley Press, Waukon, Iowa.

Cushing, Colbert E., and J. David Allan. *Streams: Their ecology and life*. Academic Press, London.

Hunt, Robert L. 1993. *Trout stream therapy*. University of Wisconsin Press, Madison.

Hynes, H.B. Noel. 1970. *The ecology of running waters*. University of Toronto Press.

Lyons, Nick. 1977. *Bright rivers*. J.B. Lippincott Company, Philadelphia and New York.

Meyer, Roy W. 1991. *Everyone's country estate: A history of Minnesota's state parks*. Minnesota Historical Society Press, St Paul.

Minnesota Department of Conservation. 1959. *Hydrologic atlas of Minnesota, Division of Waters*. Bulletin 10.

Mueller, Ross A. 1999. *Fly fishing midwestern spring creeks: Angler's guide to trouting the driftless area*. R. Mueller Publications, Appleton, Wisconsin.

Nelson, Gaylord. 2002. *Beyond earth day: Fulfilling the promise.* The University of Wisconsin, Madison.

Paddock, Joe. 2001. *Keeper of the wild: The life of Ernest Oberholtzer.* Minnesota Historical Society Press, St Paul.

Palmer, Tim. 1994. Lifelines: *The case for river conservation.* Island Press, Washington, D.C.

Perich, Shawn. 2002. *Backroads of Minnesota: Your guide to Minnesota's most scenic backroad adventures.* Voyageur Press, Inc., Stillwater.

Rosenbauer, Tom. 2007. *The orvis fly-fishing guide.* The Lyons Press, Guilford, Connecticut.

Rosgen, Dave. 1996. *Applied river morphology.* Wildland Hydrology, Pagosa Springs, Colorado.

Schara, Ron. 2003. *Ron Schara's Minnesota fishing guide.* Tristan Publishing, Inc., Golden Valley.

Smith, Lloyd L., Jr., and John B. Moyle. 1944. *A biological survey and fishery management plan for the streams of the Lake Superior North Shore watershed.* Minnesota Department of Conservation, Division of Game and Fish, Technical Bulletin No. 1, 228 pages.

Waters, Thomas F. 1987. *The Superior North Shore: A natural history of Lake Superior's northern lands and waters.* University of Minnesota Press, Minneapolis.

Waters, Thomas F. 2000. Wildstream: *A natural history of the free-flowing river.* Riparian Press, Saint Paul, Minnesota.

INDEXES

Stream Index

(Boldfaced numbers refer to illustrations.)

A

Arrowhead River
see Brule River

B

Badger Creek, 211
  fishing, 211
  tributary to South Fork
   of the Root River, 211
  PRIM map, 216
  see also color section
Baptism River, 70, **78**, 78-80
  camping, 79
  East Branch, 79
  fishing, 79
  High Falls, 78-79
  hiking, 79
  Illgen Falls, 79
  origin of name, 79
  rapids, 78, 80
  Tettegouche State Park, 78
  waterfalls, 78, 79
  PRIM map, 83
Bear Creek, **189**
  smallmouth bass fishing, 189
  tributary to Zumbro River,
   189
  PRIM map, 192
Bear Trap Creek, 66
  PRIM map, 66
Beaver Creek (Winona County),
  196, 197, 198, 201

  birdwatching, 198
  fishing, 196, 198, 201
  hiking, 198
  hunting, 197, 198
  PRIM map, 196
Beaver Creek (Houston County)
  212
  Beaver Creek Valley State
   Park, 212
  camping, 212
  East Beaver Creek, 212
  fishing, 212
  West Beaver Creek, 212
  PRIM map, 216
Beaver River, 50, 58, 70, 76-78,
  77
  fishing, 76
  origin of name, 78
  waterfalls, 77
  PRIM map, 83
Big Fork River, 331, 332,
  349, 350-352, **351**, 354,
  355, 356
  camping, 350, 351
  canoeing, 332, 349, 350, 354,
   355, 356
  fishing, 354, 355, 356
  origin of name, 355
  portaging, 350, 351, 354
  rapids, 349, 350
  waterfalls, 349, 350, 355
  PRIM map, 356
Big River, 192
  PRIM map, 192
Blackhoof River, 50, 52, **53**, 53-
  54
  fishing, 53, 54
  length, 53
  origin of name, 54
  watershed, 53, 54
  PRIM map, 54
Blue Earth River, 259, 264, 270-
  272, **271**

354, 356
fishing, 353, 354, 355, 356
plains, 349
portaging, 352, 354
rapids, 349, 350, 352, 353,
    354, 355
waterfalls, 349, 353, 354,
    355
PRIM map, 356
Little Isabella River, 37, 333
    PRIM map, 329
Lynch Creek, 211
    PRIM map, 216

M

Manitou River, 70, 80-81
    camping, 80
    fishing, 80
    George Crosby Manitou State
        Park, 80
    hiking, 80
    origin of name, 81
    rapids, 81
    waterfalls, 80, 81
    PRIM map, 83
Marshall Creek, 66
    PRIM map, 66
Mazeppa Creek, 190
    PRIM map, 192
Middle River, 310-311
    dams, 311
    old grist mill, restored, 311
    Old Mill State Park, 311
    PRIM map, 315
Minnehaha Creek, 160-161, **161**,
    169
    canoeing, 160, 161
    dams, 160, 161
    kayaking, 160, 161
    origin of name, 161
    rapids, 161

PRIM map, 171
Minneopa Creek, 270
    Minneopa State Park, 270
    PRIM map, 271
    see also color section
Minnesota River, 111, 112, 116,
    118, 120, 139, 160, 162,
    168, 169, 198, 241-256,
    244, **255**, 260, 261, 266,
    269, 270, 271, 273, 283,
    298, 303, 341
    agricultural cultivation, 247
    Big Stone Lake State Park, 243
    biking, 253, 254
    birdwatching, 245, 252, 274
    camping, 243, 245, 246, 247,
        249, 252, 253, 254, 273
    canoeing, 244, 246, 247, 252,
        253, 254, 273
    confluence with the
        Mississippi, 244, 253
    fishing, 243, 245, 250, 251,
        252, 253, 254, 273
    Fort Ridgely State Park, 249
    geological history, 241-243,
        247
    hiking, 243, 244, 245, 249,
        252, 253, 254, 274
    historical account, 249-250,
        254
    horse back riding, 245, 249,
        253
    hunting, 245, 250-251, 252,
        254, 273
    length, 244
    Minnesota River valley, 162,
        168, 241, 242, 243, 248,
        249, 254
    Minnesota Valley State Park,
        252, 253
    origin of name, 256
    rapids, 246, 251
    skiing, 253, 254

tributaries, 243, 245, 251,
259-275
Upper Sioux Agency State
Park, 246, 266
visitor center, 252
wildlife, 244, 245
PRIM map, 171, 254, 262,
264, 266, 267, 269, 270,
271
Mississippi River, 29, 38, 55,
117-125, **119, 122,** 127-
139, **130,** 142, 144,
150, 151, 160, 163-169,
167, 168, 174, 176-185,
177, 181, 186, 187, 200,
208, 211, 212, 213, 214,
218, 221, 223, 244, 246,
251, 253, 255, 257, 277,
278, 303, 336, 341, 347
backpacking, 120
Bemidji State Park, 222
biking, 120
birdwatching, 115, 117, 123,
183
campgrounds, 114, 115, 120,
121, 123, 130, 131, 167,
169
canoeing, 114, 115, 121, 123,
124, 130, 131, 169, 176,
183, 185
Charles A. Lindbergh State
Park, 130
dams, 111, 121, 128, 131,
169, 176, 177, 183
fishing, 114, 115, 120, 123,
124, 131, 132, 178, 183,
185, 336
Fort Snelling State Park, 168,
169, 247, 252, 254
hiking, 169
hunting, 114, 115, 124, 184
Itasca State Park, 120
kayaking, 114

length, 109, 115, 120, 122
Lower Mississippi, 110, 111,
176
origin of name, 109
portaging, 121
rapids, 120, 128, 131, 176,
185
Schoolcraft State Park, 123
tributaries, 117, 118, 119,
123, 139, 177, 180, 184,
185
Upper Mississippi, 110, 111,
112, 176, 181, 183
waterfalls, 128
watershed, 29, 56
yacht cruise, 120
PRIM map, 124, 139, 171,
184
Money Creek, 211
PRIM map, 216
Mons Creek, 101
PRIM map, 105
Moose River, 236-237
PRIM map, 236
Murphy Creek, 66
PRIM map, 66

N

Nemadji River, 46, 49, 50, 50-53,
51
accesses, 51
canoeing, 51
fishing, 52, 54
North Fork, 50, 51, 52, 53
origin of name, 53
South Fork, 50, 52
tributaries, 52, 53, 54
watershed area, 50, 52
PRIM map, 54
Net River, **52**
fishing, 52

R

General Index

Blackhoof River, 53
Brule River, 101
BWCWA, 331, 334
Caribou River, 81
Cascade River, 94, 96
Cloudy Spring Creek, 66
Cross River, 86
Devil Track River, 97
Diamond Creek, 212
Driftless Area, 177, 178,
    179, 184, 196, 217
Gooseberry River, 73
Gribben Creek, 212
Indian Creek, 66
Kinney Creek, 66
Murphy Creek, 66
Nemadji River, 52
Net River, 52
Root River, 212
Split Rock River, 74
Straight Lake Creek, 145
Sullivan Creek, 66
Temperance River, 90
Trappers Creek, 66
Whiteface River, 60
Whitewater River, 198,
    200
introduced above waterfalls,
    44
native to Lake Superior, 44,
    46, 178
replaced by brown trout, 178
replaced by rainbow trout,
    240
spawning of, 44, 178
stocking of, 178
brown trout, 53
    feeding of, 178
    Beaver Creek (Winona
        County), 201
    Blackhoof River, 53, 54
    Clearwater River, 323
    Crow Wing Lake (fifth),

146
Diamond Creek, 212
Driftless Area, 178, 179
Fishhook River, 144
Gilmore Creek, 180
Gribben Creek, 212
Net River, 52
Redwood River, 268
Root River, 210
Straight River (Becker
    County), 188
Temperance River, 90
Vermillion River, 162, 163
Whitewater River, 198,
    200, 202, 205, 218
Yellow Medicine River,
    266
introduction of, 178
spawning of, 54, 178
stocking of, 323
Browns Valley, Minnesota, 242,
    243, 254, 297, 298, 299,
    305
Buchanan, James W., author, *The
    Minnesota Walk Book,* 36
buffalo fish, 181
Buffalo River State Park, 309
Buffalo, Minnesota, 35
bullhead, 251, 260, 279, 303

C

Cambridge, Minnesota, 151, 153,
    155, 156
Camden State Park, Redwood
    River, 267
Camp Release, 248
Camp Ripley Junction, 130
Camp Ripley Military
    Reservation, 130
Campbell Beach, of Glacial Lake
    Agassiz, 298, 309, 311, 321

Root River, 210
St. Louis River, 57, 339
darters, 136, 288
Dayton, Minnesota, 138
DDT, 360
Dead Zone, 256
Dentaybow Landing, Little Fork
    River, 353
Des Grosseilliers, explorer, 73
Detroit, Michigan, 360
Devil's Kettle, Brule River, 101
Diebel, Lynne Smith, author
    Paddling Northern Minnesota,
    33, 57, 60, 65, 71, 115, 118,
    121, 122, 124, 143, 144, 239,
    309, 313, 321, 332, 344, 345,
    350, 351, 354
Diebel, Lynne Smith and Robert,
    authors
    Paddling Southern Minnesota,
    33, 57, 115, 118, 131, 132,
    130, 152, 153, 154, 161, 163,
    165, 169, 183, 187, 188, 190,
    192, 201, 209, 210, 222, 231,
    233, 246, 253, 261, 262, 263,
    265, 266, 269, 270, 272, 273,
    279
dispersed camping, 36, 333, 340
Dorer, Richard J., wildlife
    administrator, 361
Douglas, William O., Supreme
    Court Justice, 362
Driftless Area, 34, 35, 113, 118,
    173-192, 195-200, 207,
    208, 210, 213, 215, 216,
    275, 363
    camping, 174
    canoeing, 174, 182, 183
    fishing, 174, 176, 177, 178,
        181, 182, 185, 217
    geological history, 173
    hiking, 174, 216
    hunting, 176, 183, 216,

217
    trout water, 179
Duluth, Minnesota, District
    Court in Duluth, 76, 34, 39,
    46, 55, 57, 80, 333

E

Earth Day, 363
East Grand Forks, Minnesota,
    301, **315**, 319, 324, 328
Eden Valley, Minnesota, 134
Edmund Fitzgerald, 74
eel, American, 181-182
Elba, Minnesota, 200, 203
explorers
    English, 13, 293
    French, 102, 246, 280
Engrav, Timothy J., author,
    County Parks of Minnesota,
    36
environmental movement, 1970s,
    160
erosion
    flooding, 193, 196, 198, 201,
        206, 216, 242
    row crop cultivation, 138,
        162
    streambank erosion, 84, 140,
        165, 215, 218, 349
ethanol, 364
Europe, 181, 294
Ewing, Margaret, Copy-
    editor, University of
    Minnesota Press, 22-23
exotic species, 240

F

Fargo, North Dakota, **316**
Faribault, Minnesota, 186, 187,
    188